PRAISE FOR *RUBY UNDER A MICROSCOPE*

"Many people have dug into the Ruby source code, but few make it back out and tell the tale as elegantly as Pat does in *Ruby Under a Microscope*! I particularly love the diagrams—and there are lots of them—as they make many opaque implementation topics a lot easier to understand, especially when coupled with Pat's gentle narrative. This book is a delight for language implementation geeks and Rubyists with a penchant for digging into the guts of their tools."
—PETER COOPER (@PETERC), EDITOR OF *RUBY INSIDE* AND *RUBY WEEKLY*

"Man, this book was missing in the Ruby landscape—awesome content."
—XAVIER NORIA (@FXN), RUBY HERO, RUBY ON RAILS CORE TEAM MEMBER

"Pat Shaughnessy did a tremendous job writing THE book about Ruby internals. Definitely a must read—you won't find information like this anywhere else."
—SANTIAGO PASTORINO (@SPASTORINO), WYEWORKS CO-FOUNDER, RUBY ON RAILS CORE TEAM MEMBER

"I really enjoyed the book and now have a far better understanding of both Ruby and CS. The writing made very complex topics (at least for me) very accessible, and I found the book hard to put down. Diagrams were awesome and are already popping in my head as I code. This is by far one of my top 3 favourite Ruby books."
—VLAD IVANOVIC (@VLADIIM), DIGITAL STRATEGIST AT HOLLER SYDNEY

"While I'm not usually digging into Ruby Internals, this book was an absolutely awesome read."
—DAVID DERYL DOWNEY (@DAVIDDWDOWNEY), FOUNDER OF CYBERSPACE TECHNOLOGIES GROUP

"Nearly every Ruby expert will benefit from knowing so much about how the language and runtime operate."
—DR. DOBB'S

"Ruby isn't just a black box anymore, but rather a tool that I understand and feel good using."
—ROBERT MOSOLGO, RAILS DEVELOPER, PLANNING CENTER ONLINE

Ruby Under a Microscope

An Illustrated Guide to Ruby Internals

Pat Shaughnessy

no starch
press

Printed on demand in USA

ISBN-10: 1-59327-527-7
ISBN-13: 978-1-59327-527-3

Publisher: William Pollock
Production Editor: Riley Hoffman
Cover Illustration: Charlie Wylie
Interior Design: Octopod Studios
Developmental Editor: William Pollock
Technical Reviewer: Aaron Patterson
Copyeditor: Julianne Jigour
Compositors: Susan Glinert Stevens and Riley Hoffman
Proofreader: Elaine Merrill

For information on distribution, translations, or bulk sales, please contact No Starch Press, Inc. directly:

No Starch Press, Inc.
245 8th Street, San Francisco, CA 94103
phone: 415.863.9900; info@nostarch.com
www.nostarch.com

Library of Congress Cataloging-in-Publication Data

Shaughnessy, Pat.
   Ruby under a microscope : an illustrated guide to Ruby internals / by Pat Shaughnessy.
       pages cm
   Summary: "An under-the-hood look at how the Ruby programming language runs code. Extensively illustrated with
complete explanations and hands-on experiments. Covers Ruby 2.x"-- Provided by publisher.
     ISBN 978-1-59327-527-3 (paperback) -- ISBN 1-59327-527-7 (paperback)
   1. Ruby (Computer program language) I. Title.
   QA76.73.R83S53 2013
   005.1'17--dc23
                                                 2013030614

To my wife, Cristina; my daughter, Ana; and my son, Liam—
thanks for supporting me all along.

ABOUT THE AUTHOR

Pat Shaughnessy is a Ruby developer working at McKinsey & Co., a management consulting firm. Pat was originally trained as a physicist at MIT, but later spent more than 20 years working as a software developer using C, Java, PHP, and Ruby, among other languages. Writing *Ruby Under a Microscope* has given him an excuse to reuse bits of his scientific training while studying Ruby. A fluent Spanish speaker, Pat frequently visits his wife's family in northern Spain. He lives outside of Boston with his wife and two children.

BRIEF CONTENTS

CONTENTS IN DETAIL

6
METHOD LOOKUP AND CONSTANT LOOKUP   133

7
THE HASH TABLE: THE WORKHORSE OF RUBY INTERNALS   167

FOREWORD

Oh, hi! I didn't see you come in. I don't want to be too forward, but let me preface this by saying you should buy this book!

My name is Aaron Patterson, but my Internet friends call me "tenderlove." I am on both the Ruby core team and the Ruby on Rails core team, and I did the technical review of this book. Does that mean you should listen to me? No. Well, maybe.

Actually, when Pat approached me to do the technical review of this book, I was so excited that my top hat fell off and I dropped my monocle in my coffee! I knew about Pat's previous work on *Ruby Under a Microscope*, and the idea of making an updated and print version available made me really happy. I think many developers are intimidated by Ruby's internals and are afraid to dive in. Quite often people ask me how they can learn about how Ruby works under the hood or where to get started hacking on Ruby internals. Unfortunately I didn't have a good answer for people—until now.

Pat's style of writing, in combination with experimentation, makes Ruby internals very approachable. The experiments are combined with explanations of Ruby's internals such that you can easily understand why Ruby acts the way it does with regard to behavior *and* performance. Next time you encounter some behavior in your Ruby code, whether it be with performance, local variables and your environment, or even garbage collection, this book won't just tell you *why* your code behaves the way it does, but will even tell you *how*.

If you're someone who wants to start hacking on Ruby's internals, or if you just want to understand why Ruby acts the way it does without any hand-waving, this is the book for you. I enjoyed this book, and I hope you will too.

Aaron Patterson

<3 <3 <3 <3

FOREWORD TO
THE JAPANESE EDITION

The science fiction novel *A Connecticut Yankee in King Arthur's Court* by Mark Twain[1] is one of the books I still remember reading from my elementary school days.

It is the story of an American living in the 1880s who accidentally travels through time to King Arthur–era Britain and nonetheless survives, taking advantage of his knowledge from the modern (1880) era. Surely you would be very powerful in the 5th century if you had knowledge of telephones, bicycles, and guns. But if we travelled from the 21st century to the 5th century, how much of our knowledge could we utilize? Bicycles are okay, but how about computers? It seems almost impossible to build computers and networks from scratch by ourselves. Modern technology products are too advanced for individuals to reproduce. We don't know how technologies work even when we use them in our everyday lives.

Ruby is one such technology. Even though we use it every day, few of us know what it looks like on the inside, how it runs internally, or how one could re-create such a programming language. *Ruby Under a Microscope* sheds light on this and reveals the mystery of Ruby internals.

---

1. Mark Twain, *A Connecticut Yankee in King Arthur's Court* (Kameyama Nagarjuna translation, Iwasaki Bookstore, 1971).

This book explains the software architecture of Ruby, the structure of its object system, and tips for performance improvement. In addition to that, it covers not only CRuby but also JRuby and Rubinius. I know of few books where you can find this type of knowledge. Though we have Minero Aoki's *Ruby Hacking Guide*[2] in Japan, it's been difficult to obtain a copy for a long time. It explains a version of Ruby as old as 1.7 and naturally does not cover newer technologies like YARV. I believe *Ruby Under a Microscope* will contribute to a wider understanding of Ruby internals.

In the future someone inspired by this book may join the development of Ruby. It may be you. We will definitely welcome that. Or, someone may begin creating a next-generation programming language. I hope to see that happen.

Yukihiro Matsumoto
Matsue, Japan
October 2014

---

2. Minero Aoki, *Ruby Source Code Kanzen Kaisetsu*, known as the *Ruby Hacking Guide* (Impress, 2002); *http://i.loveruby.net/ja/rhg/book/*; *http://ruby-hacking-guide.github.io/*.

ACKNOWLEDGMENTS

I could never have finished a project like this without the support of many different people!

First of all, thanks to Satty Bhens and everyone else at McKinsey for giving me the flexibility to write a book and keep my day job at a great company. Alex Rothenberg and Daniel Higginbotham gave me invaluable advice, suffered through reading many early drafts, and helped me throughout the process. Special thanks to Xavier Noria, who took an interest in the project early on, gave me fantastic feedback on the entire rough draft, and was also the inspiration behind Experiment 6-1. Santiago Pastorino reviewed the rough draft as well. Jill Caporrimo, Prajakta Thakur, Yvannova Montalvo, Divya Ganesh, and Yanwing Wong were my "proofreading SWAT team." Self-publishing would have been much harder without your help. Finally, without the constant encouragement and support Peter Cooper has given me this year, I probably never would have attempted to write this book. Thank you, Peter.

Thanks to everyone at No Starch Press for helping me bring an expanded, updated version of *Ruby Under a Microscope* to print. The result is a book I'm proud of and one the Ruby internals topic deserves. Thanks to Julianne Jigour, my copyeditor. My writing has never been so clear and easy to follow. Thank you, Riley Hoffman and Alison Law, for your editing advice and for beautifully reproducing hundreds of diagrams for print. You've been a pleasure to work with. Thanks to Charles Nutter for the technical help and advice on JVM garbage collection. Special thanks to Aaron Patterson: This is a more interesting and accurate book because of your great suggestions and technical review. Finally, thanks to Bill Pollock for reading and editing every single line of text in the book. Your guidance and expertise have allowed me to write a book I could never have dreamed of writing on my own.

What seems complex from a distance is often quite simple when you look closely enough.

INTRODUCTION

At first glance, learning how to use Ruby can seem fairly simple. Developers around the world find Ruby's syntax to be graceful and straightforward. You can express algorithms in a very natural way, and then it's just a matter of typing ruby at the command line and pressing ENTER, and your Ruby script is running.

However, Ruby's syntax is *deceptively* simple; in fact, Ruby employs sophisticated ideas from complex languages like Lisp and Smalltalk. On top of this, Ruby is dynamic; using metaprogramming, Ruby programs can inspect and change themselves. Beneath this thin veneer of simplicity, Ruby is a very complex tool.

By looking very closely at Ruby—by learning how Ruby itself works internally—you'll discover that a few important computer science concepts underpin Ruby's many features. By studying these, you'll gain a deeper understanding of what is happening under the hood as you use the language. In the process, you'll learn how the team that built Ruby *intends* for you to use the language.

Ruby Under a Microscope will show you what happens inside Ruby when you run a simple program. You'll learn how Ruby understands and executes your code, and with the help of extensive diagrams, you'll build a mental model of what Ruby does when you create an object or call a block.

Who This Book Is For

Ruby Under a Microscope is not a beginner's guide to learning Ruby. I assume you already know how to program in Ruby and that you use it daily. There are already many great books that teach Ruby basics; the world doesn't need another one.

Although Ruby itself is written in C, a confusing, low-level language, no C programming knowledge is required to read this book. *Ruby Under a Microscope* will give you a high-level, conceptual understanding of how Ruby works without your having to understand how to program in C. Inside this book, you'll find hundreds of diagrams that make the low-level details of Ruby's internal implementation easy to understand.

NOTE *Readers familiar with C will find a few snippets of C code that give a more concrete sense of what's going on inside Ruby. I'll also tell you where the code derives from, making it easier for you to start studying the C code yourself. If you're not interested in the C code details, just skip over these sections.*

Using Ruby to Test Itself

> It doesn't matter how beautiful your theory is, it doesn't matter
> how smart you are. If it doesn't agree with experiment, it's wrong.
> —Richard Feynman

Imagine that the entire world functioned like a large computer program. To explain natural phenomena or experimental results, physicists like Richard Feynman would simply consult this program. (A scientist's dream come true!) But of course, the universe is not so simple.

Fortunately, to discover how Ruby works, all we need to do is read its internal C source code: a kind of theoretical physics that describes Ruby's behavior. Just as Maxwell's equations explain electricity and magnetism, Ruby's internal C source code explains what happens when you pass an argument to a method or include a module in a class.

Like scientists, however, we need to perform experiments to be sure our hypotheses are correct. After learning about each part of Ruby's internal implementation, we'll perform an experiment and use Ruby to test itself! We'll run small Ruby test scripts to see whether they produce the expected output or run as quickly or as slowly as we expect. We'll find out if Ruby actually behaves the way theory says it should. And since these experiments are written in Ruby, you can try them yourself.

Which Implementation of Ruby?

Ruby was invented by Yukihiro "Matz" Matsumoto in 1993, and the original, standard version of Ruby is often known as *Matz's Ruby Interpreter (MRI)*. Most of this book will discuss how MRI works; essentially, we'll learn how Matz implemented his own language.

Over the years many alternative implementations of Ruby have been written. Some, like RubyMotion, MacRuby, and IronRuby, were designed to run on specific platforms. Others, like Topaz and JRuby, were built using programming languages other than C. One version, Rubinius, was built using Ruby itself. And Matz himself is now working on a smaller version of Ruby called *mruby*, designed to run inside another application.

I explore the Ruby implementations JRuby and Rubinius in detail in Chapters 10, 11, and 12. You'll learn how they use different technologies and philosophies to implement the same language. As you study these alternative Rubies, you'll gain additional perspective on MRI's implementation.

Overview

In **Chapter 1: Tokenization and Parsing**, you'll learn how Ruby parses your Ruby program. This is one of the most fascinating areas of computer science: How can a computer language be smart enough to understand the code you give it? What does this intelligence really consist of?

Chapter 2: Compilation explains how Ruby uses a compiler to convert your program into a different language before running it.

Chapter 3: How Ruby Executes Your Code looks at the virtual machine Ruby uses to run your program. What's inside this machine? How does it work? We'll look deep inside this virtual machine to find out.

Chapter 4: Control Structures and Method Dispatch continues the description of Ruby's virtual machine, looking at how Ruby implements control structures such as if...else statements and while...end loops. It also explores how Ruby implements method calls.

Chapter 5: Objects and Classes discusses Ruby's implementation of objects and classes. How are objects and classes related? What would we find inside a Ruby object?

Chapter 6: Method Lookup and Constant Lookup examines Ruby modules and their relationship to classes. You'll learn how Ruby finds methods and constants in your Ruby code.

Chapter 7: The Hash Table: The Workhorse of Ruby Internals explores Ruby's implementation of hash tables. As it turns out, MRI uses hash tables for much of its internal data, not only for data you save in Ruby hash objects.

Chapter 8: How Ruby Borrowed a Decades-Old Idea from Lisp reveals that one of Ruby's most elegant and useful features, blocks, is based on an idea originally developed for Lisp.

In **Chapter 9: Metaprogramming** tackles one of the most difficult topics for Ruby developers. By studying how Ruby implements metaprogramming internally, you'll learn how to use metaprogramming effectively.

Chapter 10: JRuby: Ruby on the JVM introduces JRuby, an alternative version of Ruby implemented with Java. You'll learn how JRuby uses the Java Virtual Machine (JVM) to run your Ruby programs faster.

Chapter 11: Rubinius: Ruby Implemented with Ruby looks at one of the most interesting and innovative implementations of Ruby: Rubinius. You'll learn how to locate—and modify—the Ruby code in Rubinius to see how a particular Ruby method works.

Chapter 12: Garbage Collection in MRI, JRuby, and Rubinius concludes with a look at garbage collection (GC), one of the most mysterious and confusing topics in computer science. You'll see how Rubinius and JRuby use very different GC algorithms from those used by MRI.

By studying all of these aspects of Ruby's internal implementation, you'll acquire a deeper understanding of what happens when you use Ruby's complex feature set. Just as Antonie van Leeuwenhoek first saw microbes and cells looking through early microscopes in the 1600s, by looking inside of Ruby you'll discover a wide array of interesting structures and algorithms. Join me on a fascinating behind-the-scenes look at what brings Ruby to life!

*Your code has a long
road to take before
Ruby ever runs it.*

1

TOKENIZATION AND PARSING

How many times do you think Ruby reads and transforms your code before running it? Once? Twice?

The correct answer is three times. Whenever you run a Ruby script—whether it's a large Rails application, a simple Sinatra website, or a background worker job—Ruby rips your code apart into small pieces and then puts them back together in a different format *three times*! Between the time you type *ruby* and the time you start to see actual output on the console, your Ruby code has a long road to take—a journey involving a variety of different technologies, techniques, and open source tools.

Figure 1-1 shows what this journey looks like at a high level.

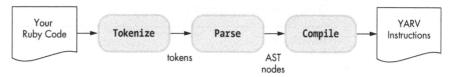

Figure 1-1: Your code's journey through Ruby

First, Ruby *tokenizes* your code, which means it reads the text characters in your code file and converts them into *tokens*, the words used in the Ruby language. Next, Ruby *parses* these tokens; that is, it groups the tokens into meaningful Ruby statements just as one might group words into sentences. Finally, Ruby compiles these statements into low-level instructions that it can execute later using a virtual machine.

I'll cover Ruby's virtual machine, called "Yet Another Ruby Virtual Machine" (YARV), in Chapter 3. But first, in this chapter, I'll describe the tokenizing and parsing processes that Ruby uses to understand your code. After that, in Chapter 2, I'll show you how Ruby compiles your code by translating it into a completely different language.

NOTE   *Throughout most of this book we'll learn about the original, standard implementation of Ruby, known as Matz's Ruby Interpreter (MRI) after Yukihiro Matsumoto, who invented Ruby in 1993. There are many other implementations of Ruby available in addition to MRI, including Ruby Enterprise Edition, MagLev, MacRuby, RubyMotion, mruby, and many, many others. Later, in Chapters 10, 11, and 12, we'll look at two of these alternative Ruby implementations: JRuby and Rubinius.*

Tokens: The Words That Make Up the Ruby Language

Suppose you write a simple Ruby program and save it in a file called *simple.rb*, shown in Listing 1-1.

```
10.times do |n|
  puts n
end
```

Listing 1-1: A very simple Ruby program (simple.rb)

Listing 1-2 shows the output you would see after executing the program from the command line.

```
$ ruby simple.rb
0
1
2
3
--snip--
```

Listing 1-2: Executing Listing 1-1

What happens after you type `ruby simple.rb` and press ENTER? Aside from general initialization, processing your command line parameters, and so on, the first thing Ruby does is open *simple.rb* and read in all the text from the code file. Next, it needs to make sense of this text: your Ruby code. How does it do this?

After reading in *simple.rb*, Ruby encounters the series of text characters shown in Figure 1-2. (To keep things simple, I'm showing only the first line of text here.)

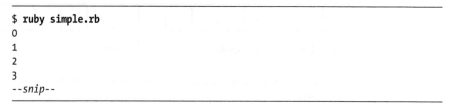

Figure 1-2: The first line of text in simple.rb

When Ruby sees these characters, it tokenizes them. That is, it converts them into a series of tokens or words that it understands by stepping through the characters one at a time. In Figure 1-3, Ruby starts scanning at the first character's position.

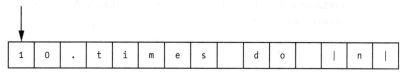

Figure 1-3: Ruby starts to tokenize your code.

The Ruby C source code contains a loop that reads in one character at a time and processes it based on what that character is.

To keep things simple, I'm describing tokenization as an independent process. In fact, the parsing engine I describe next calls this C tokenize code whenever it needs a new token. Tokenization and parsing are separate processes that actually occur at the same time. For now, let's just continue to see how Ruby tokenizes the characters in your Ruby file.

Ruby realizes that the character 1 is the start of a number and continues to iterate over the characters that follow until it finds a nonnumeric character. First, in Figure 1-4, it finds a 0.

Figure 1-4: Ruby steps to the second text character.

And stepping forward again, in Figure 1-5, Ruby finds a period character.

Figure 1-5: Ruby finds a period character.

Ruby actually considers the period character to be numeric because it might be part of a floating-point value. In Figure 1-6, Ruby steps to the next character, t.

Figure 1-6: Ruby finds the first nonnumeric character.

Now Ruby stops iterating because it has found a nonnumeric character. Because there are no more numeric characters after the period, Ruby considers the period to be part of a separate token, and it steps back one, as shown in Figure 1-7.

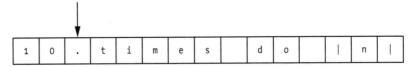

Figure 1-7: Ruby steps back one character.

Finally, in Figure 1-8, Ruby converts the numeric characters that it found into the first token from your program, called tINTEGER.

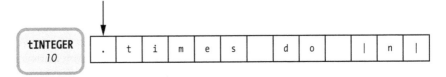

Figure 1-8: Ruby converts the first two text characters into a tINTEGER token.

Ruby continues to step through the characters in your code file, converting them into tokens and grouping characters as necessary. The second token, shown in Figure 1-9, is a single character: a period.

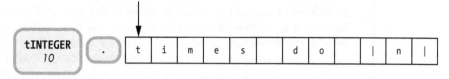

Figure 1-9: Ruby converts the period character into a token.

Next, in Figure 1-10, Ruby encounters the word *times* and creates an identifier token.

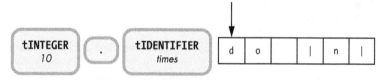

Figure 1-10: Ruby tokenizes the word times.

Identifiers are words in your Ruby code that are not reserved words. Identifiers usually refer to variable, method, or class names.

Next, Ruby sees *do* and creates a reserved word token, as indicated by keyword_do in Figure 1-11.

Figure 1-11: Ruby creates a reserved word token: keyword_do.

Reserved words are keywords that carry significant meaning in Ruby because they provide the structure, or framework, of the language. They are called *reserved words* because you can't use them as normal identifiers, although you can use them as method names, global variable names (such as $do), or instance variable names (for example, @do or @@do).

Internally, the Ruby C code maintains a constant table of reserved words. Listing 1-3 shows the first few, in alphabetical order.

```
alias
and
begin
break
case
class
```

Listing 1-3: The first few reserved words, listed alphabetically

THE PARSER_YYLEX FUNCTION

If you're familiar with C and are interested in learning more about the detailed way in which Ruby tokenizes your code file, see the *parse.y* file in your version of Ruby. The *.y* extension indicates that *parse.y* is a *grammar rule file*—one that contains a series of rules for the Ruby parser engine. (I'll discuss these in the next section.) *parse.y* is an extremely large and complex file with over 10,000 lines of code!

For now, ignore the grammar rules, and search for a C function called parser_yylex, about two-thirds of the way down the file, around line 6500. This complex C function contains the code that actually tokenizes your code. Look closely and you should see a very large switch statement that starts with the code shown in Listing 1-4.

```
❶ retry:
❷ last_state = lex_state;
❸ switch (c = nextc()) {
```

Listing 1-4: The C code inside Ruby that reads in each character from your code file

The nextc() function ❸ returns the next character in the code file text stream. Think of this function as the arrow in the previous diagrams. The lex_state variable ❷ keeps information about what state or type of code Ruby is processing at the moment.

The large switch statement inspects each character of your code file and takes a different action based on what it is. For example, the code shown in Listing 1-5 looks for whitespace characters and ignores them by jumping back up to the retry label ❶ just above the switch statement in Listing 1-4.

```
    /* white spaces */
case ' ': case '\t': case '\f': case '\r':
case '\13': /* '\v' */
  space_seen = 1;
--snip--
  goto retry;
```

Listing 1-5: This C code checks for whitespace characters in your code and ignores them.

Ruby's reserved words are defined in the file called *defs/keywords*. If you open this file, you'll see a complete list of all of Ruby's reserved words (see a partial list in Listing 1-3). The *keywords* file is used by an open source package called *gperf* to produce C code that can quickly and efficiently look up strings in a table—in this case, a table of reserved words. You can find the generated C code that looks up reserved words in *lex.c*, which defines a function named rb_reserved_word, called from *parse.y*.

One final detail about tokenization: Ruby doesn't use the Lex tokenization tool that C programmers commonly use in conjunction with a parser generator like Yacc or Bison. Instead, the Ruby core team wrote the Ruby tokenization code by hand for performance reasons.

Finally, as shown in Figure 1-12, Ruby converts the remaining characters to tokens.

Figure 1-12: Ruby finishes tokenizing the first line of text.

Ruby continues to step through your code until it has tokenized the entire Ruby script. At this point, it has processed your code for the first time, ripping it apart and putting it back together again in a completely different way. Your code began as a stream of text characters, and Ruby converted it to a stream of tokens, words that it will later combine into sentences.

Experiment 1-1: Using Ripper to Tokenize Different Ruby Scripts

Now that we've learned the basic idea behind tokenization, let's look at how Ruby actually tokenizes different Ruby scripts. After all, how else will you know that the previous explanation is actually correct?

As it turns out, a tool called *Ripper* makes it very easy to see what tokens Ruby creates for different code files. Shipped with Ruby 1.9 and Ruby 2.x, the Ripper class allows you to call the same tokenization and parsing code that Ruby uses to process text from code files. (Ripper is not available in Ruby 1.8.)

Listing 1-6 shows how simple using Ripper is.

```
require 'ripper'
require 'pp'
code = <<STR
10.times do |n|
  puts n
end
STR
puts code
❶ pp Ripper.lex(code)
```

Listing 1-6: An example of how to call `Ripper.lex` (lex1.rb)

After requiring the Ripper code from the standard library, you call it by passing some code as a string to the `Ripper.lex` method ❶. Listing 1-7 shows the output from Ripper.

```
$ ruby lex1.rb
10.times do |n|
  puts n
end
❶ [[[1, 0], :on_int, "10"],
```

```
   [[1, 2], :on_period, "."],
❷ [[1, 3], :on_ident, "times"],
   [[1, 8], :on_sp, " "],
   [[1, 9], :on_kw, "do"],
   [[1, 11], :on_sp, " "],
   [[1, 12], :on_op, "|"],
   [[1, 13], :on_ident, "n"],
   [[1, 14], :on_op, "|"],
   [[1, 15], :on_ignored_nl, "\n"],
   [[2, 0], :on_sp, "  "],
   [[2, 2], :on_ident, "puts"],
   [[2, 6], :on_sp, " "],
   [[2, 7], :on_ident, "n"],
   [[2, 8], :on_nl, "\n"],
   [[3, 0], :on_kw, "end"],
   [[3, 3], :on_nl, "\n"]]
```

Listing 1-7: The output generated by `Ripper.lex`

Each line corresponds to a single token that Ruby found in your code string. On the left, we have the line number (1, 2, or 3 in this short example) and the text column number. Next, we see the token itself displayed as a symbol, such as :on_int ❶ or :on_ident ❷. Finally, Ripper displays the text characters that correspond to each token.

The token symbols that Ripper displays are somewhat different from the token identifiers I used in Figures 1-2 through 1-12 that showed Ruby tokenizing the `10.times do` code. I used the same names you would find in Ruby's internal parse code, such as `tIDENTIFIER`, while Ripper used :on_ident instead.

Regardless, Ripper will still give you a sense of what tokens Ruby finds in your code and how tokenization works.

Listing 1-8 shows another example of using Ripper.

```
$ ruby lex2.rb
10.times do |n|
  puts n/4+6
end
--snip--
 [[2, 2], :on_ident, "puts"],
 [[2, 6], :on_sp, " "],
 [[2, 7], :on_ident, "n"],
 [[2, 8], :on_op, "/"],
 [[2, 9], :on_int, "4"],
 [[2, 10], :on_op, "+"],
 [[2, 11], :on_int, "6"],
 [[2, 12], :on_nl, "\n"],
--snip--
```

Listing 1-8: Another example of using `Ripper.lex`

This time Ruby converts the expression n/4+6 into a series of tokens in a very straightforward way. The tokens appear in exactly the same order they did inside the code file.

Listing 1-9 shows a third, slightly more complex example.

```
$ ruby lex3.rb
array = []
10.times do |n|
  array << n if n < 5
end
p array
--snip--
  [[3, 2], :on_ident, "array"],
  [[3, 7], :on_sp, " "],
❶ [[3, 8], :on_op, "<<"],
  [[3, 10], :on_sp, " "],
  [[3, 11], :on_ident, "n"],
  [[3, 12], :on_sp, " "],
  [[3, 13], :on_kw, "if"],
  [[3, 15], :on_sp, " "],
  [[3, 16], :on_ident, "n"],
  [[3, 17], :on_sp, " "],
❷ [[3, 18], :on_op, "<"],
  [[3, 19], :on_sp, " "],
  [[3, 20], :on_int, "5"],
--snip--
```

Listing 1-9: A third example of running Ripper.lex

As you can see, Ruby is smart enough to distinguish between << and < in the following line: array << n if n < 5. The characters << are converted to a single operator token ❶, while the single < character that appears later is converted into a simple less-than operator ❷. Ruby's tokenize code is smart enough to look ahead for a second < character when it finds one <.

Finally, notice that Ripper has no idea whether the code you give it is valid Ruby or not. If you pass in code that contains a syntax error, Ripper.lex will just tokenize it as usual and not complain. It's the parser's job to check syntax.

Suppose you forget the | symbol after the block parameter n ❶, as shown in Listing 1-10.

```
require 'ripper'
require 'pp'
code = <<STR
❶ 10.times do |n
  puts n
end
STR
puts code
pp Ripper.lex(code)
```

Listing 1-10: This code contains a syntax error.

Running this, you get the output shown in Listing 1-11.

```
$ ruby lex4.rb
10.times do |n
  puts n
end
--snip--
[[[1, 0], :on_int, "10"],
 [[1, 2], :on_period, "."],
 [[1, 3], :on_ident, "times"],
 [[1, 8], :on_sp, " "],
 [[1, 9], :on_kw, "do"],
 [[1, 11], :on_sp, " "],
 [[1, 12], :on_op, "|"],
 [[1, 13], :on_ident, "n"],
 [[1, 14], :on_nl, "\n"],
--snip--
```

Listing 1-11: Ripper does not detect syntax errors.

Parsing: How Ruby Understands Your Code

Once Ruby converts your code into a series of tokens, what does it do next? How does it actually understand and run your program? Does Ruby simply step through the tokens and execute each one in order?

No. Your code still has a long way to go before Ruby can run it. The next step on its journey through Ruby is called *parsing*, where words or tokens are grouped into sentences or phrases that make sense to Ruby. When parsing, Ruby takes into account the order of operations, methods, blocks, and other larger code structures.

But how can Ruby actually understand what you're telling it with your code? Like many programming languages, Ruby uses a *parser generator*. Ruby uses a parser to process tokens, but the parser itself is generated with a parser generator. Parser generators take a series of grammar rules as input that describe the expected order and patterns in which the tokens will appear.

The most widely used and well-known parser generator is Yacc (Yet Another Compiler Compiler), but Ruby uses a newer version of Yacc called *Bison*. The grammar rule file for Bison and Yacc has a *.y* extension. In the Ruby source code, the grammar rule file is *parse.y* (introduced earlier). The *parse.y* file defines the actual syntax and grammar that you have to use while writing your Ruby code; it's really the heart and soul of Ruby and where the language itself is actually defined!

Ruby uses an LALR parser generator called Bison.

Ruby uses Bison when building Ruby itself, and not to directly process tokens. In effect, there are two separate steps to the parsing process, shown in Figure 1-13.

Before you run your Ruby program, the Ruby build process uses Bison to generate the parser code (*parse.c*) from the grammar rule file (*parse.y*). Later, at run time, this generated parser code parses the tokens returned by Ruby's tokenizer code.

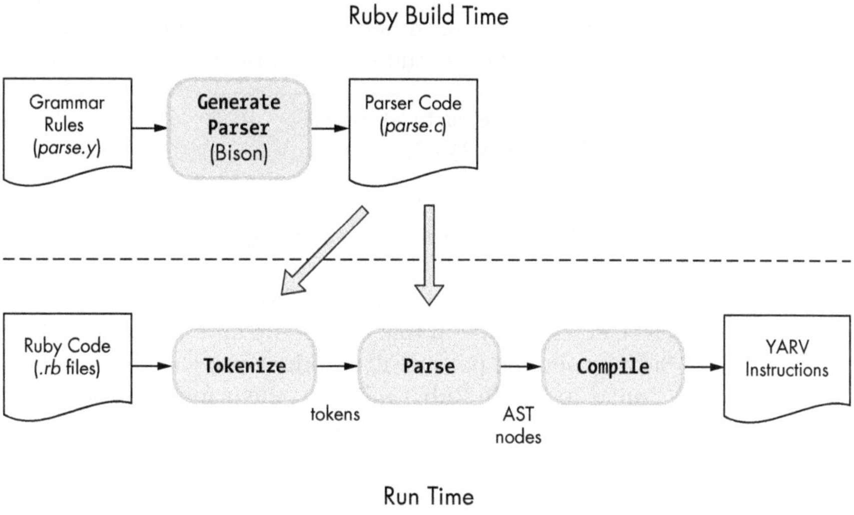

Ruby Build Time

Figure 1-13: The Ruby build process runs Bison ahead of time.

Because the *parse.y* file and the generated *parse.c* file also contain the tokenization code, Figure 1-13 has a diagonal arrow from *parse.c* to the tokenize process on the lower left. (In fact, the parse engine I'm about to describe calls the tokenization code whenever it needs a new token.) The tokenization and parsing processes actually occur simultaneously.

Understanding the LALR Parse Algorithm

How does the parser code analyze and process the incoming tokens? With an algorithm known as *LALR*, or *Look-Ahead Left Reversed Rightmost Derivation*. Using the LALR algorithm, the parser code processes the token stream from left to right, trying to match their order and the pattern in which they appear against one or more of the grammar rules from *parse.y*. The parser code also "looks ahead" when necessary to decide which grammar rule to match.

The best way to become familiar with the way Ruby grammar rules work is with an example. To keep things simple for now, we'll look at an abstract example. Later on, I'll show that Ruby actually works in precisely the same way when it parses your code.

Suppose you want to translate from the Spanish:

Me gusta el Ruby.   [Phrase 1]

to the English:

I like Ruby.

And suppose that to translate Phrase 1, you use Bison to generate a C language parser from a grammar file. Using the Bison/Yacc grammar rule syntax, you can write the simple grammar shown in Listing 1-12, with the rule name on the left and the matching tokens on the right.

```
SpanishPhrase : me gusta el ruby {
  printf("I like Ruby\n");
}
```

Listing 1-12: A simple grammar rule matching the Spanish Phrase 1

This grammar rule says the following: If the token stream is equal to me, gusta, el, and ruby—in that order—we have a match. If there's a match, the Bison generated parser will run the given C code, and the printf statement (similar to puts in Ruby) will print the translated English phrase.

Figure 1-14 shows the parsing process in action.

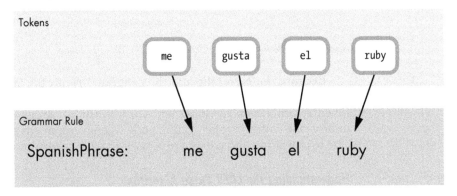

Figure 1-14: Matching tokens with a grammar rule

There are four input tokens at the top, and the grammar rule is underneath. It should be clear that there's a match because each input token corresponds directly to one of the terms on the right side of the grammar rule. We have a match on the SpanishPhrase rule.

Now let's improve on this example. Suppose you need to enhance your parser to match Phrase 1 and Phrase 2:

Me gusta el Ruby.   [Phrase 1]

and:

Le gusta el Ruby.   [Phrase 2]

In English, Phrase 2 means "She/He/It likes Ruby."

The modified grammar file in Listing 1-13 can parse both Spanish phrases.

```
SpanishPhrase: VerbAndObject el ruby {
  printf("%s Ruby\n", $1);
};
VerbAndObject: SheLikes | ILike {
  $$ = $1;
};
SheLikes: le gusta {
  $$ = "She likes";
}
ILike: me gusta {
  $$ = "I like";
}
```

Listing 1-13: These grammar rules match both Phrase 1 and Phrase 2.

As you can see, there are four grammar rules here instead of just one. Also, you're using the Bison directive $$ to return a value from a child grammar rule to a parent and $1 to refer to a child's value from a parent.

Unlike with Phrase 1, the parser can't immediately match Phrase 2 with any of the grammar rules.

In Figure 1-15, we can see the el and ruby tokens match the SpanishPhrase rule, but le and gusta do not. (Ultimately, we'll see that the child rule VerbAndObject does match le gusta, but never mind that for now.) With four grammar rules, how does the parser know which other rules to try to match against? And against which tokens?

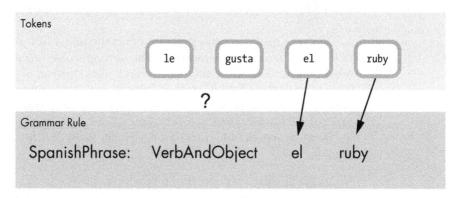

Figure 1-15: The first two tokens don't match.

This is where the intelligence of the LALR parser comes in. As I mentioned earlier, the acronym LALR stands for *Look-Ahead LR* parser, and it describes the algorithm the parser uses to find matching grammar rules. We'll get to the *look ahead* part in a minute. For now, let's start with **LR**:

- **L** (left) means the parser moves from left to right while processing the token stream. In this example, that would be le, gusta, el, and ruby, in that order.
- **R** (reversed rightmost derivation) means the parser takes a bottom-up strategy, using a shift/reduce technique, to find matching grammar rules.

Here's how the algorithm works for Phrase 2. First, the parser takes the input token stream, shown again in Figure 1-16.

Figure 1-16: The input stream of tokens

Next, it shifts the tokens to the left, creating what I'll call the *grammar rule stack*, as shown Figure 1-17.

Figure 1-17: The parser moves the first token onto the grammar rule stack.

Because the parser has processed only the token le, it places this token in the stack alone for the moment. The term *grammar rule stack* is a bit of an oversimplification; while the parser uses a stack, instead of grammar rules, it pushes numbers onto its stack to indicate which grammar rule it has just parsed. These numbers, or *states*, help the parser keep track of which grammar rules it has matched as it processes tokens.

Next, as shown in Figure 1-18, the parser shifts another token to the left.

Figure 1-18: The parser moves another token onto the stack.

Now there are two tokens in the stack on the left. At this point, the parser stops to search the different grammar rules for a match. Figure 1-19 shows the parser matching the SheLikes rule.

Figure 1-19: The parser matches the SheLikes rule and reduces.

This operation is called *reduce* because the parser is replacing the pair of tokens with a single matching rule. The parser looks through the available rules and reduces, or applies the single matching rule.

Now the parser can reduce again because there's another matching rule: VerbAndObject! The VerbAndObject rule matches because its use of the OR (|) operator matches *either* the SheLikes *or* ILike child rules.

You can see in Figure 1-20 that the parser replaces SheLikes with VerbAndObject.

Figure 1-20: The parser reduces again, matching the VerbAndObject rule.

But think about this: How did the parser know to reduce and not continue to shift tokens? Also, if in the real world there are actually many matching rules, how does the parser know which one to use? How does it decide whether to shift or reduce? And if it reduces, how does it decide which grammar rule to reduce with?

In other words, suppose at this point in the process multiple matching rules included le gusta. How would the parser know which rule to apply or whether to shift in the el token first before looking for a match? (See Figure 1-21.)

Figure 1-21: How does the parser know to shift or reduce?

Here's where the *look ahead* portion of LALR comes in. In order to find the correct matching rule, the parser looks ahead at the next token. The arrow in Figure 1-22 shows the parser looking ahead at the el token.

Figure 1-22: Looking ahead at the next token in the input stream

Additionally, the parser maintains a state table of possible outcomes depending on what the next token is and which grammar rule was just parsed. In this case, the table would contain a series of states, describing which grammar rules have been parsed so far and which states to move to next depending on the next token. (LALR parsers are complex state machines that match patterns in the token stream. When you use Bison to generate the LALR parser, Bison calculates what this state table should contain based on the grammar rules you provided.)

In this example, the state table would contain an entry indicating that if the next token was el, the parser should first reduce using the SheLikes rule before shifting a new token.

Rather than waste your time with the details of what a state table looks like (you'll find the actual LALR state table for Ruby in the generated *parse.c* file), let's continue the shift/reduce operations for Phrase 2, "Le gusta el Ruby." After matching the VerbAndObject rule, the parser would shift another token to the left, as shown in Figure 1-23.

Figure 1-23: The parser shifts another token onto the stack.

At this point, no rules would match, and the state machine would shift another token to the left (see Figure 1-24).

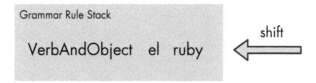

Figure 1-24: The parser shifts another token onto the stack.

Figure 1-25 shows how the parent grammar rule `SpanishPhrase` would match after a final reduce operation.

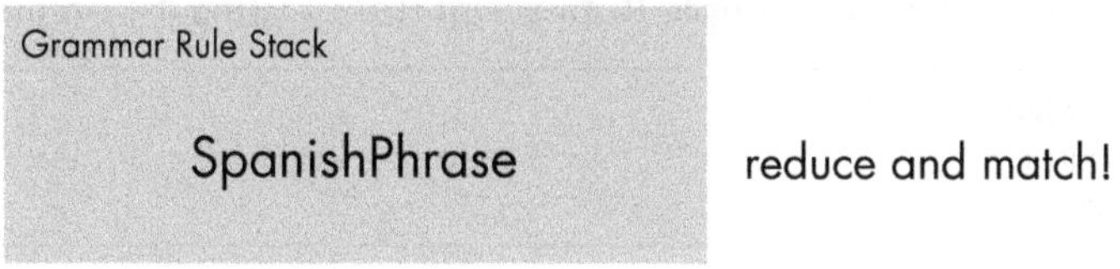

Grammar Rule Stack

SpanishPhrase   reduce and match!

Figure 1-25: The parser matches the `SpanishPhrase` rule—and the entire input stream!

I've shown you this Spanish-to-English example because Ruby parses your program in exactly the same way! Inside the Ruby *parse.y* source code file, you'll see hundreds of rules that define the structure and syntax of the Ruby language. There are parent and child rules, and the child rules return values the parent rules can refer to in exactly the same way our `SpanishPhrase` grammar rules do, using the symbols $$, $1, $2, and so on. The only real difference is scale: Our `SpanishPhrase` grammar example is trivial, really. In contrast, Ruby's grammar is very complex; it's an intricate series of interrelated parent and child grammar rules, which sometimes refer to each other in circular, recursive patterns. But this complexity just means that the generated state table in *parse.c* is quite large. The basic LALR algorithm, which describes how the parser processes tokens and uses the state table, is the same in our Spanish example as it is in Ruby.

To get a sense of just how complex the state table is for Ruby, you can try using Ruby's -y option, which displays internal debug information every time the parser jumps from one state to another. Listing 1-14 shows a small portion of the output generated when you run the `10.times` do example from Listing 1-1.

```
$ ruby -y simple.rb
Starting parse
Entering state 0
Reducing stack by rule 1 (line 850):
-> $$ = nterm @1 ()
Stack now 0
Entering state 2
Reading a token: Next token is token tINTEGER ()
Shifting token tINTEGER ()
Entering state 41
Reducing stack by rule 498 (line 4293):
   $1 = token tINTEGER ()
-> $$ = nterm numeric ()
Stack now 0 2
Entering state 109
--snip--
```

Listing 1-14: Ruby optionally displays debug information, showing how the parser jumps from one state to another.

Some Actual Ruby Grammar Rules

Let's look at some actual Ruby grammar rules from *parse.y*. Listing 1-15 contains the simple example Ruby script from Listing 1-1 on page 4.

```
10.times do |n|
  puts n
end
```

Listing 1-15: The simple Ruby program from Listing 1-1.

Figure 1-26 shows how Ruby's parsing process works with this script.

Ruby Code	Grammar Rules
10.times do |n| puts n end	program: top_compstmt top_compstmt: top_stmts opt_terms top_stmts: ... | top_stmt | ... top_stmt: stmt | ... stmt: ... | expr expr: ... | arg arg: ... | primary primary: ... | method_call brace_block | ...

Figure 1-26: The grammar rules on the right match the Ruby code on the left.

On the left is the code that Ruby is trying to parse. On the right are the actual matching grammar rules from the Ruby *parse.y* file, shown simplified. The first rule, program: top_compstmt, is the root grammar rule that matches every Ruby program in its entirety.

As you go down the list, you see a complex series of child rules that also match the entire Ruby script: top statements, a single statement, an expression, an argument, and, finally, a primary value. Once Ruby's parse reaches the primary grammar rule, it encounters a rule with two matching child rules: method_call and brace_block. Let's look at method_call first (see Figure 1-27).

Ruby Code	Grammar Rules
10.times	method_call: ... | primary_value '.' operation2 | ...

Figure 1-27: 10.times matches the method_call grammar rule.

The method_call rule matches the 10.times portion of the Ruby code—that is, where we call the times method on the 10 Fixnum object. You can see that the `method_call` rule matches another primary value, followed by a period character, followed by an `operation2` rule.

Figure 1-28 shows that the `primary_value` rule first matches the value 10.

Ruby Code	Grammar Rules
10	`primary_value: primary` `primary: literal	...`

Figure 1-28: The value 10 matches the primary_value grammar rule.

Then, in Figure 1-29, the `operation2` rule matches the method name times.

Ruby Code	Grammar Rules
times	`operation2: identifier	...`

Figure 1-29: The times method name matches the operation2 grammar rule.

How does Ruby parse the contents of the `do` ... `puts` ... `end` block that's passed to the times method? It uses the `brace_block` rule we saw in Figure 1-26. Figure 1-30 shows the definition of the `brace_block` rule.

Ruby Code	Grammar Rules
do |n| puts n end	`brace_block: ...	keyword_do opt_block_param compstmt keyword_end	...`

Figure 1-30: The entire block matches the brace_block rule.

I don't have space here to go through all the remaining child grammar rules, but you can see how this rule, in turn, contains a series of other matching child rules:

- `keyword_do` matches the do reserved keyword.
- `opt_block_param` matches the block parameter |n|.
- `compstmt` matches the contents of the block itself, puts n.
- `keyword_end` matches the end reserved keyword.

READING A BISON GRAMMAR RULE

To give you a taste of the actual Ruby *parse.y* source code, take a look at Listing 1-16, which shows part of the method_call ❶ grammar rule definition.

```
❶ method_call        :
  --snip--
        primary_value '.' operation2
        {
        /*%%%*/
            $<num>$ = ruby_sourceline;
        /*% %*/
        }
      opt_paren_args
        {
        /*%%%*/
            $$ = NEW_CALL($1, $3, $5);
            nd_set_line($$, $<num>4);
        /*%
            $$ = dispatch3(call, $1, ripper_id2sym('.'), $3);
            $$ = method_optarg($$, $5);
        %*/
        }
```

Listing 1-16: Ruby's actual method_call grammar rule from parse.y

As with the preceding Spanish-to-English example grammar file, you can see that there are snippets of complex C code after each of the terms in the grammar rule. Listing 1-17 shows one example of this.

```
        $$ = NEW_CALL($1, $3, $5);
        nd_set_line($$, $<num>4);
```

Listing 1-17: Ruby calls this C code when the opt_paren_args *grammar rule matches.*

The Bison-generated parser will execute one of these snippets when there's a match for a rule on the tokens found in the target Ruby script. However, these C code snippets also contain Bison directives, such as $$ and $1, that allow the code to create return values and to refer to values returned by other grammar rules. We end up with a confusing mix of C and Bison directives.

To make things worse, Ruby uses a trick during its build process to divide these C/Bison code snippets into separate pieces. Some of these pieces are used by Ruby, while others are used only by the Ripper tool from Experiment 1-1. Here's how that trick works:

- The C code that appears between the /*%%%*/ line and the /*% line in Listing 1-16 is actually compiled into Ruby during the Ruby build process.
- The C code between /*% and %*/ in Listing 1-16 is dropped when Ruby is built. This code is used only by the Ripper tool, which is built separately during the Ruby build process.

Ruby uses this very confusing syntax to allow the Ripper tool and Ruby itself to share the same grammar rules inside *parse.y*.

What are these snippets actually doing? As you might guess, Ruby uses the Ripper code snippets to allow the Ripper tool to display information about what Ruby is parsing. (We'll try that next, in Experiment 1-2.) There's also some bookkeeping code: Ruby uses the ruby_sourceline variable to keep track of which source code line corresponds to each portion of the grammar.

But more importantly, the snippets Ruby actually uses at run time when parsing your code create a series of *nodes*, or temporary data structures, that form an internal representation of your Ruby code. These nodes are saved in a tree structure called an *abstract syntax tree (AST)* (more about this in Experiment 1-2). You can see one example of creating an AST node in Listing 1-17, where Ruby calls the NEW_CALL C macro/function. This call creates a new NODE_CALL node, which represents a method call. (In Chapter 2 we'll see how Ruby eventually compiles this into bytecode that can be executed by a virtual machine.)

Experiment 1-2: Using Ripper to Parse Different Ruby Scripts

In Experiment 1-1, you learned how to use Ripper to display the tokens that Ruby converts your code into, and we've just seen how the Ruby grammar rules in *parse.y* are also included in the Ripper tool. Now let's learn how to use Ripper to display information about how Ruby parses your code. Listing 1-18 shows how to do it.

```
require 'ripper'
require 'pp'
code = <<STR
10.times do |n|
  puts n
end
STR
puts code
❶ pp Ripper.sexp(code)
```

Listing 1-18: An example of how to call Ripper.sexp

This is exactly the same code from Experiment 1-1, except that we call Ripper.sexp ❶ instead of Ripper.lex. Running this gives the output shown in Listing 1-19.

```
[:program,
  [[:method_add_block,
    [:call,
      [:@int, "10", [1, 0]], :".",
      [:@ident, "times", [1, 3]]],
```

```
[:do_block,
  [:block_var,
    [:params, [[:@ident, "n", [1, 13]]],
              nil, nil, nil, nil, nil, nil],
    false],
  [[:command,
    [:@ident, "puts", [2, 2]],
    [:args_add_block, [[:var_ref, [:@ident, "n", [2, 7]]]],
                      false]]]]]]
```

Listing 1-19: The output generated by `Ripper.sexp`

You can see some bits and pieces from the Ruby script in this cryptic text, but what do all of the other symbols and arrays mean?

It turns out that the output from Ripper is a textual representation of your Ruby code. As Ruby parses your code, matching one grammar rule after another, it converts the tokens in your code file into a complex internal data structure called an *abstract syntax tree (AST)*. (You can see some of the C code that produces this structure in "Reading a Bison Grammar Rule" on page 22.) The AST is used to record the structure and syntactical meaning of your Ruby code.

To see what I mean, look at Figure 1-31, which shows a graphical view of part of the output that Ripper generated for us: the `puts n` statement inside the block.

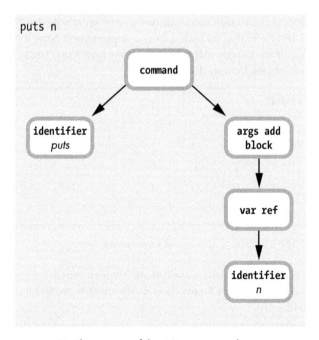

Figure 1-31: The portion of the AST corresponding to puts n

This diagram corresponds to the last three lines of the Ripper output, repeated here in Listing 1-20.

```
[[:command,
❶   [:@ident, "puts", [2, 2]],
    [:args_add_block, [[:var_ref, [:@ident, "n", [2, 7]]]],
                      false]]]
```

Listing 1-20: The last three lines of the Ripper.sexp output

As in Experiment 1-1, when we displayed token information from Ripper, you can see that the source code file line and column information are displayed as integers. For example, [2, 2] ❶ indicates that Ripper found the puts call on line 2 at column 2 of the code file. You can also see that Ripper outputs an array for each of the nodes in the AST—with [:@ident, "puts", [2, 2]] ❶, for example.

Now your Ruby program is beginning to "make sense" to Ruby. Instead of a simple stream of tokens, which could mean anything, Ruby now has a detailed description of what you meant when you wrote puts n. You see a function call (a command), followed by an identifier node that indicates which function to call.

Ruby uses the args_add_block node because you could pass a block to a command/function call like this. Even though you're not passing a block in this case, the args_add_block node is still saved into the AST. (Notice, too, how the n identifier is recorded as a :var_ref, or variable reference node, not as a simple identifier.)

Figure 1-32 represents more of the Ripper output.

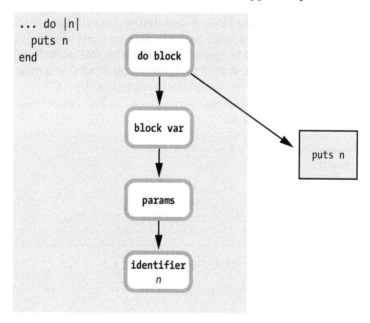

Figure 1-32: The portion of the AST corresponding to the entire block

You can see that Ruby now understands that do |n| ... end is a block, with a single block parameter called n. The puts n box on the right represents the other part of the AST shown earlier—the parsed version of the puts call.

Finally, Figure 1-33 shows the entire AST for the sample Ruby code.

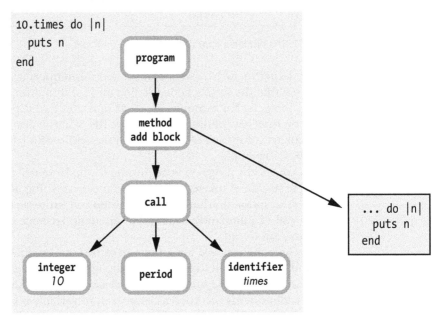

Figure 1-33: The AST for the entire Ruby program

Here, method add block means that you're calling a method, but with a block parameter: 10.times do. The call tree node obviously represents the actual method call 10.times. This is the NODE_CALL node that we saw earlier in the C code snippet. Ruby's understanding of what you meant with your code is saved in the way the nodes are arranged in the AST.

To clarify things, suppose you pass the Ruby expression 2 + 2 to Ripper, as shown in Listing 1-21.

```
require 'ripper'
require 'pp'
code = <<STR
2 + 2
STR
puts code
pp Ripper.sexp(code)
```

Listing 1-21: This code will display the AST for 2 + 2.

Running this code gives the output in Listing 1-22.

```
[:program,
 [[:binary,
    [:@int, "2", [1, 0]],
    :+,
    [:@int, "2", [1, 4]]]]]
```

Listing 1-22: The output of `Ripper.sexp` for 2 + 2

As you can see in Figure 1-34 below, the + is represented with an AST node called binary.

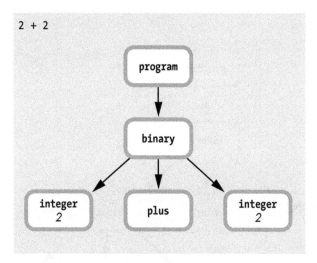

Figure 1-34: The AST for 2 + 2

But see what happens when I pass the expression 2 + 2 * 3 into Ripper, as in Listing 1-23.

```
require 'ripper'
require 'pp'
code = <<STR
2 + 2 * 3
STR
puts code
pp Ripper.sexp(code)
```

*Listing 1-23: Code to display the AST for 2 + 2 * 3*

Listing 1-24 shows that you get a second binary node for the * operator at ❶.

```
[:program,
 [[:binary,
   [:@int, "2", [1, 0]],
   :+,
❶  [:binary,
    [:@int, "2", [1, 4]],
    :*,
    [:@int, "3", [1, 8]]]]]]
```

Listing 1-24: The output of Ripper.sexp for 2 + 2 * 3

Figure 1-35 shows what that looks like.

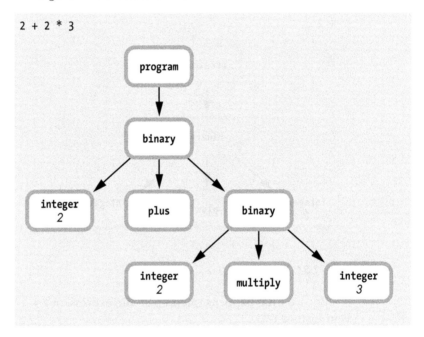

Figure 1-35: The AST for 2 + 2 * 3

Ruby was smart enough to realize that multiplication has a higher precedence than addition, but what's really interesting is how the AST tree structure captures the information about the order of operations. The token stream 2 + 2 * 3 simply indicates what you wrote in your code file. But the parsed version that's saved to the AST structure now contains the *meaning* of your code—that is, all of the information Ruby will need later to execute it.

One final note: Ruby actually contains some debug code that can display information about the AST node structure. To use it, run your Ruby script with the parsetree option (see Listing 1-25).

```
$ ruby --dump parsetree your_script.rb
```

Listing 1-25: Display debug information about your code's AST using the parsetree option.

This will display the same information we've just seen, but instead of showing symbols, the parsetree option should show the actual node names from the C source code. (In Chapter 2, I'll also use the actual node names.)

Summary

In Chapter 1, we looked at one of the most fascinating areas of computer science: how Ruby can *understand* the text that you give it—your Ruby program. In order to do this, Ruby converts your code into two different formats. First, it converts the text in your Ruby program into a series of *tokens*. Next, it uses an LALR parser to convert the input stream of tokens into a data structure called an *abstract syntax tree*.

In Chapter 2, we'll see that Ruby converts your code into a third format: a series of *bytecode instructions* that are later used when your program is actually executed.

The code Ruby actually runs looks nothing like your original code.

2

COMPILATION

Now that Ruby has tokenized and parsed your code, is it ready to run it? Will it finally get to work and iterate through the block 10 times in my simple `10.times do` example? If not, what else could Ruby possibly have to do first?

Starting with version 1.9, Ruby compiles your code before executing it. The word *compile* means to translate your code from one programming language to another. Your programming language is easy for you to understand, while usually the target language is easy for the computer to understand.

For example, when you compile a C program, the compiler translates C code to machine language, a language your computer's microprocessor hardware understands. When you compile a Java program, the compiler translates Java code to Java bytecode, a language the Java Virtual Machine understands.

Ruby's compiler is no different. It translates your Ruby code into another language that Ruby's virtual machine understands. The only difference is that you don't use Ruby's compiler directly; unlike in C or Java,

Ruby's compiler runs automatically without you ever knowing. Here in Chapter 2, I'll explain how Ruby does this and what language it translates your code into.

No Compiler for Ruby 1.8

The Ruby core team introduced a compiler with version 1.9. Ruby 1.8 and earlier versions of Ruby don't contain a compiler. Instead, Ruby 1.8 immediately executes your code after the tokenizing and parsing processes are finished. It does this by walking through the nodes in the AST tree and executing each one. Figure 2-1 shows another way of looking at the Ruby 1.8 tokenizing and parsing processes.

The top of Figure 2-1 shows your Ruby code. Below this are the different internal formats Ruby converts your Ruby code into. These are the tokens and AST nodes we saw in Chapter 1—the different

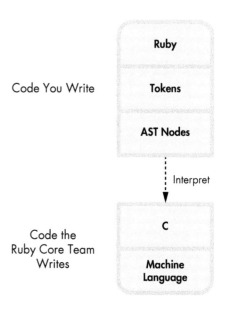

Figure 2-1: In Ruby 1.8, your code is converted into AST nodes and then interpreted.

forms your code takes when you run it using Ruby. The lower section of the diagram shows the code the Ruby core team wrote: the C source code for the Ruby language and the machine language it is converted into by the C compiler.

The dotted line between the two code sections indicates that Ruby interprets your code. The Ruby C code, the lower section, reads and executes your code, the top section. Ruby 1.8 doesn't compile or translate your code into any form beyond AST nodes. After converting it into AST nodes, it proceeds to iterate over the nodes in the AST, taking whatever action each node represents as it executes each node.

The gap in the middle of the diagram shows that your code is never completely compiled into machine language. If you were to disassemble and inspect the machine language that your CPU actually runs, you would not see instructions that directly map to your original Ruby code. Instead, you would find instructions that tokenize, parse, and execute your code, or, in other words, that implement the Ruby interpreter.

Ruby 1.9 and 2.0 Introduce a Compiler

If you've upgraded to Ruby 1.9 or 2.0, Ruby is still not quite ready to run your code. It needs to compile it first.

With Ruby 1.9, Koichi Sasada and the Ruby core team introduced Yet Another Ruby Virtual Machine (YARV), which actually executes your Ruby code. At a high level, this is the same idea behind the Java Virtual Machine (JVM) used by Java and many other languages. (I'll cover YARV in more detail in Chapters 3 and 4.)

When using YARV (as with the JVM), you first compile your code into *bytecode*, a series of low-level instructions that the virtual machine understands. The only differences between YARV and the JVM are the following:

- Ruby doesn't expose the compiler to you as a separate tool. Instead, it automatically compiles your Ruby code into bytecode instructions internally.
- Ruby never compiles your Ruby code all the way to machine language. As you can see in Figure 2-2, Ruby interprets the bytecode instructions. The JVM, on the other hand, can compile some of the bytecode instructions all the way into machine language using its "hotspot" or just-in-time (JIT) compiler.

Figure 2-2 shows how Ruby 1.9 and 2.0 handle your code.

Notice that this time, unlike in the process shown in Figure 2-1, your code is translated into a third format. After parsing the tokens and producing the AST, Ruby 1.9 and 2.0 continue to compile your code into a series of low-level instructions called *YARV instructions.*

The primary reason for using YARV is speed: Ruby 1.9 and 2.0 run much faster than Ruby 1.8 due to the use of YARV instructions. Like Ruby 1.8, YARV is an interpreter—just a faster one. Your Ruby code ultimately is still not converted directly into machine language by Ruby 1.9 or 2.0. There is still a gap in Figure 2-2 between the YARV instructions and Ruby's C code.

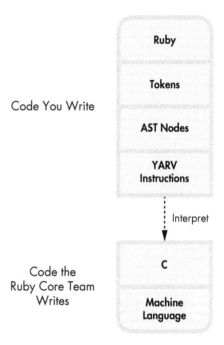

Figure 2-2: Ruby 1.9 and 2.0 compile the AST nodes into YARV instructions before interpreting them.

How Ruby Compiles a Simple Script

In this section, we'll look at the last step along your code's journey through Ruby: how Ruby compiles your code into the instructions that YARV expects. Let's explore how Ruby's compiler works by stepping through an example compilation. Listing 2-1 shows a simple Ruby script that calculates 2 + 2 = 4.

```
puts 2+2
```

Listing 2-1: A one-line Ruby program we will compile as an example

Figure 2-3 shows the AST structure that Ruby will create after tokenizing and parsing this simple program. (This is a more detailed view of the AST than you would get from the Ripper tool that we saw in Experiment 1-2 on page 23.)

NOTE   *The technical names shown in Figure 2-3 (NODE_SCOPE, NODE_FCALL, and so on) are taken from the actual Ruby C source code. To keep things simple, I'm omitting some AST nodes—specifically, ones that represent arrays of the arguments to each method call, which in this simple example would be arrays of only one element.*

puts 2+2

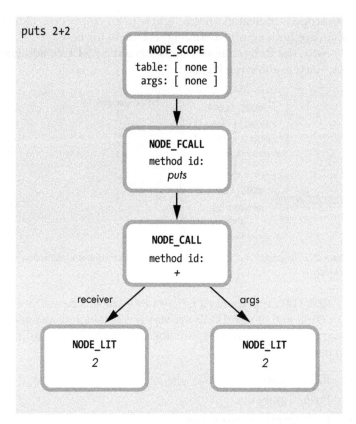

Figure 2-3: The AST Ruby produces after parsing the code in Listing 2-1

Before we cover the details of how Ruby compiles the puts 2+2 script, let's look at one very important attribute of YARV: It's a *stack-oriented virtual machine.* That means when YARV executes your code, it maintains a stack of values—mainly arguments and return values for the YARV instructions. (I'll explain this in more detail in Chapter 3.) Most of YARV's instructions either push values onto the stack or operate on the values that they find on the stack, leaving a result value on the stack as well.

In order to compile the puts 2+2 AST structure into YARV instructions, Ruby will iterate over the tree recursively from the top down, converting each AST node into instructions. Figure 2-4 shows how this works, beginning with NODE_SCOPE.

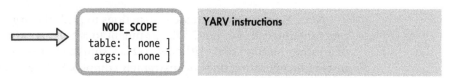

Figure 2-4: Ruby starts the compile process at the root of the AST.

NODE_SCOPE tells the Ruby compiler that it is starting to compile a new *scope,* or section of Ruby code, which, in this case, is a whole new program.

This scope is indicated on the right with an empty box. (The table and args values are both empty, so we'll ignore them for now.)

Next, the Ruby compiler steps down the AST tree and encounters NODE_FCALL, as shown in Figure 2-5.

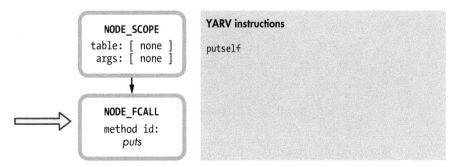

Figure 2-5: To compile a function call, Ruby first creates an instruction to push the receiver.

NODE_FCALL represents a *function call*—in this case, the call to puts. (Function and method calls are very important and very common in Ruby programs.) Ruby compiles function calls for YARV according to the following pattern:

- Push receiver.
- Push arguments.
- Call the method/function.

In Figure 2-5, the Ruby compiler first creates a YARV instruction called putself to indicate that the function call uses the current value of the self pointer as the receiver. Because I call puts from the top-level scope—that is, the top section—of this simple script, self is set to point to the top self object. (The top self object is an instance of the Object class that is automatically created when Ruby starts up. One purpose of top self is to serve as the receiver for function calls like this one in the top-level scope.)

Next, Ruby needs to create instructions to push the arguments of the puts function call. But how? The argument to puts is 2+2, which is the result of another method call. Although 2+2 is a simple expression, puts could instead be operating on some extremely complex Ruby expression involving many operators, method calls, and so on. How can Ruby know which instructions to create here?

The answer lies in the structure of the AST. By simply following the tree nodes down recursively, Ruby can take advantage of all the parser's earlier work. In this case, it can now just step down to the NODE_CALL node, as shown in Figure 2-6.

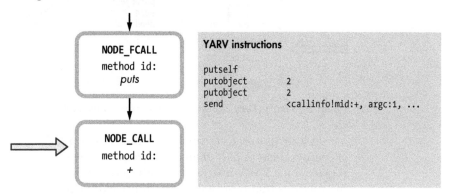

Figure 2-6: Next, Ruby writes instructions for calculating 2+2, the argument to puts.

Here Ruby will compile the + method call, which theoretically is the process of sending the + message to the 2 integer object. Again, following the same receiver, arguments, method call pattern, Ruby performs these actions in order:

1. Creates a YARV instruction to push the receiver onto the stack (the object 2 in this case).

2. Creates a YARV instruction to push the argument or arguments onto the stack (again, 2 in this example).

3. Creates a method call YARV instruction send <callinfo!mid:+, argc:1, ARGS_SKIP> that means "send the + message" to the receiver, which is the object previously pushed onto the YARV stack (in this case, the first Fixnum 2 object). mid:+ means "method id = +" and is the name of the method we want to call. The argc:1 parameter tells YARV there is one argument to this method call (the second Fixnum 2 object). ARGS_SKIP indicates the arguments are simple values (not blocks or arrays of unnamed arguments), allowing YARV to skip some work it would have to do otherwise.

When Ruby executes the send <callinfo!mid:+... instruction it adds 2+2, fetching those arguments from the stack, and leaves the result, 4, as a new value on top of the stack. What's fascinating about this is that YARV's stack-oriented nature also helps Ruby compile the AST nodes more easily, as you can see when it finishes compiling the NODE_FCALL, as shown in Figure 2-7.

Now Ruby can assume that the return value of the 2+2 operation—that is, 4—will be left at the top of the stack, just where it needs to be as the argument to the puts function call. Ruby's stack-oriented virtual machine goes hand in hand with the way that it recursively compiles the AST nodes! As you can see at the right of Figure 2-7, Ruby has added the send <callinfo!mid:puts, argc:1 instruction, which calls puts and indicates that there is one argument to puts.

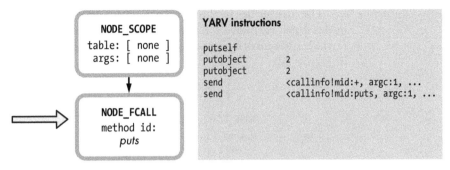

Figure 2-7: Finally, Ruby can write an instruction for the call to puts.

As it turns out, Ruby further modifies these YARV instructions before executing them as part of an optimize step. One of its optimizations is to replace some YARV instructions with *specialized instructions*, which are YARV instructions that represent commonly used, primitive operations, such as size, not, less than, greater than, and so on. One such instruction, opt_plus, is used for adding two numbers together. During optimization, Ruby replaces send <callinfo!mid:+... with opt_plus, as shown in Figure 2-8.

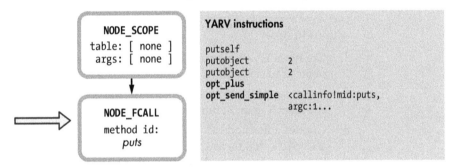

Figure 2-8: Ruby replaces some instructions with specialized instructions.

As you can see in Figure 2-8, Ruby also replaces the second send with opt_send_simple, which runs a bit faster when none of the arguments needs special treatment, such as expansion.

Compiling a Call to a Block

Next, let's compile my 10.times do example from Listing 1-1 in Chapter 1 (see Listing 2-2).

```
10.times do |n|
  puts n
end
```

Listing 2-2: A simple script that calls a block

Notice that this example contains a block parameter to the `times` method. This is interesting because it will give us a chance to see how the Ruby compiler handles blocks. Figure 2-9 shows the AST for the `10.times do` example again, using the actual node names rather than the simplified output from Ripper.

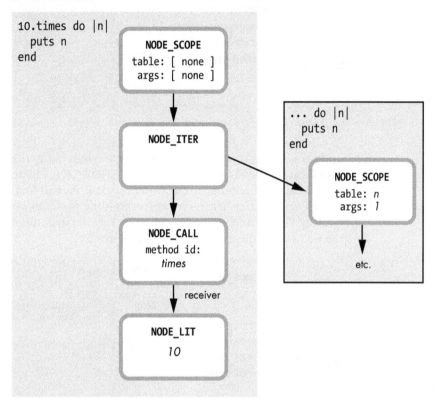

Figure 2-9: The AST for the call to `10.times`, passing a block

This looks very different than `puts 2+2`, mostly because of the inner block shown at the right. (Ruby handles the inner block differently, as we'll see shortly.)

Let's break down how Ruby compiles the main portion of the script shown on the left of Figure 2-9. As before, Ruby starts with the first `NODE_SCOPE` and creates a new snippet of YARV instructions, as shown in Figure 2-10.

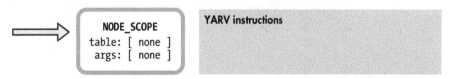

Figure 2-10: Each `NODE_SCOPE` is compiled into a new snippet of YARV instructions.

Next, Ruby steps down the AST nodes to NODE_ITER, as shown in Figure 2-11.

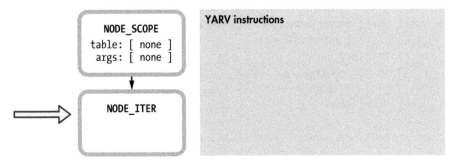

Figure 2-11: Ruby stepping through an AST

At this point, there is still no code generated, but notice in Figure 2-9 that two arrows lead from NODE_ITER: one to NODE_CALL, which represents the 10.times call, and another to the inner block. Ruby will first continue down the AST and compile the nodes corresponding to the 10.times code. The resulting YARV code, following the same receiver-arguments-message pattern we saw in Figure 2-6, is shown in Figure 2-12.

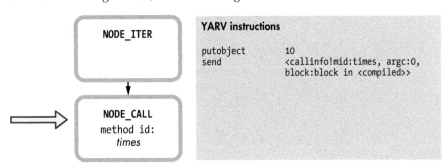

Figure 2-12: Ruby compiles the 10.times method call.

Notice that the new YARV instructions shown in Figure 2-12 push the receiver (the integer object 10) onto the stack first, after which Ruby generates an instruction to execute the times method call. But notice, too, the block:block in <compiled> argument in the send instruction. This indicates that the method call also contains a block argument: my do |n| puts n end block. In this example, NODE_ITER has caused the Ruby compiler to include this block argument because the AST above shows an arrow from NODE_ITER to the second NODE_SCOPE.

Ruby continues by compiling the inner block, beginning with the second NODE_SCOPE shown at right in Figure 2-9. Figure 2-13 shows what the AST for that inner block looks like.

This looks simple enough—just a single function call and a single argument n. But notice the value for table and args in NODE_SCOPE. These values were empty in the parent NODE_SCOPE, but they're set here in the inner NODE_SCOPE. As you might guess, these values indicate the presence of the block parameter n.

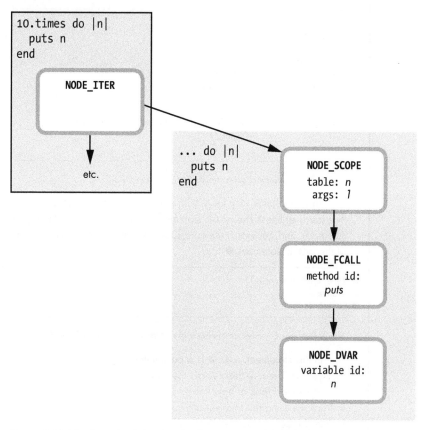

Figure 2-13: The branch of the AST for the contents of the block

Also notice that the Ruby parser created NODE_DVAR instead of NODE_LIT, which we saw earlier in Figure 2-9. This is the case because n is not just a literal string; it's a block parameter passed in from the parent scope.

From a relatively high level, Figure 2-14 shows how Ruby compiles the inner block.

HOW RUBY ITERATES THROUGH THE AST

Let's look more closely at how Ruby actually iterates through the AST structure, converting each node into YARV instructions. The MRI C source code file that implements the Ruby compiler is called *compile.c*. To learn how the code in *compile.c* works, we first look for the function iseq_compile_each. Listing 2-3 shows the beginning of that function.

```
/**
  compile each node

  self:  InstructionSequence
  node:  Ruby compiled node
  poped: This node will be poped
 */
static int
iseq_compile_each(rb_iseq_t *iseq, LINK_ANCHOR *ret, NODE * node,
                  int poped)
{
```

Listing 2-3: This C function compiles each node in the AST.

This function is very long, with a very, very long switch statement that runs to thousands of lines! The switch statement branches based on the type of the current AST node and generates the corresponding YARV code. Listing 2-4 shows the start of the switch statement ❷.

```
❶ type = nd_type(node);
  --snip--
❷ switch (type) {
```

Listing 2-4: This C switch statement looks at the type of each AST node.

In this statement, node ❶ is a parameter passed into iseq_compile_each, and nd_type is a C macro that returns the type from the given node structure.

Now we'll look at how Ruby compiles function or method call nodes into YARV instructions using the receiver-arguments-function call pattern. First, search *compile.c* for the C case statement shown in Listing 2-5.

```
case NODE_CALL:
case NODE_FCALL:
case NODE_VCALL:{                    /* VCALL: variable or call */
  /*
    call:  obj.method(...)
    fcall: func(...)
    vcall: func
  */
```

Listing 2-5: This case of the switch compiles method calls in your Ruby code.

NODE_CALL represents a real method call (like 10.times), NODE_FCALL is a function call (like puts), and NODE_VCALL is a variable or function call. Skipping over some of the C code details (including the optional SUPPORT_JOKE code used for implementing the goto statement), Listing 2-6 shows what Ruby does next to compile these AST nodes.

```
/* receiver */
if (type == NODE_CALL) {
❶    COMPILE(recv, "recv", node->nd_recv);
}
else if (type == NODE_FCALL || type == NODE_VCALL) {
❷    ADD_CALL_RECEIVER(recv, nd_line(node));
}
```

Listing 2-6: This C code compiles the receiver value for a method call.

Here, Ruby calls either COMPILE or ADD_CALL_RECEIVER as follows:

- In the case of real method calls (like NODE_CALL), Ruby calls COMPILE ❶ to recursively call into iseq_compile_each again, processing the next AST node down the tree that corresponds to the receiver of the method call or message. This will create YARV instructions to evaluate whatever expression was used to specify the target object.

- If there is no receiver (NODE_FCALL or NODE_VCALL), Ruby calls ADD_CALL_RECEIVER ❷, which creates a putself YARV instruction.

Next, as shown in Listing 2-7, Ruby creates YARV instructions to push each argument of the method/function call onto the stack.

```
/* args */
if (nd_type(node) != NODE_VCALL) {
❶    argc = setup_args(iseq, args, node->nd_args, &flag);
}
else {
❷    argc = INT2FIX(0);
}
```

Listing 2-7: This snippet of C code compiles the arguments to every Ruby method call.

For NODE_CALL and NODE_FCALL, Ruby calls into the setup_args function ❶, which will recursively call into iseq_compile_each again as needed in order to compile each argument to the method/function call. For NODE_VCALL, there are no arguments, so Ruby simply sets argc to 0 ❷.

Finally, Ruby creates YARV instructions to execute the actual method or function call, as shown here:

```
ADD_SEND_R(ret, nd_line(node), ID2SYM(mid),
           argc, parent_block, LONG2FIX(flag));
```

This C macro will create the new send YARV instruction, which will cause the actual method call to occur when YARV executes it.

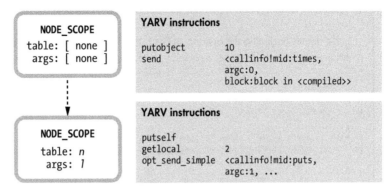

Figure 2-14: How Ruby compiles a call to a block

You can see the parent NODE_SCOPE at the top, along with the YARV code from Figure 2-12. Below that I've listed the YARV code compiled from the inner block's AST.

The key point here is that Ruby compiles each distinct scope in your Ruby program—methods, blocks, classes, or modules, for example—into a separate snippet of YARV instructions.

Experiment 2-1: Displaying YARV Instructions

One easy way to see how Ruby compiles your code is with RubyVM::InstructionSequence, which gives you access to Ruby's YARV engine from your Ruby program! Like the Ripper tool, its use is very straightforward, as you can see in Listing 2-8.

```
code = <<END
puts 2+2
END
puts RubyVM::InstructionSequence.compile(code).disasm
```

Listing 2-8: How to view the YARV instructions for puts 2+2

The challenge lies in understanding what the output actually means. For example, Listing 2-9 shows the output for puts 2+2.

```
== disasm: <RubyVM::InstructionSequence:<compiled>@<compiled>>==========
❶ 0000 trace            1                                        (   1)
  0002 putself
  0003 putobject        2
  0005 putobject        2
  0007 opt_plus         <callinfo!mid:+, argc:1, ARGS_SKIP>
  0009 opt_send_simple  <callinfo!mid:puts, argc:1, FCALL|ARGS_SKIP>
❷ 0011 leave
```

Listing 2-9: The YARV instructions for puts 2+2

As you can see in Listing 2-9, the output contains all of the same instructions from Figures 2-5 to 2-8 and two new ones: trace ❶ and leave ❷. The trace instruction is used to implement the set_trace_func feature,[1] which will call a given function for each Ruby statement executed in your program. The leave function is like a return statement. The line numbers on the left show the position of each instruction in the bytecode array that the compiler actually produces.

RubyVM::InstructionSequence makes it easy to explore how Ruby compiles different Ruby scripts. For example, Listing 2-10 shows how to compile my 10.times do example.

```
code = <<END
10.times do |n|
  puts n
end
END
puts RubyVM::InstructionSequence.compile(code).disasm
```

Listing 2-10: Displaying the YARV instructions for a call to a block

The output that I get now is shown below in Listing 2-11. Notice that the send <callinfo!mid:times YARV instruction shows block:block in <compiled> ❷, which indicates that I'm passing a block to the 10.times method call.

```
❶ == disasm: <RubyVM::InstructionSequence:<compiled>@<compiled>>==========
== catch table
| catch type: break  st: 0002 ed: 0006 sp: 0000 cont: 0006
|------------------------------------------------------------------------
0000 trace              1                                           (   1)
0002 putobject          10
❷ 0004 send              <callinfo!mid:times, argc:0, block:block in <compiled>>
0006 leave
❸ == disasm: <RubyVM::InstructionSequence:block in <compiled>@<compiled>>=
== catch table
| catch type: redo   st: 0000 ed: 0011 sp: 0000 cont: 0000
| catch type: next   st: 0000 ed: 0011 sp: 0000 cont: 0011
|------------------------------------------------------------------------
local table (size: 2, argc: 1 [opts: 0, rest: -1, post: 0, block: -1] s3)
[ 2] n<Arg>
0000 trace              256                                         (   1)
0002 trace              1                                           (   2)
0004 putself
0005 getlocal_OP__WC__0 2
0007 opt_send_simple    <callinfo!mid:puts, argc:1, FCALL|ARGS_SKIP>
0009 trace              512                                         (   3)
0011 leave                                                          (   2)
```

Listing 2-11: The YARV instructions for a call to a block and for the block itself

---

1. For Ruby 2.x, the Ruby core team recommends using TracePoint instead of set_trace_func.

As you can see, Ruby displays the two YARV instruction snippets separately. The first corresponds to the global scope ❶ and the second to the inner block scope ❸.

The Local Table

In Figures 2-3 through 2-14, you may have noticed that each NODE_SCOPE element in the AST contained information I labeled table and args. These values in the inner NODE_SCOPE structure contain information about the block's parameter n (see Figure 2-9 on page 39).

Ruby generated the information about this block parameter during the parsing process. As I discussed in Chapter 1, Ruby parses the block parameter along with the rest of my Ruby code using grammar rules. In fact, I showed the specific rule for parsing block parameters back in Figure 1-30 (page 21): opt_block_param.

Once Ruby's compiler runs, however, the information about the block parameter is copied out of the AST and into another data structure called the *local table*, saved nearby the newly generated YARV instructions. Each snippet of YARV instructions, each scope in your Ruby program, has its own local table.

Figure 2-15 shows the local table attached to the YARV instructions that Ruby generated for the sample block code from Listing 2-2.

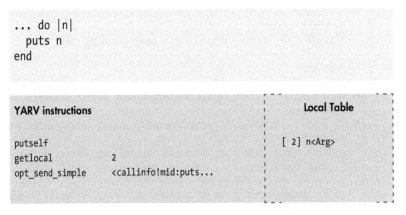

Figure 2-15: A snippet of YARV instructions with a local table

Notice on the right side of Figure 2-15 that Ruby has associated the number 2 with the block parameter n. As we'll see in Chapter 3, the YARV instructions that refer to n will use this index 2. The getlocal instruction is an example of this. The <Arg> notation indicates that this value is an argument to the block.

As it turns out, Ruby also saves information about local variables in this table, hence the name *local table*. Figure 2-16 shows the YARV instructions and local table Ruby will generate when compiling a method that uses one local variable and takes two arguments.

```
def add_two(a, b)
  sum = a+b
end
```

YARV instructions		Local Table
getlocal	4	[2] sum
getlocal	3	[3] b<Arg>
opt_plus	<callinfo!mid:+...	[4] a<Arg>
dup		
setlocal	2	

Figure 2-16: This local table contains one local variable and two arguments.

Here, you can see that Ruby lists all three values in the local table. As we'll see in Chapter 3, Ruby treats local variables and method arguments in the same way. (Notice that the local variable sum does not have the <Arg> label.)

Think of the local table as a key to help you understand what the YARV instructions do, similar to the legend on a map. As you can see in Figure 2-16, local variables have no label, but Ruby uses the following labels to describe different types of method and block arguments:

<Arg>   A standard method or block argument

<Rest>   An array of unnamed arguments that are passed together using a * (splat) operator

<Post>   A standard argument that appears after the splat array

<Block>   A Ruby proc object that is passed using the & operator

<Opt=i>   A parameter defined with a default value. Internally, this value is a pointer to YARV instructions that set the default value. The local table does not contain the actual default values.

Understanding the information displayed by the local table can help you understand how Ruby's complex argument syntax works and how to take full advantage of the language.

To help you understand what I mean, let's look at how Ruby compiles a method call that uses an array of unnamed arguments, as shown Listing 2-12.

```
def complex_formula(a, b, *args, c)
  a + b + args.size + c
end
```

Listing 2-12: A method that takes standard arguments and an array of unnamed arguments

Here a, b, and c are standard arguments, and args is an array of other arguments that appear between b and c. Figure 2-17 shows how the local table saves all of this information.

As in Figure 2-16, <Arg> refers to a standard argument. But now Ruby uses <Rest> to indicate that value 3 contains the "rest" of the arguments and <Post> to indicate that value 2 contains the argument that appears after the unnamed array, the last one.

```
def complex_formula (a, b, *args, c)
  a + b + args.size + c
end
```

YARV instructions		Local Table
getlocal	5	[2] c<Post>
getlocal	4	[3] args<Rest>
opt_plus	<callinfo!mid:+...	[4] b<Arg>
getlocal	3	[5] a<Arg>
opt_size	<callinfo!mid:size...	
opt_plus	<callinfo!mid:+...	
getlocal	2	
opt_plus	<callinfo!mid:+...	

Figure 2-17: Ruby saves information about special arguments in the local table.

Compiling Optional Arguments

As you probably know, you can make an argument optional by specifying a default value for it in the argument list. Later, Ruby will use the default value if you don't provide a value for that argument when you call the method or block. Listing 2-13 shows a simple example.

```
def add_two_optional(a, b = 5)
  sum = a+b
end
```

Listing 2-13: A method that takes an optional argument

If you provide a value for b, the method will use that value as follows:

```
puts add_two_optional(2, 2)
=> 4
```

But if you don't, Ruby will assign the default value of 5 to b:

```
puts add_two_optional(2)
=> 7
```

Ruby has a bit more work to do in this situation. Where does the default value go? Where does the Ruby compiler put it? Figure 2-18 shows how Ruby generates a few extra YARV instructions during the compile process that set the default value.

```
def add_two_optional (a, b = 5)
  sum = a+b
end
```

YARV instructions		Local Table
putobject	**5**	[2] sum
setlocal	**3**	[3] b<Opt=0>
getlocal	4	[4] a<Arg>
getlocal	3	
opt_plus	<callinfo!mid:+...	
dup		
setlocal	2	

Figure 2-18: Ruby's compiler generates extra code to handle optional arguments.

Ruby's compiler generates the bolded YARV instructions, putobject and setlocal, to set the value of b to 5 when you call the method. (As we'll see in Chapter 3, YARV will call these instructions if you don't provide a value for b but skip them if you do.) You can also see that Ruby lists the optional argument b in the local table as b<Opt=0>. The 0 here refers to YARV instructions that set the default value.

Compiling Keyword Arguments

In Ruby 2.x, we can specify a name along with a default value for each method or block argument. Arguments written this way are known as *keyword arguments*. For example, Listing 2-14 shows the same argument b declared using Ruby 2.0's new keyword argument syntax.

```
def add_two_keyword(a, b: 5)
  sum = a+b
end
```

Listing 2-14: A method that takes a keyword argument

Now to provide a value for b, I need to use its name:

```
puts add_two_keyword(2, b: 2)
 => 4
```

Or, if I don't specify b at all, Ruby will use the default value:

```
puts add_two_keyword(2)
 => 7
```

How does Ruby compile keyword arguments? Figure 2-19 shows Ruby needs to add quite a bit of additional code to the method's YARV snippet.

```
def add_two_keyword (a, b: 5)
   sum = a+b
end
```

YARV instructions		Local Table
getlocal	3	[2] sum
dup		[3] ?
putobject	:b	[4] b
opt_send_simple	<callinfo!mid:key?...	[5] a<Arg>
branchunless	18	
dup		
putobject	:b	
opt_send_simple	<callinfo!mid:delete...	
setlocal	4	
jump	22	
putobject	5	
setlocal	4	
pop		
getlocal	5	
getlocal	4	
opt_plus	<callinfo!mid:+...	
dup		
setlocal	2	

Figure 2-19: The Ruby compiler generates many more instructions to handle keyword arguments.

The Ruby compiler generates all of the YARV instructions in bold—13 new instructions—to implement the keyword argument b. In Chapters 3 and 4, I'll cover how YARV works in detail and what these instructions actually mean, but for now, we can guess what's going on here:

- In the local table, we can see a new mystery value shown as [3]?.
- To the left of Figure 2-19, new YARV instructions call the key? and delete methods.

Which Ruby class contains the key? and delete methods? The Hash. Figure 2-19 shows evidence that Ruby must implement keyword arguments using an internal, hidden hash object. All of these additional YARV instructions automatically add some logic to my method that checks this hash for the argument b. If Ruby finds the value of b in the hash, it uses it. If not, it uses the default value of 5. The mystery element [3]? in the local table must be this hidden hash object.

Experiment 2-2: Displaying the Local Table

Along with YARV instructions, RubyVM::InstructionSequence will also display the local table associated with each YARV snippet or scope. Finding and understanding the local table for your code will help you to understand what the corresponding YARV instructions do. In this experiment, we'll look at where the local table appears in the output generated by the RubyVM::InstructionSequence object.

Listing 2-15 repeats Listing 2-10 from Experiment 2-1.

```
code = <<END
10.times do |n|
  puts n
end
END

puts RubyVM::InstructionSequence.compile(code).disasm
```

Listing 2-15: Displaying the YARV instructions for a call to a block

And Listing 2-16 repeats the output we saw earlier in Experiment 2-1.

```
== disasm: <RubyVM::InstructionSequence:<compiled>@<compiled>>==========
== catch table
| catch type: break  st: 0002 ed: 0006 sp: 0000 cont: 0006
|------------------------------------------------------------------------
0000 trace            1                                              (   1)
0002 putobject        10
0004 send             <callinfo!mid:times, argc:0, block:block in <compiled>>
0006 leave
== disasm: <RubyVM::InstructionSequence:block in <compiled>@<compiled>>=
```

```
== catch table
| catch type: redo   st: 0000 ed: 0011 sp: 0000 cont: 0000
| catch type: next   st: 0000 ed: 0011 sp: 0000 cont: 0011
|------------------------------------------------------------------------
❶ local table (size: 2, argc: 1 [opts: 0, rest: -1, post: 0, block: -1] s3)
❷ [ 2] n<Arg>
0000 trace             256                                        (   1)
0002 trace             1                                          (   2)
0004 putself
0005 getlocal_OP__WC__0 2
0007 opt_send_simple   <callinfo!mid:puts, argc:1, FCALL|ARGS_SKIP>
0009 trace             512                                        (   3)
0011 leave                                                        (   2)
```

Listing 2-16: Along with the YARV instructions, RubyVM::InstructionSequence displays the local table.

Just above the YARV snippet for the inner scope—the block—we see information about its local table at ❶. This displays the total size of the table (size: 2), the argument count (argc: 1), and other information about the types of parameters (opts: 0, rest: -1, post: 0).

The second line ❷ shows the actual contents of the local table. In this example, we have just one argument, n.

Listing 2-17 shows how to use RubyVM::InstructionSequence in the same way to compile my unnamed arguments example from Listing 2-12.

```
code = <<END
def complex_formula(a, b, *args, c)
  a + b + args.size + c
end
END

puts RubyVM::InstructionSequence.compile(code).disasm
```

Listing 2-17: This method uses unnamed arguments with a splat operator.

And Listing 2-18 shows the output.

```
❶ == disasm: <RubyVM::InstructionSequence:<compiled>@<compiled>>==========
0000 trace             1                                          (   1)
0002 putspecialobject  1
0004 putspecialobject  2
0006 putobject         :complex_formula
0008 putiseq           complex_formula
❷ 0010 opt_send_simple <callinfo!mid:core#define_method, argc:3, ARGS_SKIP>
0012 leave
== disasm: <RubyVM::InstructionSequence:complex_formula@<compiled>>=====
❸ local table (size: 5, argc: 2 [opts: 0, rest: 2, post: 1, block: -1] s0)
❹ [ 5] a<Arg>     [ 4] b<Arg>    [ 3] args<Rest> [ 2] c<Post>
0000 trace             8                                          (   1)
0002 trace             1                                          (   2)
```

```
0004 getlocal_OP__WC__0 5
0006 getlocal_OP__WC__0 4
0008 opt_plus           <callinfo!mid:+, argc:1, ARGS_SKIP>
0010 getlocal_OP__WC__0 3
0012 opt_size           <callinfo!mid:size, argc:0, ARGS_SKIP>
0014 opt_plus           <callinfo!mid:+, argc:1, ARGS_SKIP>
0016 getlocal_OP__WC__0 2
0018 opt_plus           <callinfo!mid:+, argc:1, ARGS_SKIP>
0020 trace              16                                        (   3)
0022 leave                                                        (   2)
```

Listing 2-18: Displaying the YARV instructions for a call to a block

The top YARV scope, around ❶, shows the instructions YARV uses to define a new method. Notice the call to `core#define_method` at ❷, an internal C function that YARV uses to create new Ruby methods. This corresponds to calling `def complex_formula` in my script. (I'll discuss how Ruby implements methods in more detail in Chapters 5, 6, and 9.)

Notice the local table for the lower YARV snippet at ❸. This line now shows more information about the unnamed arguments (`rest: 2`) and the last standard argument following them (`post: 1`). Finally, the line at ❹ shows the contents of the local table that I showed back in Figure 2-17.

Summary

In this chapter, we learned how Ruby compiles our code. You may think of Ruby as a dynamic scripting language, but, in fact, it uses a compiler just like C, Java, and many other programming languages. The obvious difference is that Ruby's compiler runs automatically behind the scenes; you never need to worry about compiling your Ruby code.

We've learned that Ruby's compiler works by iterating through the AST produced by the tokenizing and parsing processes, generating a series of bytecode instructions along the way. Ruby translates your code from Ruby into a language tailored for the YARV virtual machine, and it compiles every scope or section of your Ruby program into a different snippet or set of these YARV instructions. Every block, method, lambda, or other scope in your program has a corresponding set of bytecode instructions.

We've also seen how Ruby handles different types of arguments. We were able to use the local table as a key or legend for understanding which YARV instructions accessed which arguments or local variables. And we saw how Ruby's compiler generates additional, special YARV instructions to handle optional and keyword parameters.

In Chapter 3, I'll begin to explain how YARV executes the instructions produced by the compiler—that is, how YARV executes your Ruby program.

YARV is not just a stack machine—it's a double-stack machine!

3

HOW RUBY EXECUTES
YOUR CODE

Now that Ruby has tokenized, parsed, and compiled
your code, it's finally ready to execute it. But just how
does it do that? We've seen how the Ruby compiler
creates YARV (Yet Another Ruby Virtual Machine)
instructions, but how does YARV actually run them?
How does it track variables and return values and
arguments? How does it implement if statements and
other control structures?

Koichi Sasada and the Ruby core team designed YARV to use a stack
pointer and a program counter—that is, to function like your computer's
actual microprocessor. In this chapter, I'll examine the basics of YARV
instructions; namely, how they pop arguments off of and push return
values onto an internal stack. We'll also see how YARV keeps track of

your Ruby call stack along with its own internal stack. I'll explain how Ruby accesses local variables and how it can find variables farther down your call stack using dynamic access. We'll finish with a look at how Ruby implements special variables. In Chapter 4 I'll continue the discussion of YARV by examining how it implements control structures and method dispatch.

YARV's Internal Stack and Your Ruby Stack

As we'll see in a moment, YARV uses a stack internally to track intermediate values, arguments, and return values. YARV is a stack-oriented virtual machine.

In addition to its own internal stack, YARV keeps track of your Ruby program's *call stack*, recording which methods call which other methods, functions, blocks, lambdas, and so on. In fact, YARV is not just a stack machine—it's a double-stack machine! It has to track the arguments and return values not only for its own internal instructions but also for your Ruby program.

Figure 3-1 shows YARV's basic registers and internal stack.

YARV instructions

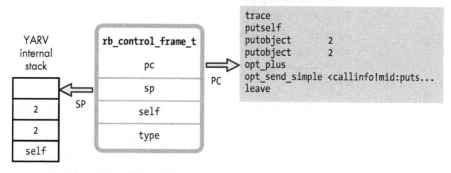

Figure 3-1: Some of YARV's internal registers, including the program counter and stack pointer

YARV's internal stack is on the left. The SP label is the *stack pointer*, or the location of the top of the stack. On the right are the instructions that YARV is executing. PC is the *program counter*, or the location of the current instruction.

You can see the YARV instructions that Ruby compiled from the puts 2+2 example on the right side of Figure 3-1. YARV stores both the SP and PC registers in a C structure called rb_control_frame_t, along with a type field, the current value of Ruby's self variable, and some other values not shown here.

At the same time, YARV maintains another stack of these rb_control_frame_t structures, as shown in Figure 3-2.

This second stack of rb_control_frame_t structures represents the path that YARV has taken through your Ruby program, and YARV's current location. In other words, this is your Ruby call stack—what you would see if you ran puts caller.

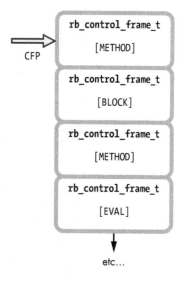

Figure 3-2: YARV keeps track of your Ruby call stack using a series of rb_control_frame_t structures.

The CFP pointer indicates the *control frame pointer*. Each stack frame in your Ruby program stack contains, in turn, a different value for the self, PC, and SP registers, as shown in Figure 3-1. The type field in each rb_control_frame_t structure indicates the type of code running at this level in your Ruby call stack. As Ruby calls into the methods, blocks, or other structures in your program, the type might be set to METHOD, BLOCK, or one of a few other values.

Stepping Through How Ruby Executes a Simple Script

In order to help you understand this a bit better, here are a couple of examples. I'll begin with the simple 2+2 example from Chapters 1 and 2, shown again in Listing 3-1.

```
puts 2+2
```

Listing 3-1: A one-line Ruby program that we'll execute as an example

This one-line Ruby script doesn't have a Ruby call stack, so I'll focus on the internal YARV stack for now. Figure 3-3 shows how YARV will execute this script, beginning with the first instruction, trace.

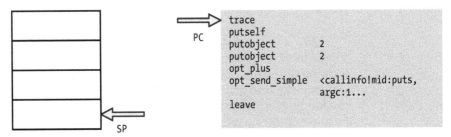

Figure 3-3: On the left is YARV's internal stack, and on the right is the compiled version of my puts 2+2 program.

As you can see in Figure 3-3, YARV starts the program counter (PC) at the first instruction, and initially the stack is empty. Now YARV will execute the trace instruction, incrementing the PC register, as shown in Figure 3-4.

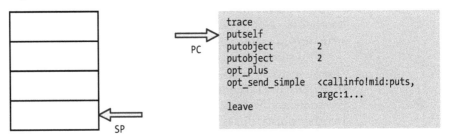

Figure 3-4: Ruby executes the first instruction, trace.

Ruby uses the trace instruction to support the set_trace_func feature. If you call set_trace_func and provide a function, Ruby will call it each time it executes a line of Ruby code.

Next, YARV executes putself and pushes the current value of self onto the stack, as shown in Figure 3-5.

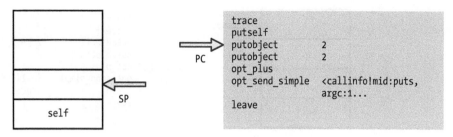

Figure 3-5: putself pushes the top self value onto the stack.

Because this simple script contains no Ruby objects or classes, the self pointer is set to the default top self object. This is an instance of the Object class that Ruby automatically creates when YARV starts. It serves as the receiver for method calls and the container for instance variables in the top-level scope. The top self object contains a single, predefined to_s method, which returns the string main. You can call this method by running the following command in the console:

```
$ ruby -e 'puts self'
=> main
```

YARV will use this self value on the stack when it executes the opt_send_simple instruction: self is the receiver of the puts method because I didn't specify a receiver for this method call.

Next, YARV executes putobject 2. It pushes the numeric value 2 onto the stack and increments the PC again, as shown in Figure 3-6.

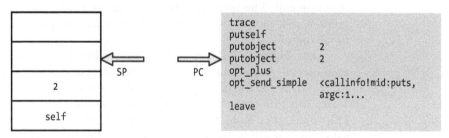

Figure 3-6: Ruby pushes the value 2 onto the stack, the receiver of the + method.

This is the first step of the receiver (arguments) operation pattern described in "How Ruby Compiles a Simple Script" on page 34. First, Ruby pushes the receiver onto the internal YARV stack. In this example, the Fixnum object 2 is the receiver of the message/method +, which takes a single argument, also a 2. Next, Ruby pushes the argument 2, as shown in Figure 3-7.

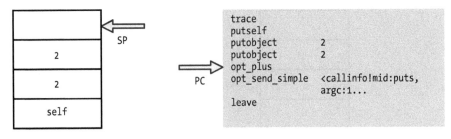

Figure 3-7: Ruby pushes another value 2 onto the stack, the argument of the + method.

Finally, Ruby executes the + operation. In this case, opt_plus is an optimized instruction that will add two values: the receiver and the argument, as shown in Figure 3-8.

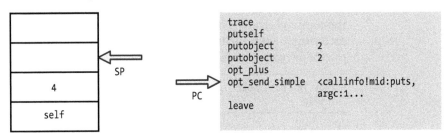

Figure 3-8: The opt_plus instruction calculates 2 + 2 = 4.

As you can see in Figure 3-8, the opt_plus instruction leaves the result, 4, at the top of the stack. Now Ruby is perfectly positioned to execute the puts function call: The receiver self is first on the stack, and the single argument, 4, is at the top of the stack. (I'll describe how method lookup works in Chapter 6.)

Next, Figure 3-9 shows what happens when Ruby executes the puts method call. As you can see, the opt_send_simple instruction leaves the return value, nil, at the top of the stack. Finally, Ruby executes the last instruction, leave, which finishes the execution of our simple, one-line Ruby program. Of course, when Ruby executes the puts call, the C code implementing the puts function will actually display the value 4 in the console output.

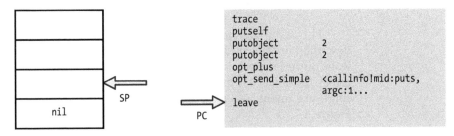

Figure 3-9: Ruby calls the puts method on the top self object.

Executing a Call to a Block

Now let's see how the Ruby call stack works. In Listing 3-2, a slightly more complicated example, you see a simple Ruby script that calls a block 10 times, printing out a string.

```
10.times do
  puts "The quick brown fox jumps over the lazy dog."
end
```

Listing 3-2: This example program calls a block 10 times.

Let's skip over a few steps and start where YARV is about to call the times method, as shown in Figure 3-10.

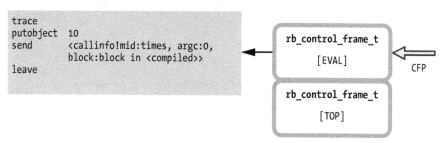

Figure 3-10: Every Ruby program starts with these two control frames.

On the left side of the diagram are the YARV instructions that Ruby is executing. On the right, you see two control frame structures.

At the bottom of the stack, you see a control frame with the type set to TOP. Ruby always creates this frame first when starting a new program. At the top of the stack, at least initially, a frame of type EVAL corresponds to the top level or main scope of the Ruby script.

Next, Ruby calls the times message on the Fixnum object 10—the receiver of the times message. When it does so, it adds a new level to the control frame stack, as shown in Figure 3-11.

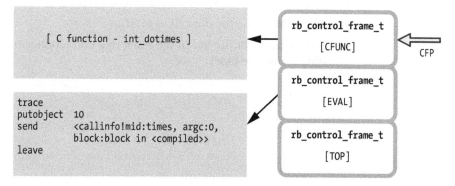

Figure 3-11: Ruby uses the CFUNC frame when you call built-in functions implemented in C.

This new entry (at the right of Figure 3-11) represents a new level in the program's Ruby call stack, and the CFP pointer has moved up to point at the new control frame structure. Also, notice that because the Integer#times method is built into Ruby, there are no YARV instructions for it. Instead, Ruby will call some internal C code to pop the argument 10 off the stack and call the provided block 10 times. Ruby gives this control frame a type of CFUNC.

Finally, Figure 3-12 shows what the YARV and control frame stacks will look like if we interrupt the program inside the inner block.

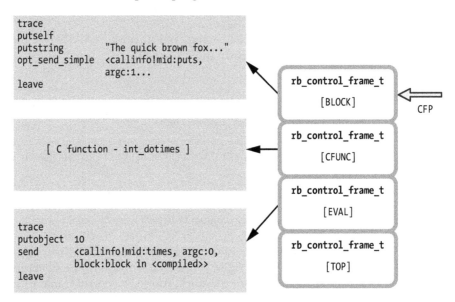

Figure 3-12: The CFP stack when we pause the code from Listing 3-2 inside the block

There will now be four entries, as follows, in the control frame stack on the right:

- The TOP and EVAL frames that Ruby always starts with
- The CFUNC frame for the call to 10.times
- A BLOCK frame at the top of the stack that corresponds to the code running inside the block

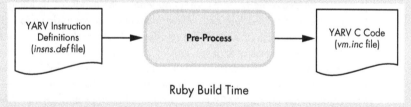

Ruby processes the *insns.def* file using Ruby: The build process first uses Ruby[1] to generate *vm.inc* and a few similar files. Then it uses these C source code files to compile *Miniruby*, a small version of Ruby, which later helps compile the complete version of Ruby. The other generated C files are related to encodings and C extension libraries.

Listing 3-4 shows what the snippet for putself looks like in *vm.inc* once Ruby has processed it.

```
INSN_ENTRY(putself){
{
  VALUE val;
  DEBUG_ENTER_INSN("putself");
❶  ADD_PC(1+0);
  PREFETCH(GET_PC());
  #define CURRENT_INSN_putself 1
  #define INSN_IS_SC()      0
  #define INSN_LABEL(lab)  LABEL_putself_##lab
  #define LABEL_IS_SC(lab) LABEL_##lab##_##t
  COLLECT_USAGE_INSN(BIN(putself));
{
#line 282 "insns.def"
❷    val = GET_SELF();
#line 408 "vm.inc"
  CHECK_VM_STACK_OVERFLOW(REG_CFP, 1);
❸  PUSH(val);
#undef CURRENT_INSN_putself
#undef INSN_IS_SC
#undef INSN_LABEL
#undef LABEL_IS_SC
  END_INSN(putself);}}}
```

Listing 3-4: The definition of putself is transformed into this C code during the Ruby build process.

The single line val = GET_SELF() appears in the middle of the listing at ❷. Above and below this line, Ruby calls a few different C macros to do various things, like add 1 to the program counter (PC) register at ❶ and push the val value onto the YARV internal stack at ❸. If you look through *vm.inc*, you'll see this same C code repeated over and over again for the definition of each YARV instruction.

The *vm.inc* C source code file, in turn, is included by the *vm_exec.c* file, which contains the primary YARV instruction loop that steps through the YARV instructions in your program one after another and calls the C code corresponding to each one.

---

1. That is, Ruby is required to build Ruby. This design is based on the assumption that Ruby developers have Ruby in their development environments. The public source distribution includes the generated *vm.inc*, so you do not need Ruby if you use it.

Experiment 3-1: Benchmarking Ruby 2.0 and Ruby 1.9 vs. Ruby 1.8

The Ruby core team introduced the YARV virtual machine with Ruby 1.9. Earlier versions of Ruby executed programs by directly stepping through the nodes of the *abstract syntax tree (AST)*. There was no compile step: Ruby just tokenized, parsed, and then immediately executed your code.

Ruby 1.8 worked just fine. In fact, for years it was the most commonly used version. Then why did the Ruby core team do all of the extra work required to write a compiler and a new virtual machine? Speed. Executing a compiled Ruby program using YARV is much faster than walking through the AST directly.

How much faster is YARV? Let's take a look! In this experiment, we'll measure how much faster Ruby 2.0 and 1.9 are compared to Ruby 1.8 by executing the very simple Ruby script shown in Listing 3-5.

```
i = 0
while i < ARGV[0].to_i
  i += 1
end
```

Listing 3-5: A simple test script for benchmarking Ruby 2.0 and Ruby 1.9 vs. Ruby 1.8

This script receives a count value from the command line via the `ARGV` array and then just iterates in a `while` loop counting up to that value. This Ruby script is very, very simple: By measuring the time it takes to execute this script for different values of `ARGV[0]`, we should get a good sense of whether executing YARV instructions is actually faster than iterating over AST nodes. (There are no database calls or other external code involved.)

We can use the Unix `time` command to measure how long it takes Ruby to iterate one time:

```
$ time ruby benchmark1.rb 1
ruby benchmark1.rb 1  0.02s user 0.00s system 92% cpu 0.023 total
```

ten times:

```
$ time ruby benchmark1.rb 10
ruby benchmark1.rb 10  0.02s user 0.00s system 94% cpu 0.027 total
```

and so on.

Figure 3-14 shows a plot of the measured times on a logarithmic scale for Ruby 1.8.7, 1.9.3, and 2.0.

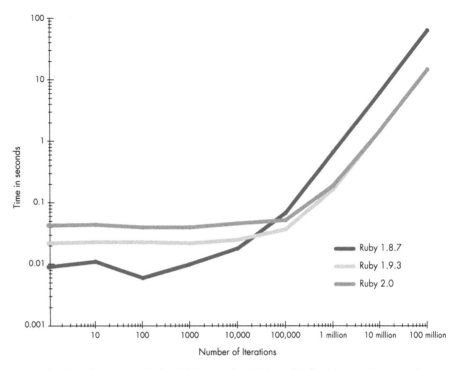

Figure 3-14: Performance of Ruby 1.8.7 vs. Ruby 1.9.3 and Ruby 2.0; time (in seconds) vs. number of iterations on a logarithmic scale

Looking at the chart, you can see that for short-lived processes, such as loops with a small number of iterations (see the left side of Figure 3-14), Ruby 1.8.7 is actually faster than Ruby 1.9.3 and 2.0 because there is no need to compile the Ruby code into YARV instructions. Instead, after tokenizing and parsing the code, Ruby 1.8.7 immediately executes it. The time difference between Ruby 1.8.7 and Ruby 1.9.3 and 2.0 at the left side of the chart, about 0.01 seconds, tells us how long it takes Ruby 1.9.3 or 2.0 to compile the script into YARV instructions. You can also see that Ruby 2.0 is actually a bit slower than Ruby 1.9.3 for short loops.

However, after about 11,000 iterations, Ruby 1.9.3 and 2.0 are faster. This crossover occurs when the additional speed provided by executing YARV instructions begins to pay off and make up for the additional time spent compiling. For long-lived processes, such as loops with a large number of iterations (see the right side of Figure 3-14), Ruby 1.9 and 2.0 are about 4.25 times faster! Also, we can see that Ruby 2.0 and 1.9.3 execute YARV instructions at exactly the same speed for many iterations.

This speed up doesn't look like much on the logarithmic chart in Figure 3-14, but notice what happens if we redraw the right side of this chart using a linear scale instead, as shown in Figure 3-15.

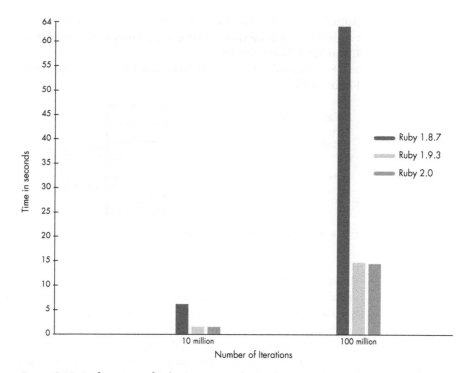

Figure 3-15: Performance of Ruby 1.8.7 vs. Ruby 1.9.3 vs. Ruby 2.0; time (in seconds) for 10 or 100 million iterations on a linear scale

The difference is dramatic! Executing this simple Ruby script using Ruby 1.9.3 or Ruby 2.0 with YARV is about 4.25 times faster than it is using Ruby 1.8.7 without YARV.

Local and Dynamic Access of Ruby Variables

In the previous section, we saw how Ruby maintained an internal stack used by YARV as well as your Ruby program's call stack. But something obvious was missing from both of the code examples: variables. Neither script used any Ruby variables. A more realistic example program would have used variables many times. How does Ruby handle variables internally? And where are they stored?

Ruby stores all of the values you save in variables on YARV's stack, along with the parameters to and return values from the YARV instructions. However, accessing these variables is not so simple. Internally, Ruby uses two very different methods for saving and retrieving a value you save in a variable: *local access* and *dynamic access*.

Local Variable Access

Whenever you make a method call, Ruby sets aside some space on the YARV stack for any local variables declared inside the method you are calling.

Ruby knows how many variables you are using by consulting the *local table* created for each method during the compilation step discussed in "The Local Table" on page 46.

For example, suppose we write the silly Ruby function you see in Figure 3-16.

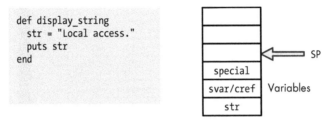

Figure 3-16: An example Ruby script that uses a local variable

The Ruby code is at the left of the figure; on the right is a diagram showing the YARV stack and stack pointer. You can see that Ruby stores the variables on the stack just under the stack pointer. (Notice that a space is reserved for the str value on the stack, three slots under SP, at SP-3.)

Ruby uses svar/cref to contain one of two things: either a pointer to a table of the special variables in the current method (values such as $! for *last exception message* or $& for *last regular expression match*) or to the current lexical scope. In this context, *lexical scope* indicates which class or module you are currently adding methods to. (In Experiment 3-2 we'll explore special variables in more detail, and I'll discuss lexical scope further in Chapter 6.) Ruby uses the first slot—the special variable—to track information related to blocks. (More in a moment when we discuss dynamic variable access.)

When the example code saves a value into str, Ruby just needs to write the value into that space on the stack, as shown in Figure 3-17.

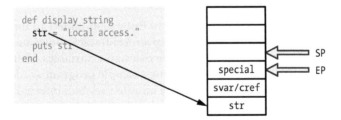

Figure 3-17: Ruby saves local variables on its stack near the environment pointer (EP).

To implement this internally, YARV uses another pointer similar to the stack pointer, called the EP or *environment pointer*. This points to where the local variables for the current method are located on the stack. Initially, EP is set to SP-1. Later on, the value of SP will change as YARV executes instructions, while the EP value will normally remain constant.

Figure 3-18 shows the YARV instructions that Ruby compiled my display_string function into.

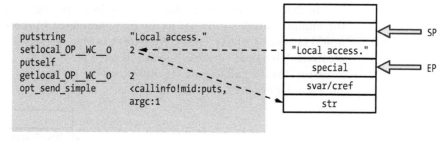

Figure 3-18: The display_string *method compiled into YARV instructions*

Ruby uses the setlocal YARV instruction to set the value of a local variable. However, instead of setlocal in Figure 3-18, I show an instruction called setlocal_OP__WC__0.

As it turns out, beginning with version 2.0, Ruby uses an optimized instruction with this confusing name instead of the simple setlocal. The difference is that Ruby 2.0 includes one of the parameters of the instruction, 0, in the instruction name itself.

Internally, Ruby 2.0 calls this the *operand* optimization. (In the optimized instruction name, *OP* stands for *operand* and *WC* for *wildcard*.) In other words, getlocal_OP__WC__0 is equivalent to getlocal *, 0, and setlocal_ OP__WC__0 is the same as setlocal *, 0. The instruction now requires only one parameter, as indicated by *. This trick allows Ruby 2.0 to save a bit of time because it doesn't need to pass the 0 argument separately.

But to keep things simple, let's ignore the operand optimization. Figure 3-19 repeats the YARV instructions for my example but shows getlocal and setlocal with the second operand listed normally.

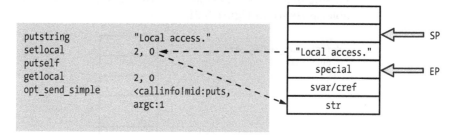

Figure 3-19: The compiled version of display_string *shown without operand optimization*

This a bit easier to understand. As you can see, first the putstring instruction saves the Local access string on top of the stack, incrementing the SP pointer. Then, YARV uses the setlocal instruction to get the value at the top of the stack and save it in the space allocated on the stack for the str local variable. The two dashed arrows on the left side of Figure 3-19 show the setlocal instruction copying the value. This type of operation is called *local variable access.*

To determine which variable to set, setlocal uses the EP pointer and the numerical index provided as the first parameter. In this example, that would be address of str = EP-2. We'll discuss what the second parameter, 0, means in "Dynamic Variable Access" on page 71.

Next, for the call to puts str, Ruby uses the getlocal instruction, as shown in Figure 3-20.

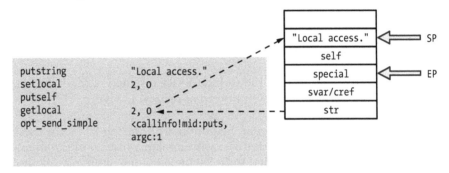

Figure 3-20: Getting the value of a local variable using getlocal

Here, Ruby has pushed the string value back onto the top of the stack, where it can be used as an argument for the call to the puts function. Again, the first parameter to getlocal, 2, indicates which local variable to access. Ruby uses the local table for this snippet at compile time to find out 2 corresponds to the variable str.

Method Arguments Are Treated Like Local Variables

Passing in a *method argument* works the same way as accessing a local variable, as shown in Figure 3-21.

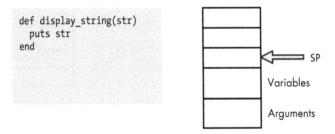

Figure 3-21: Ruby stores method arguments on the stack just like local variables.

Method arguments are essentially the same as local variables. The only difference between the two is that the calling code pushes the arguments onto the stack before the method call even occurs. In this example there are no local variables, but the single argument appears on the stack just like a local variable, as shown in Figure 3-22.

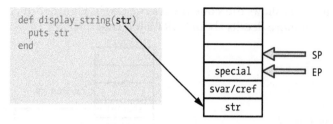

Figure 3-22: The calling code saves the argument values before the method is called.

Dynamic Variable Access

Now let's see how dynamic variable access works and what that special value is. Ruby uses dynamic access when you use a variable that's defined in a different scope—for example, when you write a block that references values in the surrounding code. Listing 3-6 shows an example.

```
def display_string
  str = "Dynamic access."
  10.times do
    puts str
  end
end
```

Listing 3-6: The code inside the block accesses str in the surrounding method.

Here, str is a local variable in display_string. As you can see in Figure 3-23, Ruby will save str using the setlocal instruction in just the same way we saw in Figure 3-18.

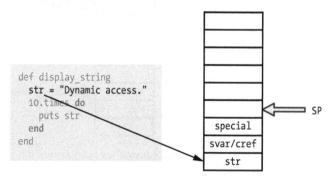

Figure 3-23: Ruby saves the value of the str local variable on the stack as usual.

Next, Ruby will call the 10.times method, passing a block in as an argument. Let's step through the process of calling a method with a block.

Figure 3-24 shows the same process we saw in Figures 3-10, 3-11, and 3-12 but with more details about YARV's internal stack.

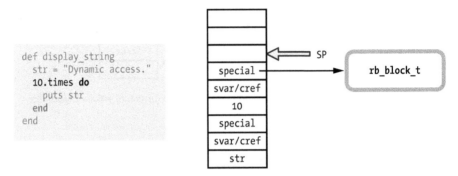

```
def display_string
  str = "Dynamic access."
  10.times do
    puts str
  end
end
```

Figure 3-24: When Ruby calls a method passing in a block, it saves a pointer to a new rb_block_t structure as the special value in the new stack frame.

Notice the value 10 on the stack: This is the actual receiver of the times method. Notice too that Ruby has created a new stack frame with svar/cref and special above the value 10 for the C code that implements Integer#times to use. Because we passed a block into the method call, Ruby saves a pointer to this block in the special variable in the new stack frame. Each frame on the YARV stack corresponding to a method call tracks whether there was a block argument using this special variable. (I'll discuss blocks and the rb_block_t structure in more detail in Chapter 8.)

Now the Integer#times method yields to or calls the block's code 10 times. Figure 3-25 shows how the YARV stack appears when Ruby is executing the code inside the block.

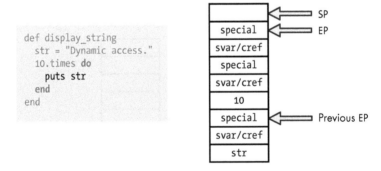

```
def display_string
  str = "Dynamic access."
  10.times do
    puts str
  end
end
```

Figure 3-25: How YARV's stack would appear if we halted execution inside the block

Just as we saw in Figures 3-17 through 3-22, Ruby sets EP to point to the location of the special value in each stack frame. Figure 3-25 shows one value of EP for the new stack frame used by the block near the top of the stack and a second value of EP in the original method's stack frame near the bottom. In Figure 3-25 this second pointer is labeled *Previous EP*.

Now, what happens when Ruby executes the puts str code inside the block? Ruby needs to obtain the value of the local variable str and pass it to the puts function as an argument. But notice in Figure 3-25 that str is located farther down the stack. It's not a local variable inside the block; rather, it's a variable in the surrounding method, display_string. How does Ruby obtain the value from farther down the stack while executing code inside the block?

This is where dynamic variable access comes in and why Ruby needs those special values in each stack frame. Figure 3-26 shows how dynamic variable access works.

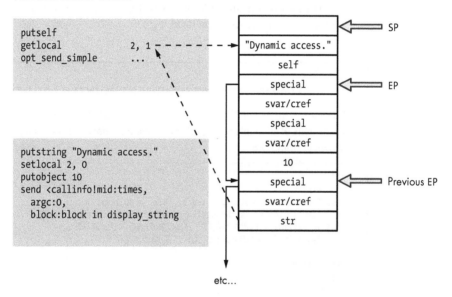

Figure 3-26: Ruby using dynamic variable access to obtain the value of str from farther down the stack

The dashed arrows indicate dynamic variable access: The getlocal YARV instruction copies the value of str from the lower stack frame (from the parent or outer Ruby scope) to the top of the stack, where the block can access it. Notice how the EP pointers form a kind of ladder that Ruby can climb to access the local variables in the parent scope, the grandparent scope, and so on.

In the getlocal 2, 1 call in Figure 3-26, the second parameter, 1, tells Ruby where to find the variable. In this example, Ruby will follow the ladder of EP pointers one level down the stack to find str. That is, 1 means step once from the block's scope to the surrounding method's scope.

Listing 3-7 shows another example of dynamic variable access.

```
def display_string
  str = "Dynamic access."
  10.times do
    10.times do
      puts str
    end
  end
end
```

Listing 3-7: In this example, Ruby would step two levels down the stack to find str *using dynamic variable access.*

If I had two nested blocks, as in Listing 3-7, Ruby would have used getlocal 2, 2 instead of getlocal 2, 1.

CLIMBING THE ENVIRONMENT POINTER LADDER IN C

Let's look at the actual C implementation of getlocal. As it does with most YARV instructions, Ruby implements getlocal in the *insns.def* code file, using the code shown in Listing 3-8.

```
/**
  @c variable
  @e Get local variable (pointed by `idx' and `level').
     'level' indicates the nesting depth from the current block.
  @j level, idx で指定されたローカル変数の値をスタックに置く。
     level はブロックのネストレベルで、何段上かを示す。
 */
DEFINE_INSN
getlocal
(lindex_t idx, rb_num_t level)
()
(VALUE val)
{
    int i, lev = (int)level;
❶   VALUE *ep = GET_EP();

    for (i = 0; i < lev; i++) {
❷       ep = GET_PREV_EP(ep);
    }
❸   val = *(ep - idx);
}
```

Listing 3-8: The C implementation of the getlocal *YARV instruction*

First, the GET_EP macro ❶ returns the EP from the current scope. (This macro is defined in the *vm_insnhelper.h* file along with a number of other macros related to

---

YARV instructions.) Next, Ruby iterates over the EP pointers, moving from the current to the parent scope and then from the parent to the grandparent scope by repeatedly dereferencing the EP pointers. Ruby uses the GET_PREV_EP macro at ❷ (also defined in *vm_insnhelper.h*) to move from one EP to another. The level parameter tells Ruby how many times to iterate or how many rungs of the ladder to climb.

Finally, Ruby obtains the target variable using the idx parameter at ❸, which is the index of the target variable. As a result, this line of code gets the value from the target variable.

```
val = *(ep - idx);
```

This code means the following:

- Start from the address of the EP for the target scope ep, obtained previously from the GET_PREV_EP iterations.

- Subtract idx from this address. The integer value idx gives getlocal the index of the local variable that you want to load from the local table. In other words, it tells getlocal how far down the stack the target variable is located.

- Get the value from the YARV stack at the adjusted address.

Therefore, in the call to getlocal in Figure 3-26, YARV will take the EP from the scope one level down on the YARV stack and subtract the index value str (in this case, 2) to obtain a pointer to the str variable.

```
getlocal 2, 1
```

Experiment 3-2: Exploring Special Variables

In Figures 3-16 through 3-26, I showed you a value called svar/cref in the EP-1 position on the stack. What are these two values, and how can Ruby save two values in one location on the stack? For that matter, why does it do this? Let's find out.

Usually, the EP-1 slot in the stack will contain the svar value, which is a pointer to a table of any special variables defined in this stack frame. In Ruby the term *special variables* refers to values that Ruby automatically creates as a matter of convenience, based on the environment or on recent operations. For example, Ruby sets $* to the ARGV array and $! to the last exception raised.

All special variables begin with the dollar sign ($) character, which usually indicates a global variable. Does that mean that special variables are global variables? If so, then why does Ruby save a pointer to them on the stack?

To answer this question, let's create a simple Ruby script to match a string using a regular expression.

```
/fox/.match("The quick brown fox jumped over the lazy dog.\n")
puts "Value of $& in the top level scope: #{$&}"
```

Here I match the word fox in the string using a regex, and then I print the matching string using the $& special variable. Here's the output I get running this at the console.

```
$ ruby regex.rb
Value of $& in the top level scope: fox
```

Listing 3-9 shows another example, this time searching for the same string twice: first in the top-level scope and then again from inside a method call.

```
  str = "The quick brown fox jumped over the lazy dog.\n"
❶ /fox/.match(str)

  def search(str)
❷   /dog/.match(str)
❸   puts "Value of $& inside method: #{$&}"
  end
  search(str)

❹ puts "Value of $& in the top level scope: #{$&}"
```

Listing 3-9: Referring to $& from two different scopes

This is simple Ruby code, but it still may be a bit confusing. Here's how this works:

- We search the string in the top scope for fox at ❶. This matches and saves fox into the $& special variable.
- We call the search method and search for dog at ❷. I immediately print the match using the same $& variable inside the method at ❸.
- Finally, we return to the top-level scope and print the value of $& again at ❹.

Running this test gives the following output.

```
$ ruby regex_method.rb
Value of $& inside method: dog
Value of $& in the top level scope: fox
```

This is what we expect, but consider the following for a moment. The $& variable is obviously not global because it has different values at different places in my Ruby script. Ruby preserves the value of $& from the top-level scope when executing the search method, which allows me to print the matching word fox from the original search. Ruby provides for this behavior by saving a separate set of special variables at each level of the stack using the svar value, as shown in Figure 3-27.

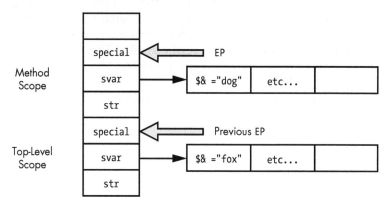

Figure 3-27: Each stack frame has its own set of special variables.

Notice that Ruby saved the fox string in a table referred to by the svar pointer for the top-level scope and saved the dog string in a different table for the inner-method scope. Ruby finds the proper special variable table using the EP pointer for each stack frame.

Ruby saves actual global variables (variables you define using a dollar sign prefix) in a single, global hash table. Regardless of where you save or retrieve the value of a normal global variable, Ruby accesses the same global hash table.

Now for one more test: What if I perform the search inside a block and not a method? Listing 3-10 shows this new search.

```
str = "The quick brown fox jumped over the lazy dog.\n"
/fox/.match(str)

2.times do
  /dog/.match(str)
  puts "Value of $& inside block: #{$&}"
end

puts "Value of $& in the top-level scope: #{$&}"
```

Listing 3-10: Displaying the value of $& from inside a block

Here's the output I get at the console this time.

```
$ ruby regex_block.rb
Value of $& inside block: dog
Value of $& inside block: dog
Value of $& in the top-level scope: dog
```

Notice that now Ruby has overwritten the value of $& in the top scope with the matching word dog from the search I performed inside the block! This is by design: Ruby considers the top-level and inner-block scope to be the same with regard to special variables. This is similar to how dynamic variable access works; we expect variables inside the block to have the same values as those in the parent scope.

Figure 3-28 shows how Ruby implements this behavior.

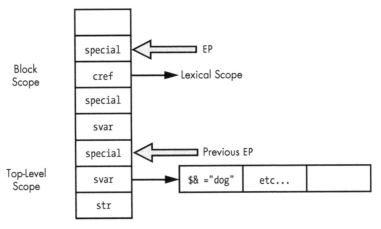

Figure 3-28: Ruby uses the EP-1 stack position for cref in blocks and for svar otherwise.

As you can see in Figure 3-28, Ruby has just a single special variable table for the top-level scope. It finds the special variables using the previous EP pointer, which points to the top-level scope. Inside the block scope (because there is no need for a separate copy of the special variables), Ruby takes advantage of the EP-1 open slot and saves the value cref there instead. Ruby uses the cref value to keep track of which lexical scope this block belongs to. *Lexical scope* refers to a section of code within the syntactical structure of your program and is used by Ruby to look up constant values. (See Chapter 6 for more on lexical scope.) Specifically, Ruby uses the cref value here to implement metaprogramming API calls, such as eval and instance_eval. The cref value indicates whether the given block should be executed in a different lexical scope compared to the parent scope. (See "instance_eval Creates a Singleton Class for a New Lexical Scope" on page 243.)

A DEFINITIVE LIST OF SPECIAL VARIABLES

One place to find an accurate list of all the special variables that Ruby supports is the C source itself. For example, Listing 3-11 is a piece of Ruby's C source code that tokenizes your Ruby program, as snipped from the parser_yylex function located in *parse.y*:

```
❶ case '$':
   lex_state = EXPR_END;
   newtok();
   c = nextc();
❷ switch (c) {
❸   case '_':              /* $_: last read line string */
       c = nextc();
       if (parser_is_identchar()) {
           tokadd('$');
           tokadd('_');
           break;
       }
       pushback(c);
       c = '_';
       /* fall through */
❹   case '~':              /* $~: match-data */
     case '*':             /* $*: argv */
     case '$':             /* $$: pid */
     case '?':             /* $?: last status */
     case '!':             /* $!: error string */
     case '@':             /* $@: error position */
     case '/':             /* $/: input record separator */
     case '\\':            /* $\: output record separator */
     case ';':             /* $;: field separator */
     case ',':             /* $,: output field separator */
     case '.':             /* $.: last read line number */
     case '=':             /* $=: ignorecase */
     case ':':             /* $:: load path */
     case '<':             /* $<: reading filename */
     case '>':             /* $>: default output handle */
     case '\"':            /* $": already loaded files */
       tokadd('$');
       tokadd(c);
       tokfix();
       set_yylval_name(rb_intern(tok()));
       return tGVAR;
```

Listing 3-11: Consulting parse.y is a good way to find a definitive list of Ruby's many special variables.

Notice at ❶ that Ruby matches a dollar sign character ($). This is part of the large C switch statement that tokenizes your Ruby code—the process I discussed in "Tokens: The Words That Make Up the Ruby Language" on page 4. This is

continued

followed by an inner `switch` statement at ❷ that matches on the following character. Each of these characters and each of the `case` statements that follow (at ❸ and after ❹) correspond to one of Ruby's special variables.

Just a bit farther down in the function, more C code (see Listing 3-12) parses other special variable tokens that you write in your Ruby code, such as $& and related special variables.

```
❶ case '&':                    /* $&: last match */
  case '`':                    /* $`: string before last match */
  case '\'':                   /* $': string after last match */
  case '+':                    /* $+: string matches last paren. */
    if (last_state == EXPR_FNAME) {
        tokadd('$');
        tokadd(c);
        goto gvar;
    }
    set_yylval_node(NEW_BACK_REF(c));
    return tBACK_REF;
```

Listing 3-12: These case statements correspond to Ruby's regex-related special variables.

At ❶ you can see four more `case` statements corresponding to the special variables $&, $`, $/, and $+, all related to regular expressions.

Finally, the code in Listing 3-13 tokenizes $1, $2, and so on, producing the special variables that return the nth back reference from the last regular expression operation.

```
❶ case '1': case '2': case '3':
  case '4': case '5': case '6':
  case '7': case '8': case '9':
    tokadd('$');
❷   do {
        tokadd(c);
        c = nextc();
    } while (c != -1 && ISDIGIT(c));
    pushback(c);
    if (last_state == EXPR_FNAME) goto gvar;
    tokfix();
    set_yylval_node(NEW_NTH_REF(atoi(tok()+1)));
    return tNTH_REF;
```

Listing 3-13: This C code tokenizes Ruby's nth back reference special variables: $1, $2, and so forth.

The `case` statements at ❶ match the numerical digits 1 through 9, while the C `do...while` loop at ❷ continues to process digits until an entire number is read in. This allows you to create special variables with multiple digits, such as $12.

Summary

We've covered a lot of ground in this chapter. We began by looking at how Ruby keeps track of two stacks: an internal stack YARV uses and your Ruby call stack. Next, we saw how YARV executed two simple Ruby programs: one that calculated 2 + 2 = 4 and another that called a block 10 times. In Experiment 3-1 we learned that executing YARV instructions in Ruby 2.0 and 1.9 is almost four times faster than in Ruby 1.8, which executes your program directly from the AST.

We moved on to look at how Ruby saves variables on the internal YARV stack using two methods: local and dynamic variable access. We also saw how method arguments are handled by Ruby in just the same way as local variables. In Experiment 3-2 we finished with a look at how Ruby handles special variables.

When you run any Ruby program, you are actually using a virtual machine designed specifically to execute Ruby programs. By examining how this machine works on a detailed level, we've acquired a deeper understanding of how the Ruby language works and, for example, what happens when you call a method or save a value in a local variable. In Chapter 4 we'll continue to explore this virtual machine by looking at how control structures work and at YARV's method dispatch process.

*YARV uses its own internal set
of control structures, like the
structures you use in Ruby.*

4

CONTROL STRUCTURES AND METHOD DISPATCH

In Chapter 3 I explained how YARV uses a stack while executing its instruction set and how it can access variables locally or dynamically. Controlling the flow of execution is another fundamental requirement for any programming language, and Ruby has a rich set of control structures, too. How does YARV implement control structures?

Like Ruby, YARV has its own control structures, albeit at a much lower level. Instead of if or unless statements, YARV uses two low-level instructions called branchif and branchunless. Instead of using control structures such as while...end or until...end loops, YARV has a single low-level function called jump that allows it to change the program counter and move through your compiled program. By combining the branchif or branchunless instruction with the jump instruction, YARV can execute most of Ruby's simple control structures.

When your code calls a method, YARV uses the *send* instruction. This process is known as *method dispatch*. You can consider *send* to be another one of Ruby's control structures—the most complex and sophisticated one of all.

In this chapter we'll learn more about YARV by exploring how it controls execution flow in your program. We'll also look at the method dispatch process as we learn how Ruby categorizes methods into types, calling each method type differently.

How Ruby Executes an if Statement

In order to understand how YARV controls execution flow, let's see how the if...else statement works. The left side of Figure 4-1 shows a simple Ruby script that uses both if and else. On the right side of the figure, you can see the corresponding snippet of compiled YARV instructions. Reading the YARV instructions, you see that Ruby follows a pattern for implementing the if...else statement. It goes like this:

1. Evaluate condition
2. Jump to false code if condition is false
3. True code; jump past false code
4. False code

```
i = 0                        0000 trace           1
if i < 10                    0002 putobject       0
  puts "small"               0003 setlocal        2, 0
else                         0005 trace           1
  puts "large"               0007 getlocal        2, 0
end                          0009 putobject       10
puts "done"                  0011 opt_lt          <callinfo!mid:<, argc:1
                             0013 branchunless    25
                             0015 trace           1
                             0017 putself
                             0018 putstring       "small"
                             0020 opt_send_simple <callinfo!mid:puts, argc:1
                             0022 pop
                             0023 jump            33
                             0025 trace           1
                             0027 putself
                             0028 putstring       "large"
                             0030 opt_send_simple <callinfo!mid:puts, argc:1
                             0032 pop
                             0033 trace           1
                             0035 putself
                             0036 putstring       "done"
                             0038 opt_send_simple <callinfo!mid:puts, argc:1
                             0040 leave
```

Figure 4-1: How Ruby compiles an if...else statement

This pattern should be a bit easier to follow in the flowchart shown in Figure 4-2 on the next page. The branchunless instruction in the center of the figure is the key to how Ruby implements if statements. It works as follows:

1. Ruby evaluates the condition of the if statement, i < 10, using the opt_lt (optimized less-than) instruction. This evaluation leaves either a true or false value on the stack.

2. branchunless jumps down to the else code if the condition is false. That is, it "branches unless" the condition is true. Ruby uses branchunless, not branchif, for if...else conditions because the positive case is compiled to appear right after the condition code. Therefore, YARV needs to jump if the condition is false.

3. If the condition is true, Ruby does not branch and just continues to execute the positive case code. Once it's finished, it jumps down to the instructions following the if...else statement using the jump instruction.

4. Whether or not it branches, Ruby continues to execute the subsequent code.

YARV implements the unless statement similarly to how it implements if, except that the positive and negative code snippets are in reverse order. For looping control structures like while...end and until...end, YARV uses the branchif instruction instead, but the idea is the same: Calculate the loop condition, execute branchif to jump as necessary, and then use jump statements to implement the loop.

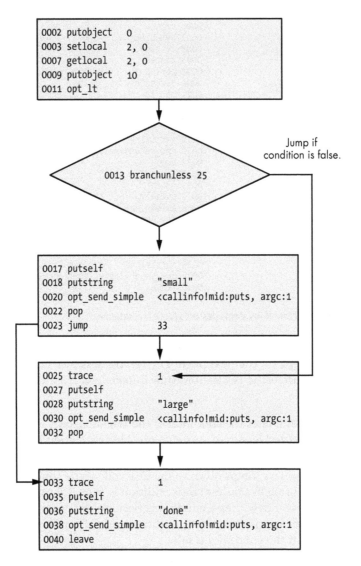

```
0002 putobject   0
0003 setlocal    2, 0
0007 getlocal    2, 0
0009 putobject   10
0011 opt_lt
```

Jump if
condition is false.

0013 branchunless 25

```
0017 putself
0018 putstring       "small"
0020 opt_send_simple  <callinfo!mid:puts, argc:1
0022 pop
0023 jump             33
```

```
0025 trace            1
0027 putself
0028 putstring        "large"
0030 opt_send_simple  <callinfo!mid:puts, argc:1
0032 pop
```

```
0033 trace            1
0035 putself
0036 putstring        "done"
0038 opt_send_simple  <callinfo!mid:puts, argc:1
0040 leave
```

Figure 4-2: This flowchart shows the pattern Ruby uses to compile
if...else statements.

Jumping from One Scope to Another

One of the challenges YARV has in implementing some control structures
is that, as with dynamic variable access, Ruby can jump from one scope to
another. For example, break can be used to exit a simple loop like the one
in Listing 4-1.

```
i = 0
while i<10
  puts i
  i += 1
  break
end
```

Listing 4-1: break used to exit a simple loop

And it can also be used to exit a block iteration, like the one in Listing 4-2.

```
10.times do |n|
  puts n
  break
end
puts "continue from here"
```

Listing 4-2: break used to exit a block

In the first listing, YARV can exit the while loop using simple jump instructions. But exiting a block like the one in the second listing is not so simple: In this case, YARV needs to jump to the parent scope and continue execution after the call to 10.times. How does YARV know where to jump to? And how does it adjust both its internal stack and your Ruby call stack in order to continue execution properly in the parent scope?

To implement jumping from one place to another in the Ruby call stack (that is, outside the current scope), Ruby uses the throw YARV instruction. This instruction resembles the Ruby throw method: It sends, or throws, the execution path back up to a higher scope. For example, Figure 4-3 shows how Ruby compiles Listing 4-2, with the block containing a break statement. The Ruby code is on the left, and the compiled version is on the right.

```
10.times do |n|              putself
  puts n                     getlocal        2, 0
  break                      opt_send_simple <callinfo!mid:puts, argc:1
end                          pop
puts "continue from here"    putnil
                             throw           2
                             leave


                             putobject       10
                             send            <callinfo!mid:times, argc:0
                             pop
                             putself
                             putstring       "continue from here"
                             opt_send_simple <callinfo!mid:puts, argc:1
                             leave
```

Figure 4-3: How Ruby compiles a break statement used inside a block

Catch Tables

At the top right of Figure 4-3, the throw 2 in the compiled code for the block throws an exception at the YARV instruction level using a *catch table*, or a table of pointers that may be attached to any YARV code snippet. Conceptually, a catch table might look like Figure 4-4.

```
YARV instructions                                          Catch Table

putobject          10
send               <callinfo!mid:times, argc:0
pop ◄───────────────────────────────────────── BREAK
putself
putstring          "continue from here"
opt_send_simple    <callinfo!mid:puts, argc:1
leave
```

Figure 4-4: Each snippet of YARV code can contain a catch table.

This catch table contains just a single pointer to the pop statement, where execution would continue after an exception. Whenever you use a break statement in a block, Ruby compiles the throw instruction into the block's code. And whenever you call a block or write a loop using while, for, and so on, Ruby adds the BREAK entry into the parent scope's catch table. If you wrote a nested loop, Ruby would add the BREAK entry to the outer loop scope's catch table.

Later, when YARV executes the throw instruction, it checks to see whether there's a catch table containing a break pointer for the current YARV instruction sequence, as shown in Figure 4-5.

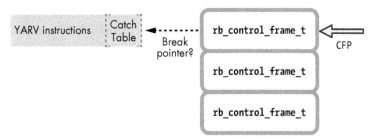

Figure 4-5: While executing a throw instruction, YARV starts iterating down the Ruby call stack.

If it doesn't find a catch table, Ruby starts to iterate down through the stack of rb_control_frame_t structures in search of a catch table containing a break pointer, as shown in Figure 4-6.

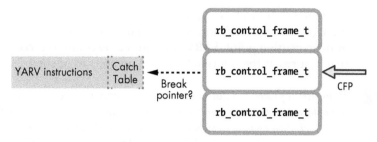

Figure 4-6: Ruby continues to iterate down the call stack looking for a catch table with a break pointer.

As you can see in Figure 4-7, Ruby continues to iterate until it finds a catch table with a break pointer.

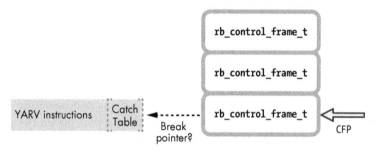

Figure 4-7: Ruby keeps iterating until it finds a catch table with a break pointer or reaches the end of the call stack.

In this simple example, there is only one level of block nesting, so Ruby finds the catch table and break pointer after just one iteration, as shown in Figure 4-8.

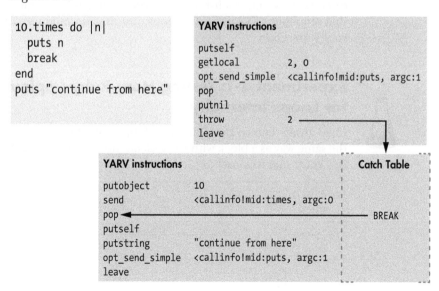

Figure 4-8: Ruby finds a catch table with a break pointer.

Once Ruby finds the catch table pointer, it resets both the Ruby call stack (the CFP pointer) and the internal YARV stack to reflect the new program execution point. YARV continues to execute your code from there—that is, it resets the internal PC and SP pointers as needed.

> **NOTE** *Ruby uses a process similar to raising and rescuing an exception internally in order to implement a very commonly used control structure: the break keyword. In other words, what in more verbose languages is an exceptional occurrence becomes in Ruby a common, everyday action. Ruby has wrapped up a confusing, unusual syntax—the raising/rescuing of exceptions—into a simple keyword, break, and made it very easy to understand and use. (Of course, Ruby needs to use exceptions because of the way blocks work. On the one hand, they're like separate functions or subroutines, but on the other, they're just part of the surrounding code.)*

Other Uses for Catch Tables

The return keyword is another ordinary Ruby control structure that also uses catch tables. Whenever you call return from inside a block, Ruby raises an internal exception that it rescues with a catch table pointer in the same way it does when you call break. In fact, break and return are implemented with the same YARV instructions with one exception: For return, Ruby passes a 1 to the throw instruction (for example, throw 1), while for break, it passes a 2 (throw 2). The return and break keywords are really two sides of the same coin.

Besides break, Ruby uses the catch table to implement the control structures rescue, ensure, retry, redo, and next. For example, when you explicitly raise an exception in your Ruby code using the raise keyword, Ruby implements the rescue block using the catch table, but with a rescue pointer. The catch table is simply a list of event types that can be caught and handled by that sequence of YARV instructions, just as you would use a rescue block in your Ruby code.

Experiment 4-1: Testing How Ruby Implements for Loops Internally

I had always known that Ruby's for loop control structure worked essentially the same way as a block with the each method of the Enumerable module. That is, I knew that this code:

```
for i in 0..5
  puts i
end
```

worked like this code:

```
(0..5).each do |i|
  puts i
end
```

But I never suspected that internally Ruby actually implements for loops using each! In other words, Ruby has no for loop control structure. Instead, the for keyword is really just syntactical sugar for calling each with a range.

To prove this, simply inspect the YARV instructions produced by Ruby when you compile a for loop. In Listing 4-3, let's use the same RubyVM::InstructionSequence.compile method to display the YARV instructions.

```
code = <<END
for i in 0..5
  puts i
end
END
puts RubyVM::InstructionSequence.compile(code).disasm
```

Listing 4-3: This code will display how Ruby compiles a for loop.

Running this code gives the output shown in Listing 4-4.

```
== disasm: <RubyVM::InstructionSequence:<compiled>@<compiled>>==========
== catch table
| catch type: break  st: 0002 ed: 0006 sp: 0000 cont: 0006
|------------------------------------------------------------------------
local table (size: 2, argc: 0 [opts: 0, rest: -1, post: 0, block: -1] s1)
[ 2] i
0000 trace              1                                          (   1)
0002 putobject          0..5
0004 send               <callinfo!mid:each, argc:0, block:block in <compiled>>
0006 leave
== disasm: <RubyVM::InstructionSequence:block in <compiled>@<compiled>>=
== catch table
| catch type: redo   st: 0004 ed: 0015 sp: 0000 cont: 0004
| catch type: next   st: 0004 ed: 0015 sp: 0000 cont: 0015
|------------------------------------------------------------------------
local table (size: 2, argc: 1 [opts: 0, rest: -1, post: 0, block: -1] s3)
[ 2] ?<Arg>
0000 getlocal_OP__WC__0 2                                          (   3)
0002 setlocal_OP__WC__1 2                                          (   1)
0004 trace              256
0006 trace              1                                          (   2)
0008 putself
0009 getlocal_OP__WC__1 2
0011 opt_send_simple    <callinfo!mid:puts, argc:1, FCALL|ARGS_SKIP>
0013 trace              512                                        (   3)
0015 leave
```

Listing 4-4: The output generated by Listing 4-3

Figure 4-9 shows the Ruby code on the left and YARV instructions on the right. (I've removed some of the technical details, like the trace statements, in order to simplify things a bit.)

```
for i in 0..5
  puts i
end
```

```
putobject   0..5
send        <callinfo!mid:each, argc:0
leave
```

```
getlocal        2, 0
setlocal        2, 1
putself
getlocal        2, 1
opt_send_simple <callinfo!mid:puts, argc:1
leave
```

Figure 4-9: A simplified display of the YARV instructions in Listing 4-4

Notice that there are two separate YARV code blocks: The outer scope calls each on the range 0..5, and an inner block makes the puts i call. The getlocal 2, 0 instruction in the inner block loads the implied block parameter value, and the setlocal instruction that follows saves it into the local variable i, located back in the parent scope using dynamic variable access.

In effect, Ruby has automatically done the following:

- Converted the for i in 0..5 code into (0..5).each do
- Created a block parameter to hold each value in the range
- Copied the block parameter, or the iteration counter, back into the local variable i each time around the loop

The send Instruction: Ruby's Most Complex Control Structure

We've seen how YARV controls the execution flow of our Ruby program using low-level instructions such as branchunless and jump. However, the most commonly used and important YARV instruction for controlling Ruby program execution flow is the send instruction. The send instruction tells YARV to jump to another method and start executing it.

Method Lookup and Method Dispatch

How does send work? How does YARV know which method to call, and how does it actually call the method? Figure 4-10 shows a high-level overview of the process.

This seems very simple, but the algorithm Ruby uses to find and call the target method is actually very complex. First, in *method lookup*, Ruby searches for the method your code actually should call. This involves looping through the classes and modules that make up the receiver object.

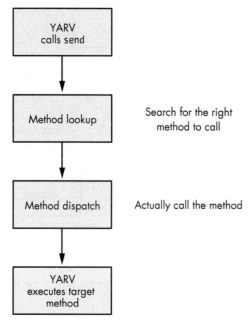

```
┌─────────────────┐
│      YARV       │
│   calls send    │
└─────────────────┘
         │
         ▼
┌─────────────────┐
│  Method lookup  │        Search for the right
└─────────────────┘           method to call
         │
         ▼
┌─────────────────┐
│ Method dispatch │        Actually call the method
└─────────────────┘
         │
         ▼
┌─────────────────┐
│      YARV       │
│ executes target │
│     method      │
└─────────────────┘
```

Figure 4-10: Ruby uses method lookup to find which method to call, and uses method dispatch to call it.

Once Ruby finds the method your code is trying to call, it uses *method dispatch* to actually execute the method call. This involves preparing the arguments to the method, pushing a new frame onto YARV's internal stack, and changing YARV's internal registers in order to actually start executing the target method. Like method lookup, method dispatch is a complex process because of the way Ruby categorizes your methods.

During the rest of this chapter I'll discuss the method dispatch process. We'll see how method lookup works in Chapter 6, once we have learned more about how Ruby implements objects, classes, and modules.

Eleven Types of Ruby Methods

Internally, Ruby categorizes your methods into 11 different types! During the method dispatch process, Ruby determines which type of method your code is trying to call. It then calls each type of method differently depending on its type, as shown in Figure 4-11.

Most methods—including all methods you write with Ruby code in your program—are referred to as ISEQ, or *instruction sequence* methods, by YARV's internal source code because Ruby compiles your code into a series of YARV bytecode instructions. But internally, YARV uses 10 other method types as well. These other method types are required because Ruby needs to call certain methods in a special way in order to speed up method dispatch, because these methods are implemented with C code or for various internal, technical reasons.

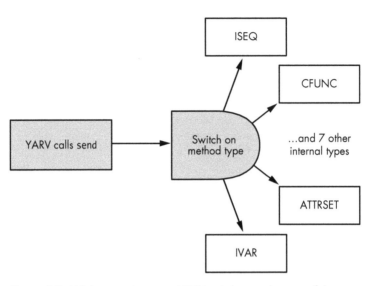

Figure 4-11: While executing send, YARV switches on the type of the target method.

Here's a quick description of all 11 method types. We'll explore some of these in more detail in the following sections.

ISEQ A normal method that you write using Ruby code, this is the most common method type. ISEQ stands for *instruction sequence.*

CFUNC Using C code included directly inside the Ruby executable, these are the methods that Ruby implements rather than you. CFUNC stands for *C function.*

ATTRSET A method of this type is created by the `attr_writer` method. ATTRSET stands for *attribute set.*

IVAR Ruby uses this method type when you call `attr_reader`. IVAR stands for *instance variable.*

BMETHOD Ruby uses this method type when you call `define_method` and pass in a proc object. Because the method is represented internally by a proc, Ruby needs to handle this method type in a special way.

ZSUPER Ruby uses this method type when you set a method to be public or private in a particular class or module when it was actually defined in some superclass. This method is not commonly used.

UNDEF Ruby uses this method type internally when it needs to remove a method from a class. Also, if you remove a method using `undef_method`, Ruby creates a new method of the same name using the UNDEF method type.

NOTIMPLEMENTED Like UNDEF, Ruby uses this method type to mark certain methods as not implemented. This is necessary, for example, when you run Ruby on a platform that doesn't support a particular operating system call.

OPTIMIZED Ruby speeds up some important methods using this type, like the `Kernel#send` method.

MISSING Ruby uses this method type if you ask for a method object from a module or class using `Kernel#method` and the method is missing.

REFINED Ruby uses this method type in its implementation of refinements, a new feature introduced in version 2.0.

Now let's focus on the most important and frequently used method types: ISEQ, CFUNC, ATTRSET, and IVAR.

Calling Normal Ruby Methods

Most methods in your Ruby code are identified by the constant `VM_METHOD_TYPE_ISEQ` inside Ruby's source code. This means that they consist of a sequence of YARV instructions.

You define standard Ruby methods in your code with the `def` keyword, as shown here.

```
def display_message
  puts "The quick brown fox jumps over the lazy dog."
end
display_message
```

`display_message` is a standard method because it's created using the `def` keyword followed by normal Ruby code. Figure 4-12 shows how Ruby calls the `display_message` method.

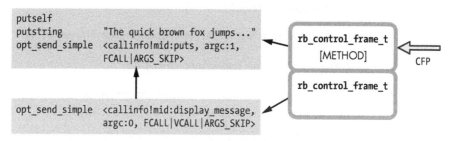

Figure 4-12: A normal method is comprised of YARV instructions.

On the left are two snippets of YARV code: the calling code at the bottom and the target method at the top. On the right you can see that Ruby created a new stack frame using a new `rb_control_frame_t` structure, set to type METHOD.

The key idea in Figure 4-12 is that both the calling code and the target method are comprised of YARV instructions. When you call a standard method, YARV creates a new stack frame and then starts executing the instructions in the target method.

Preparing Arguments for Normal Ruby Methods

When Ruby compiles your code, it creates a table of local variables and arguments for each method. Each argument listed in the local table is labeled as standard (<Arg>) or as one of a few different special types, such as block, optional, and so on. Ruby records the type of each method's arguments in this way so it can tell whether any additional work is required when your code calls the method. Listing 4-5 shows a single Ruby method that uses each type of argument.

```ruby
def five_argument_types(a, b = 1, *args, c, &d)
  puts "Standard argument #{a.inspect}"
  puts "Optional argument #{b.inspect}"
  puts "Splat argument array #{args.inspect}"
  puts "Post argument #{c.inspect}"
  puts "Block argument #{d.inspect}"
end

five_argument_types(1, 2, 3, 4, 5, 6) do
  puts "block"
end
```

Listing 4-5: Ruby's argument types (argument_types.rb)

Listing 4-6 shows the result when we call the example method with the numbers 1 through 6 and a block.

```
$ ruby argument_types.rb
Standard argument 1
Optional argument 2
Splat argument array [3, 4, 5]
Post argument 6
Block argument #<Proc:0x007ff4b2045ac0@argument_types.rb:9>
```

Listing 4-6: The output generated by Listing 4-5

To make this behavior possible, YARV does some additional processing on each type of argument when you call a method:

Block arguments   When you use the & operator in an argument list, Ruby needs to convert the provided block into a proc object.

Optional arguments   Ruby adds additional code to the target method when you use an optional argument with a default value. This code sets the default value into the argument. When you later call a method with an optional argument, YARV resets the program counter or PC register to skip this added code when a value is provided.

Splat argument array   For these, YARV creates a new array object and collects the provided argument values into it. (See the array [3, 4, 5] in Listing 4-6.)

Standard and post arguments   Because these need no special treatment, YARV has no additional work to do.

Then there are keyword arguments. Whenever Ruby calls a method that uses keyword arguments, YARV has even more work to do. ("Experiment 4-2: Exploring How Ruby Implements Keyword Arguments" on page 99 explores this in more detail.)

Calling Built-In Ruby Methods

Many of the methods built into the Ruby language are CFUNC methods (VM_METHOD_TYPE_CFUNC in Ruby's C source code). Ruby implements these using C code rather than Ruby code. For example, consider the Integer#times method from "Executing a Call to a Block" on page 61. The Integer class is included in the Ruby interpreter, and the times method is implemented by C code in the file *numeric.c*.

The classes you use every day have many examples of CFUNC methods, such as String, Array, Object, Kernel, and so on. For example, the String#upcase method is implemented by C code in *string.c*, and Struct#each is implemented by C code in *struct.c*.

When Ruby calls a built-in CFUNC method, it doesn't need to prepare the method arguments in the same way it does with normal ISEQ methods; it simply creates a new stack frame and calls the target method, as shown in Figure 4-13.

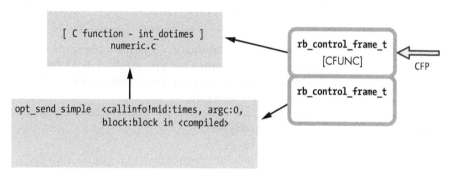

Figure 4-13: Ruby implements CFUNC methods using C code in one of Ruby's C source files.

As we saw with ISEQ methods in Figure 4-12, calling a CFUNC method involves creating a new stack frame. This time, however, Ruby uses a rb_control_frame_t structure with type CFUNC instead.

Calling attr_reader and attr_writer

Ruby uses two special method types, IVAR and ATTRSET, to speed up the process of accessing and setting instance variables in your code. Before I explain what these method types mean and how method dispatch works with them, have a look at Listing 4-7, which retrieves and sets the value of an instance variable.

```
  class InstanceVariableTest
❶   def var
      @var
    end
❷   def var=(val)
      @var = val
    end
  end
```

Listing 4-7: A Ruby class with an instance variable and accessor methods

In this listing, the class `InstanceVariableTest` contains an instance variable, `@var`, and two methods, var ❶ and var= ❷. Because I wrote these methods using Ruby code, both will be standard Ruby methods with the type set to `VM_METHOD_TYPE_ISEQ`. As you can see, they allow you to get or set the value of `@var`.

Ruby actually provides a shortcut for creating these methods: `attr_reader` and `attr_writer`. The following code shows a shorter way of writing the same class, using these shortcuts.

```
class InstanceVariableTest
  attr_reader :var
  attr_writer :var
end
```

Here, `attr_reader` automatically defines the same var method, and `attr_writer` automatically defines the var= method, both from Listing 4-7.

And here's an even simpler, more concise way of defining the same two methods using `attr_accessor`.

```
class InstanceVariableTest
  attr_accessor :var
end
```

As you can see, `attr_accessor` is shorthand for calling `attr_reader` and `attr_writer` together for the same instance variable.

Method Dispatch Optimizes attr_reader and attr_writer

Since Ruby developers use `attr_reader` and `attr_writer` so often, YARV uses two special method types, IVAR and ATTRSET, to speed up method dispatch and make your program run faster.

Let's begin with the ATTRSET method type. Whenever you define a method using `attr_writer` or `attr_accessor`, Ruby marks the generated method with the `VM_METHOD_TYPE_ATTRSET` method type internally. When Ruby executes the code and calls the method, it uses a C function, `vm_setivar`, to set the instance variable in a fast, optimized manner. Figure 4-14 shows how YARV calls the generated var= method to set var.

```
opt_send_simple  <callinfo!mid:var=, argc:1, ARGS_SKIP> ──▶ [ C function - vm_setivar ]
```

Figure 4-14: VM_METHOD_TYPE_ATTRSET methods call vm_setivar directly.

Notice that this figure is similar to Figure 4-13. In both cases, Ruby calls an internal C function when executing our code. But notice in Figure 4-14 that when executing an ATTRSET method, Ruby doesn't even create a new stack frame. It doesn't need to because the method is so short and simple. Also, because the generated var= method will never raise an exception, Ruby doesn't need a new stack frame to display in error messages. The vm_setivar C function can very quickly set the value and return.

The IVAR method type works similarly. When you define a method using attr_reader or attr_accessor, Ruby marks the generated method with the VM_METHOD_TYPE_IVAR method type internally. When it executes IVAR methods, Ruby calls an internal C function called vm_getivar to get and return the instance variable's value quickly, as shown in Figure 4-15.

```
opt_send_simple  <callinfo!mid:var, argc:0, ARGS_SKIP> ──▶ [ C function - vm_getivar ]
```

Figure 4-15: VM_METHOD_TYPE_IVAR methods call vm_getivar directly.

Here, the opt_send_simple YARV instruction on the left calls the vm_getivar C function on the right. As in Figure 4-14, when calling vm_setivar, Ruby doesn't need to create a new stack frame or execute YARV instructions. It simply returns the value of var immediately.

Experiment 4-2: Exploring How Ruby Implements Keyword Arguments

Beginning with Ruby 2.0, you can specify labels for method arguments. Listing 4-8 shows a simple example.

❶ ```
def add_two(a: 2, b: 3)
  a+b
end
```

❷ ```
puts add_two(a: 1, b: 1)
  => 2
```

Listing 4-8: A simple example of using keyword arguments

We use the labels a and b for the keyword arguments to add_two ❶. When we call the function ❷, we get the result 2. I hinted in Chapter 2 that Ruby uses a hash to implement keyword arguments. Let's prove this is the case using Listing 4-9.

```
   class Hash
❶   def key?(val)
❷     puts "Looking for key #{val}"
      false
    end
  end

  def add_two(a: 2, b: 3)
    a+b
  end

  puts add_two (a: 1, b: 1)
```

Listing 4-9: Demonstrating that Ruby uses a hash to implement keyword arguments

We override the key? method ❶ of the Hash class, which displays a message ❷ and then returns false. Here's the output we get when we run Listing 4-9.

```
Looking for key a
Looking for key b
5
```

As you can see, Ruby is calling Hash#key? twice: once to find the key a and a second time to find the key b. For some reason, Ruby has created a hash even though we never used a hash in the code. Also, Ruby is now ignoring the values we pass into add_two. Instead of 2, we get 5. It looks like Ruby is using the default values for a and b, not the values we provided. Why did Ruby create a hash, and what does it contain? And why did Ruby ignore my parameter values when I overrode Hash#key??

To learn how Ruby implements keyword arguments and to explain the results we see running Listing 4-9, we can examine the YARV instructions generated by Ruby's compiler for add_two. Running Listing 4-10 displays the YARV instructions that correspond to Listing 4-9.

```
code = <<END
def add_two(a: 2, b: 3)
  a+b
end

puts add_two(a: 1, b: 1)
END

puts RubyVM::InstructionSequence.compile(code).disasm
```

Listing 4-10: Displaying the YARV instructions for the code in Listing 4-9

Figure 4-16 shows a simplified version of the output generated by Listing 4-10.

```
def add_two(a: 2, b: 3)
  a+b
end

puts add_two(a: 1, b: 1)  ──▶
```

```
putself
putself
putspecialobject 1
putobject        [:a, 1, :b, 1]
opt_send_simple  <callinfo!
                 mid:core#hash_from_ary, argc:1
opt_send_simple  <callinfo!mid:add_two, argc:1
opt_send_simple  <callinfo!mid:puts, argc:1
```

Figure 4-16: Part of the output generated by Listing 4-10

On the right of Figure 4-16, you can see that Ruby first pushes an array onto the stack: [:a, 1, :b, 1]. Next, it calls the internal C function hash_from_ary, which we can guess will convert the [:a, 1, :b, 1] array into a hash. Finally, Ruby calls the add_two method to add the numbers and the puts method to display the result.

Now let's look at the YARV instructions for the add_two method itself, shown in Figure 4-17.

YARV instructions	Local Table
0000 getlocal 2, 0	
0002 dup	
0003 putobject :a	
0005 opt_send_simple <callinfo!mid:key?...	[2] ?
0007 branchunless 18	[3] b
0009 dup	[4] a
▶0010 putobject :a	
0012 opt_send_simple <callinfo!mid:delete...	
0014 setlocal 4, 0	
0016 jump 22	
0018 putobject 2	
0020 setlocal 4, 0	
0022 dup	
etc...	

```
def add_two(a: 2, b: 3)
  a+b
end

puts add_two(a: 1, b: 1)
```

Figure 4-17: The YARV instructions compiled from the beginning of the add_two method

What are these YARV instructions doing? The Ruby method add_two didn't contain any code similar to this! (All add_two does is add a and b together and return the sum.)

To find out, let's walk through Figure 4-17. On the left side, we see the Ruby add_two method, and on the right, the YARV instructions for add_two. On the far right, you see the local table for add_two. Notice that there are three values listed there: [2] ?, [3] b, and [4] a. It should be clear that a and b correspond to the two arguments to add_two, but what does [2] ? mean? This appears to be some sort of mystery value.

The mystery value is the hash we saw created in Figure 4-16! In order to implement keyword arguments, Ruby has created this third, hidden argument to add_two.

The YARV instructions in Figure 4-17 show that getlocal 2, 0 followed by dup places this hash onto the stack as a receiver. Next, putobject :a puts the symbol :a onto the stack as a method parameter, and opt_send_simple <callinfo!mid:key? calls the key? method on the receiver, which is the hash.

These YARV instructions are equivalent to the following line of Ruby code. Ruby is querying the hidden hash object to see whether it contains the key :a.

```
hidden_hash.key?(:a)
```

Reading the rest of the YARV instructions from Figure 4-17, we see that if the hash contains the key, Ruby calls the delete method, which removes the key from the hash and returns the corresponding value. Next, setlocal 4, 0 saves this value into the a argument. If the hash didn't contain the key :a, Ruby would call putobject 2 and setlocal 4, 0 to save the default value 2 into the argument.

To summarize, all of the YARV instructions shown in Figure 4-17 implement the snippet of Ruby code shown in Listing 4-11.

```
if hidden_hash.key?(:a)
  a = hidden_hash.delete(:a)
else
  a = 2
end
```

Listing 4-11: The YARV instructions shown in Figure 4-17 are equivalent to this Ruby code.

Now we can see that Ruby stores the keyword arguments and their values in the hidden hash argument. When the method starts, it first loads each argument's value from the hash or uses the default value if there is none. The behavior indicated by the Ruby code in Figure 4-14 explains the results we saw when running Listing 4-9. Remember that we changed the Hash#key? method to always return false. If hidden_hash.key? always returns false, Ruby will ignore the value of each argument and use the default value instead, even if a value was provided.

One last detail about keyword arguments: Whenever you call any method and use keyword arguments, YARV checks to see whether the keyword arguments you provide are expected by the target method. Ruby raises an exception if there is an unexpected argument, as shown in Listing 4-12.

```
def add_two(a: 2, b: 3)
  a+b
end

puts add_two(c: 9)
 => unknown keyword: c (ArgumentError)
```

Listing 4-12: Ruby throws an exception if you pass an unexpected keyword argument.

Because the argument list for add_two didn't include the letter c, Ruby throws an exception when we try to call the method with c. This special check happens during the method dispatch process.

Summary

This chapter began with a look at how YARV controls the execution flow of your Ruby program using a series of low-level control structures. By displaying the YARV instructions produced by Ruby's compiler, we saw some of YARV's control structures and learned how they work. In Experiment 4-1, we discovered that Ruby implements for loops internally using the each method with a block.

We also learned that internally Ruby categorizes methods into 11 types. We saw that Ruby creates a standard ISEQ method when you write a method using the def keyword and that Ruby labels its own built-in methods as CFUNC methods because they are implemented using C code. We learned about the ATTRSET and IVAR method types and saw how Ruby switches on the type of the target method during the method dispatch process.

Finally, in Experiment 4-2, we looked at how Ruby implements keyword arguments, and we discovered along the way that Ruby uses a hash to track the argument labels and default values.

In Chapter 5 we'll switch gears and explore objects and classes. We'll return to YARV internals again in Chapter 6 when we look at how the method lookup process works and discuss the concept of lexical scope.

Every Ruby object is the combination of a class pointer and an array of instance variables.

5

OBJECTS AND CLASSES

We learn early on that Ruby is an object-oriented language, descended from languages like Smalltalk and Simula. Every value is an object, and all Ruby programs consist of a set of objects and the messages sent between them. Typically, we learn about object-oriented programming by looking at how to use objects and what they can do: how they can group together data values and behavior related to those values; how each class should have a single responsibility or purpose; and how different classes can be related to each other through encapsulation or inheritance.

But what are Ruby objects? What information does an object contain? If we were to look at a Ruby object through a microscope, what would we see? Are there any moving parts inside? And what about Ruby classes? What exactly is a class?

I'll answer these questions in this chapter by exploring how Ruby works internally. By looking at how Ruby implements objects and classes, you'll learn how to use them and how to write object-oriented programs using Ruby.

ROADMAP

Inside a Ruby Object

Ruby saves each of your custom objects in a C structure called RObject, which looks like Figure 5-1 in Ruby 1.9 and 2.0.

At the top of the figure is a pointer to the RObject structure. (Internally, Ruby always refers to any value with a VALUE pointer.) Below this pointer, the RObject structure contains an inner RBasic structure and information specific to custom objects. The RBasic section contains information that all objects use: a set of Boolean values called flags that store a variety of internal technical values, and a class pointer called klass. The class pointer indicates

If I could slice open a Ruby object, what would I see?

which class an object is an instance of. In the RObject section, Ruby saves an array of instance variables that each object contains, using numiv, the instance variable count, and ivptr, a pointer to an array of values.

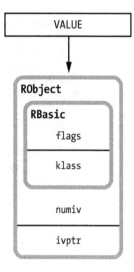

If we were to define the Ruby object structure in technical terms, we could say

> Every Ruby object is the combination of a class pointer and an array of instance variables.

At first glance, this definition doesn't seem very useful because it doesn't help us understand the meaning or purpose behind objects or how to use them in a Ruby program.

Figure 5-1: The RObject structure

Inspecting klass and ivptr

To understand how Ruby uses RObject in programs, we'll create a simple Ruby class and then inspect an instance of this class using IRB. For example, suppose I have the simple Ruby class shown in Listing 5-1.

```
class Mathematician
  attr_accessor :first_name
  attr_accessor :last_name
end
```

Listing 5-1: A simple Ruby class

Ruby needs to save the class pointer in RObject because every object must track the class you used to create it. When you create an instance of a class, Ruby internally saves a pointer to that class inside RObject, as shown in Listing 5-2.

```
$ irb
> euler = Mathematician.new
❶ => #<Mathematician:0x007fbd738608c0>
```

Listing 5-2: Creating an object instance in IRB

By displaying the class name #<Mathematician at ❶, Ruby displays the value of the class pointer for the euler object. The hex string that follows is actually the VALUE pointer for the object. (This will differ for every instance of Mathematician.)

Ruby also uses the instance variable array to track the values you save in an object, as shown in Listing 5-3.

```
> euler.first_name = 'Leonhard'
 => "Leonhard"
> euler.last_name  = 'Euler'
 => "Euler"
> euler
❶ => #<Mathematician:0x007fbd738608c0 @first_name="Leonhard", @last_name="Euler">
```

Listing 5-3: Inspecting instance variables in IRB

As you can see, in IRB Ruby also displays the instance variable array for euler at ❶. Ruby needs to save this array of values in each object because every object instance can have different values for the same instance variables, as shown at ❶ in Listing 5-4.

```
> euclid = Mathematician.new
> euclid.first_name = 'Euclid'
> euclid
❶ => #<Mathematician:0x007fabdb850690 @first_name="Euclid">
```

Listing 5-4: A different instance of the Mathematician class

Visualizing Two Instances of One Class

Let's look at Ruby's C structures in a bit more detail. When you run the Ruby code shown in Figure 5-2, Ruby creates one RClass structure and two RObject structures.

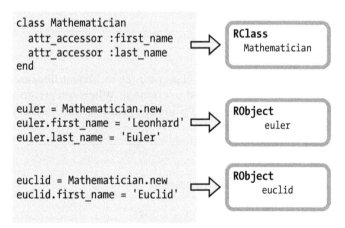

Figure 5-2: Creating two instances of one class

I'll discuss how Ruby implements classes with the RClass structure in the next section. For now, let's look at Figure 5-3, which shows how Ruby saves the Mathematician information in the two RObject structures.

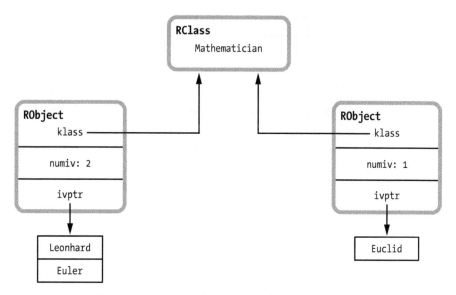

Figure 5-3: Visualizing two instances of one class

As you can see, each `klass` value points to the `Mathematician` `RClass` structure, and each `RObject` structure has a separate array of instance variables. Both arrays contain `VALUE` pointers—the same pointer that Ruby uses to refer to the `RObject` structure. (Notice that one of the objects contains two instance variables, while the other contains only one.)

Generic Objects

Now you know how Ruby saves custom classes, like the `Mathematician` class, in `RObject` structures. But remember that every Ruby value—including basic data types such as integers, strings, and symbols—is an object. The Ruby source code internally refers to these built-in types as "generic" types. How does Ruby store these generic objects? Do they also use the `RObject` structure?

The answer is no. Internally, Ruby uses a different C structure, not `RObject`, to save values for each of its generic data types. For example, Ruby saves string values in `RString` structures, arrays in `RArray` structures, regular expressions in `RRegexp` structures, and so on. Ruby uses `RObject` only to save instances of custom object classes that you create and a few custom object classes that Ruby creates internally. However, all of these different structures share the same `RBasic` information that we saw in `RObject`, as shown in Figure 5-4.

Since the `RBasic` structure contains the class pointer, each of these generic data types is also an object. Each is an instance of some Ruby class, as indicated by the class pointer saved inside `RBasic`.

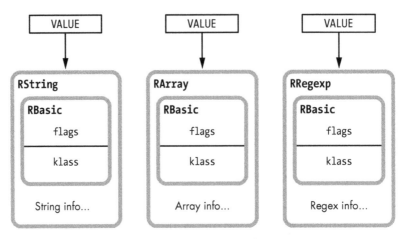

Figure 5-4: Different Ruby object structures all use the RBasic structure.

Simple Ruby Values Don't Require a Structure at All

As a performance optimization, Ruby saves small integers, symbols, and a few other simple values without any structure at all, placing them right inside the VALUE pointer, as shown in Figure 5-5.

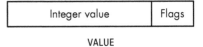

Figure 5-5: Ruby saves integers in the VALUE pointer.

These VALUEs are not pointers at all; they're values themselves. For these simple data types, there is no class pointer. Instead, Ruby remembers the class using a series of bit flags saved in the first few bits of the VALUE. For example, all small integers have the FIXNUM_FLAG bit set, as shown in Figure 5-6.

Whenever the FIXNUM_FLAG is set, Ruby knows that this VALUE is really a small integer, an instance of the

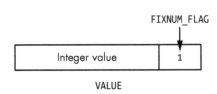

Figure 5-6: FIXNUM_FLAG indicates this is an instance of the Fixnum class.

Fixnum class, and not a pointer to a value structure. (A similar bit flag indicates whether the VALUE is a symbol, and values such as nil, true, and false also have their own flags.)

It's easy to see that integers, strings, and other generic values are all objects by using IRB, as you can see in Listing 5-5.

```
$ irb
> "string".class
 => String
> 1.class
 => Fixnum
> :symbol.class
 => Symbol
```

Listing 5-5: Inspecting classes for some generic values

Here, we see that Ruby saves a class pointer or the equivalent bit flag for all values by calling the class method on each. In turn, the class method returns the class pointer, or at least the name of the class that each klass pointer refers to.

Do Generic Objects Have Instance Variables?

Let's go back to our definition of a Ruby object:

> Every Ruby object is the combination of a class pointer and an array of instance variables.

What about instance variables for generic objects? Do integers, strings, and other generic data values have instance variables? That would seem odd, but if integers and strings are objects, this must be true! And if it is true, where does Ruby save these values if it doesn't use the RObject structure?

Using the instance_variables method, shown in Listing 5-6, you can see that each of these basic values can also contain an array of instance variables, strange as that may seem.

```
$ irb
> str = "some string value"
 => "some string value"
> str.instance_variables
 => []
> str.instance_variable_set("@val1", "value one")
 => "value one"
> str.instance_variables
 => [:@val1]
> str.instance_variable_set("@val2", "value two")
 => "value two"
> str.instance_variables
 => [:@val1, :@val2]
```

Listing 5-6: Saving instance variables in a Ruby string object

Repeat this exercise using symbols, arrays, or any Ruby value, and you'll find that every Ruby value is an object and every object contains a class pointer and an array of instance variables.

READING THE RBASIC AND ROBJECT C STRUCTURE DEFINITIONS

Listing 5-7 shows the definitions of the RBasic and RObject C structures. (You can find this code in the *include/ruby/ruby.h* header file.)

```
    struct RBasic {
❶    VALUE flags;
❷    const VALUE klass;
    };

    #define ROBJECT_EMBED_LEN_MAX 3
    struct RObject {
❸    struct RBasic basic;
      union {
        struct {
❹        long numiv;
❺        VALUE *ivptr;
❻        struct st_table *iv_index_tbl;
❼      } heap;
❽      VALUE ary[ROBJECT_EMBED_LEN_MAX];
      } as;
    };
```

Listing 5-7: The definitions of the RBasic and RObject C structures

At the top, you see the definition of RBasic. This definition contains the two values: flags ❶ and klass ❷. Below, you see the RObject definition. Notice that it contains a copy of the RBasic structure at ❸. Following this, the union keyword contains a structure called heap at ❼, followed by an array called ary at ❽.

The heap structure at ❼ contains the following values:

- First, the value numiv at ❹ tracks the number of instance variables contained in this object.

- Next, ivptr at ❺ is a pointer to an array containing the values of this object's instance variables. Notice that the names, or IDs, of the instance variables are not stored here; only the values are stored.

- iv_index_tbl at ❻ points to a hash table that maps between the name, or ID, of each instance variable and its location in the ivptr array. This value is actually stored in the RClass structure for this object's class; this pointer is simply a cache, or shortcut, that Ruby uses to obtain that hash table quickly. (The st_table type refers to Ruby's implementation of hash tables, which I'll discuss in Chapter 7.)

The last member of the RObject structure, ary at ❽, occupies the same memory space as all previous values because of the union keyword at the top. Using this ary value, Ruby can save all of the instance variables right inside the RObject structure—if they'll fit. This eliminates the need to call malloc to allocate extra memory to hold the instance variable value array. (Ruby also uses this sort of optimization for the RString, RArray, RStruct, and RBignum structures.)

Where Does Ruby Save Instance Variables for Generic Objects?

Internally, Ruby uses a bit of a hack to save instance variables for generic objects—that is, for objects that don't use an RObject structure. When you save an instance variable in a generic object, Ruby saves it in a special hash called generic_iv_tbl. This hash maintains a map between generic objects and pointers to other hashes that contain each object's instance variables. Figure 5-7 shows how this would look for the str string example in Listing 5-6.

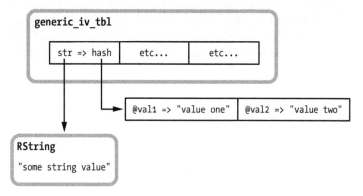

Figure 5-7: generic_iv_tbl stores instance variables for generic objects.

Experiment 5-1: How Long Does It Take to Save a New Instance Variable?

To learn more about how Ruby saves instance variables internally, let's measure how long it takes Ruby to save one in an object. To do this, I'll create a large number of test objects, as shown in Listing 5-8.

```
ITERATIONS = 100000
❶ GC.disable
❷ obj = ITERATIONS.times.map { Class.new.new }
```

Listing 5-8: Creating test objects using Class.new

Here, I'm using Class.new at ❷ to create a unique class for each new object in order to make sure they're all independent. I've also disabled garbage collection at ❶ to avoid skewing the results with GC operations. Then, in Listing 5-9, I add instance variables to each.

```
Benchmark.bm do |bench|
  20.times do |count|
    bench.report("adding instance variable number #{count+1}") do
      ITERATIONS.times do |n|
        obj[n].instance_variable_set("@var#{count}", "value")
```

```
        end
      end
    end
  end
```

Listing 5-9: Adding instance variables to each test object

Listing 5-9 iterates 20 times, repeatedly saving one more new instance variable to each of the objects. Figure 5-8 shows the time that it takes Ruby 2.0 to add each variable: The first bar on the left is the time it takes to save the first instance variable in all the objects, and each subsequent bar is the additional time taken to save one more instance variable in each object.

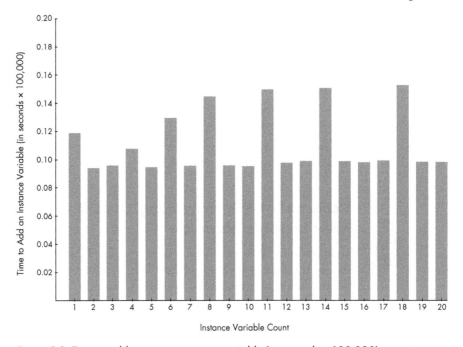

Figure 5-8: Time to add one more instance variable (in seconds x 100,000) vs. instance variable count

Figure 5-8 shows a strange pattern. Sometimes it takes Ruby longer to add a new instance variable. What's going on here?

The reason for this behavior has to do with the ivptr array where Ruby stores the instance variables, as shown in Figure 5-9.

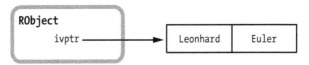

Figure 5-9: Two instance variables saved in an object

In Ruby 1.8 this array is a hash table containing both the variable names (the hash keys) and the values, which will automatically expand to accommodate any number of elements.

Ruby 1.9 and later save memory by storing the values in a simple array. The instance variable names are saved in the object's class instead, because they're the same for all instances of a class. As a result, Ruby 1.9 and 2.0 need to either preallocate a large array to handle any number of instance variables or repeatedly increase the size of this array as you save more variables.

In fact, as you can see in Figure 5-8, Ruby 1.9 and 2.0 repeatedly increase the array size. For example, suppose you have seven instance variables in a given object, as shown in Figure 5-10.

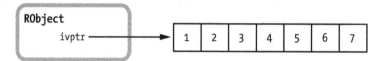

Figure 5-10: Seven instance variables in an object

When you add the eighth variable—bar 8 in Figure 5-8—Ruby 1.9 and 2.0 increase the array size by three, anticipating that you will soon add more variables, as shown in Figure 5-11.

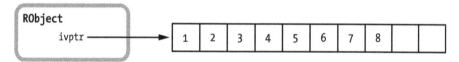

Figure 5-11: Adding an eighth value allocates extra space.

Allocating more memory takes extra time, which is why bar 8 is higher. Now if you add two more instance variables, Ruby 1.9 and 2.0 won't need to reallocate memory for this array because the space will already be available. This explains the shorter times for bars 9 and 10.

What's Inside the RClass Structure?

Every object remembers its class by saving a pointer to an RClass structure. What information does each RClass structure contain? What would we see if we could look inside a Ruby class? Let's build a model of the information that must be present in RClass. This model will give us a technical definition of what a Ruby class is, based on what we know classes can do.

Two objects, one class

Every Ruby developer knows how to write a class: You type the class keyword, specify a name for the new class, and then type in the class's methods. Listing 5-10 shows a familiar example.

```ruby
class Mathematician
  attr_accessor :first_name
  attr_accessor :last_name
end
```

Listing 5-10: The same simple Ruby class we saw in Listing 5-1

attr_accessor is shorthand for defining get and set methods for an attribute. (The methods defined by attr_accessor also check for nil values). Listing 5-11 shows a more verbose way of defining the same Mathematician class.

```ruby
class Mathematician
  def first_name
    @first_name
  end
  def first_name=(value)
    @first_name = value
  end
  def last_name
    @last_name
  end
  def last_name=(value)
    @last_name = value
  end
end
```

Listing 5-11: The same class written without attr_accessor

It appears that this class—and every Ruby class—is just a group of method definitions. You can assign behavior to an object by adding methods to its class, and when you call a method on an object, Ruby looks for the method in the object's class. This leads to our first definition of a Ruby class:

A Ruby class is a group of method definitions.

Therefore, the RClass structure for Mathematician must save a list of all the methods defined in the class, as shown in Figure 5-12.

Notice in Listing 5-11 that I've also created two instance variables: @first_name and @last_name. We saw earlier how Ruby stores these values in each RObject structure, but you may have noticed that only the *values* of these variables are stored in RObject, not their names. (Ruby 1.8 does store the names in RObject.) Ruby must store the attribute names in RClass, which makes sense because the names will be the same for every Mathematician instance.

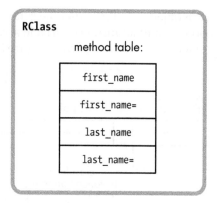

Figure 5-12: Ruby classes contain a method table.

Let's redraw `RClass` again and include a table of attribute names this time, as shown in Figure 5-13.

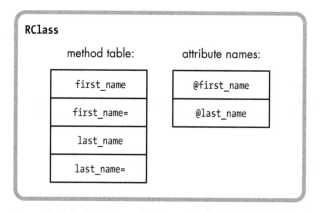

Figure 5-13: Ruby classes also contain a table of attribute names.

Now our definition of a Ruby class is as follows:

> A Ruby class is a group of method definitions and a table of attribute names.

At the beginning of this chapter, I mentioned that every value in Ruby is an object. This might be true for classes, too. Let's prove this using IRB.

```
> p Mathematician.class
=> Class
```

As you can see, Ruby classes are all instances of the `Class` class; therefore, classes are also objects. Now to update our definition of a Ruby class again:

> A Ruby class is a Ruby object that also contains method definitions and attribute names.

Because Ruby classes are objects, we know that the RClass structure must also contain a class pointer and an instance variable array, the values that we know every Ruby object contains, as shown in Figure 5-14.

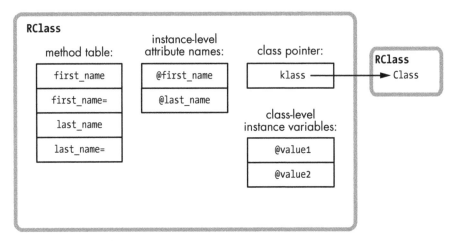

Figure 5-14: Ruby classes also contain a class pointer and instance variables.

As you can see, I've added a pointer to the Class class, which is in theory the class of every Ruby class object. However, in Experiment 5-2 on page 127, I'll show that this diagram is in fact not accurate—that klass actually points to something else! I've also added a table of instance variables.

NOTE *These are the class-level instance variables. Don't confuse these with the table of attribute names for the object-level instance variables.*

This is rapidly getting out of control! The RClass structure seems to be much more complex than the RObject structure. But don't worry—we're getting close to an accurate picture of the RClass structure. Next we need to consider two more important types of information contained in each Ruby class.

Inheritance

Inheritance is an essential feature of object-oriented programming. Ruby implements single inheritance by allowing us to optionally specify one superclass when we create a class. If we don't specify a superclass, Ruby assigns the Object class as the superclass. For example, we could rewrite the Mathematician class using a superclass like this:

```
class Mathematician < Person
--snip--
```

Now every instance of Mathematician will include the same methods that instances of Person have. In this example, we might want to move the first_name and last_name accessor methods into Person. We could also move the @first_name and @last_name attributes into the Person class. Every instance of Mathematician will contain these methods and attributes, even though we moved them to the Person class.

The Mathematician class must contain a reference to the Person class (its superclass) so that Ruby can find any methods or attributes defined in the superclass.

Let's update our definition again, assuming that Ruby tracks the superclass using another pointer similar to klass:

> A Ruby class is a Ruby object that also contains method definitions, attribute names, and a superclass pointer.

And let's redraw the RClass structure to include the new superclass pointer, as shown in Figure 5-15.

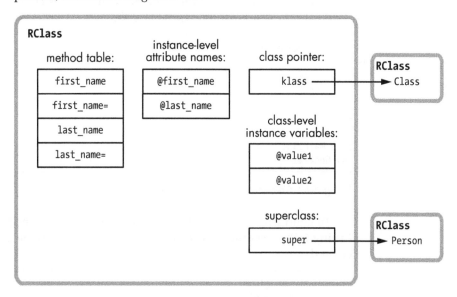

Figure 5-15: Ruby classes also contain a superclass pointer.

At this point, it is critical to understand the difference between the klass pointer and the super pointer. The klass pointer indicates which class the Ruby class object is an instance of. This will always be the Class class:

```
> p Mathematician.class
=> Class
```

Ruby uses the klass pointer to find the methods of the Mathematician class object, such as the new method that every Ruby class implements. However, the super pointer records the class's superclass:

```
> p Mathematician.superclass
=> Person
```

Ruby uses the super pointer to help find methods contained in each Mathematician instance, such as first_name= or last_name. As we'll see next, Ruby also uses the super pointer when getting or setting class variables.

Class Instance Variables vs. Class Variables

One confusing bit of Ruby syntax is the concept of *class variables*. You might think that these are simply the instance variables of a class (the class-level instance variables from Figure 5-14), but class instance variables and class variables are distinctly different.

To create a class instance variable, you simply create an instance variable using the @ symbol, but in the context of a class rather than an object. For example, Listing 5-12 shows how we could use an instance variable of Mathematician to indicate a branch of mathematics this class corresponds to. We create the @type instance variable at ❶.

```
   class Mathematician
❶    @type = "General"
     def self.type
       @type
     end
   end

   puts Mathematician.type
    => General
```

Listing 5-12: Creating a class-level instance variable

In contrast, to create a class variable, you would use the @@ notation. Listing 5-13 shows the same example, with the class variable @@type ❶ created.

```
   class Mathematician
❶    @@type = "General"
     def self.type
       @@type
     end
   end

   puts Mathematician.type
    => General
```

Listing 5-13: Creating a class variable

What's the difference? When you create a class variable, Ruby creates a single value for you to use in that class and in any subclasses you might define. On the other hand, using a class *instance* variable causes Ruby to create a separate value for each class or subclass.

Let's review Listing 5-14 to see how Ruby handles these two types of variables differently. First, I define a class instance variable called `@type` in the `Mathematician` class and set its value to the string `General`. Next, I create a second class called `Statistician`, which is a subclass of `Mathematician`, and change the value of `@type` to the string `Statistics`.

```ruby
class Mathematician
  @type = "General"
  def self.type
    @type
  end
end

class Statistician < Mathematician
  @type = "Statistics"
end

puts Statistician.type
❶ => Statistics
puts Mathematician.type
❷ => General
```

Listing 5-14: Each class and subclass has its own instance variables.

Notice that the values of `@type` in `Statistician` at ❶ and `Mathematician` at ❷ are different. Each class has its own separate copy of `@type`.

However, if I use a class variable instead, Ruby shares that value between `Mathematician` and `Statistician`, as demonstrated in Listing 5-15.

```ruby
class Mathematician
  @@type = "General"
  def self.type
    @@type
  end
end

class Statistician < Mathematician
  @@type = "Statistics"
end

puts Statistician.type
❶ => Statistics
puts Mathematician.type
❷ => Statistics
```

Listing 5-15: Ruby shares class variables among a class and all of its subclasses.

Here, Ruby shows the same value for `@@type` in `Statistician` at ❶ and in `Mathematician` at ❷.

Internally, however, Ruby actually saves both class variables and class instance variables in the same table inside the RClass structure. Figure 5-16 shows how the Mathematician class would save the @type and @@type values if you created both of them. The extra @ symbol in the name allows Ruby to distinguish between the two types of variables.

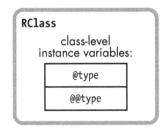

Figure 5-16: Ruby saves class variables and class instance variables in the same table.

Getting and Setting Class Variables

It's true: Ruby saves both class variables and class instance variables in the same table. However, the ways Ruby gets or sets these two types of variables are quite different.

When you get or set a class instance variable, Ruby looks up the variable in the RClass structure corresponding to the target class and either saves or retrieves the value. Figure 5-17 shows how Ruby saves the class instance variables from Listing 5-14.

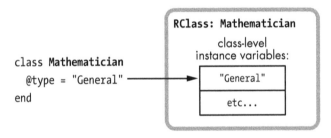

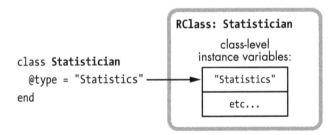

Figure 5-17: Ruby saves class instance variables in the RClass structure of the target class.

At the top of the figure, you can see a line of code that saves a class instance variable in Mathematician. Below that is a similar line of code that saves a value in Statistician. In both cases, Ruby saves the class instance variable in the RClass structure for the current class.

Ruby uses a more complex algorithm for class variables. To produce the behavior we saw in Listing 5-15, Ruby needs to search through all the superclasses to see whether any of them define the same class variable. Figure 5-18 shows an example.

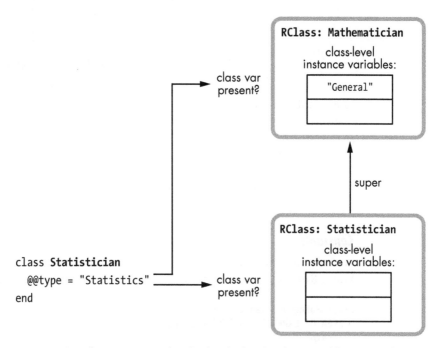

Figure 5-18: Before saving it, Ruby checks whether the class variable exists in the target class or any of its superclasses.

When you save a class variable, Ruby looks in the target class and all of its superclasses for an existing variable. It will find @@type in the highest superclass. In Figure 5-18 you can see Ruby checks both the Statistician and Mathematician classes when saving the @@type class variable in Statistician. Because I already saved the same class variable in Mathematician (Listing 5-15), Ruby will use that and overwrite it with the new value, as shown in Figure 5-19.

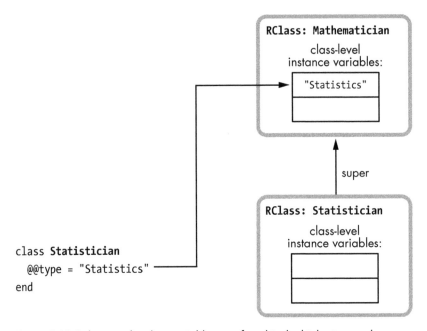

```
class Statistician
  @@type = "Statistics"
end
```

Figure 5-19: Ruby uses the class variable copy found in the highest superclass.

Constants

We have one more feature of Ruby classes to cover: *constants*. As you may know, Ruby allows you to define constant values inside a class, like this:

```
class Mathematician < Person
  AREA_OF_EXPERTISE = "Mathematics"
  --snip--
```

Constant values must start with a capital letter, and they are valid within the scope of the current class. (Curiously, Ruby allows you to change a constant value, but it will display a warning when you do so.) Let's add a constant table to our RClass structure, because Ruby must save these values inside each class, as shown in Figure 5-20.

Now we can write a complete, technical definition of a Ruby class:

> A Ruby class is a Ruby object that also contains method definitions, attribute names, a superclass pointer, and a constants table.

Granted, this isn't as concise as the simple definition we had for a Ruby object, but each Ruby class contains much more information than each Ruby object. Ruby classes are obviously fundamental to the language.

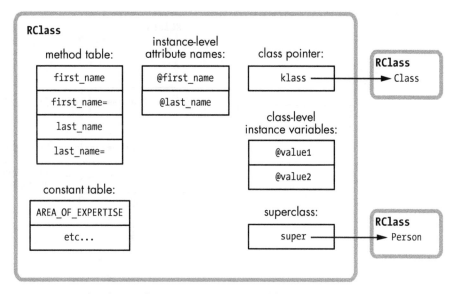

Figure 5-20: Ruby classes also contain a constants table.

The Actual RClass Structure

Having built up a conceptual model for what information must be stored in RClass, let's look at the actual structure that Ruby uses to represent classes, as shown in Figure 5-21.

As you can see, Ruby uses two separate structures to represent each class: RClass and rb_classext_struct. But these two structures act as one large structure because each RClass always contains a pointer (ptr) to a corresponding rb_classext_struct. You might guess that the Ruby core team decided to use two different structures because there are so many different values to save, but in fact they probably created rb_classext_struct to save internal values that they didn't want to expose in the public Ruby C extension API.

Like RObject, RClass has a VALUE pointer (shown on the left of Figure 5-21). Ruby always accesses classes using these VALUE pointers. The right side of the figure shows the technical names for the fields:

- flags and klass are the same RBasic values that every Ruby value contains.
- m_tbl is the method table, a hash whose keys are the names, or IDs, of each method and whose values are pointers to the definition of each method, including the compiled YARV instructions.
- iv_index_tbl is the attribute names table, a hash that maps each instance variable name to the index of the attribute's value in each RObject instance variable array.
- super is a pointer to the RClass structure for this class's superclass.

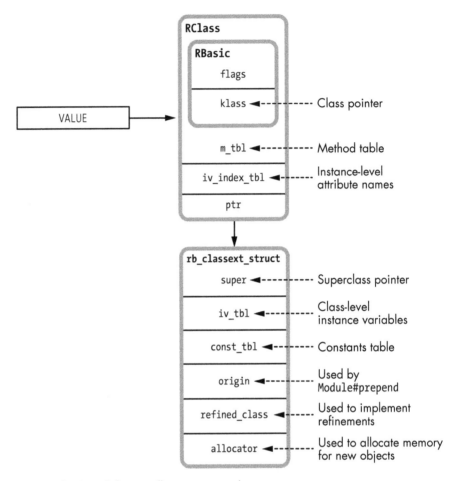

Figure 5-21: How Ruby actually represents a class

- iv_tbl contains the class-level instance variables and class variables, including both their names and values.
- const_tbl is a hash containing all of the constants (names and values) defined in this class's scope. You can see that Ruby implements iv_tbl and const_tbl in the same way: Class-level instance variables and constants are almost the same thing.
- Ruby uses origin to implement the Module#prepend feature. I'll discuss what prepend does and how Ruby implements it in Chapter 6.
- Ruby uses the refined_class pointer to implement the new experimental refinements feature, which I'll discuss further in Chapter 9.
- Finally, Ruby uses allocator internally to allocate memory for new instances of this class.

Now for a quick look at the actual RClass structure definition, as shown in Listing 5-16.

```
typedef struct rb_classext_struct rb_classext_t;
struct RClass {
    struct RBasic basic;
    rb_classext_t *ptr;
    struct st_table *m_tbl;
    struct st_table *iv_index_tbl;
};
```

Listing 5-16: The definition of the RClass C structure

Like the RObject definition we saw in Listing 5-7, this structure definition—including all of the values shown in Figure 5-21—can be found in the *include/ruby/ruby.h* file.

The rb_classext_struct structure definition, on the other hand, can be found in the *internal.h* C header file, as shown in Listing 5-17.

```
struct rb_classext_struct {
    VALUE super;
    struct st_table *iv_tbl;
    struct st_table *const_tbl;
    VALUE origin;
    VALUE refined_class;
    rb_alloc_func_t allocator;
};
```

Listing 5-17: The definition of the rb_classext_struct C structure

Again, you can see the values from Figure 5-21. Notice that the st_table C type appears four times in Listings 5-16 and 5-17; this is Ruby's hash table data structure. Internally, Ruby saves much of the information for each class using hash tables: the attribute names table, the method table, the class-level instance variable table, and the constants table.

Experiment 5-2: Where Does Ruby Save Class Methods?

We've seen how each RClass structure saves all methods defined in a certain class. In this example, Ruby stores information about the first_name method inside the RClass structure for Mathematician using the method table:

```
class Mathematician
  def first_name
    @first_name
  end
end
```

But what about class methods? It's common in Ruby to save methods in a class directly, using the syntax shown in Listing 5-18.

```
class Mathematician
  def self.class_method
    puts "This is a class method."
  end
end
```

Listing 5-18: Defining a class method using def self

Alternatively, you can use the syntax shown in Listing 5-19.

```
class Mathematician
  class << self
    def class_method
      puts "This is a class method."
    end
  end
end
```

Listing 5-19: Defining a class method using class << self

Are they saved in the RClass structure along with the normal methods for each class, perhaps with a flag to indicate they are class methods and not normal methods? Or are they saved somewhere else? Let's find out!

It's easy to see where class methods are *not* saved. They are obviously not saved in the RClass method table along with normal methods, because instances of Mathematician cannot call them, as demonstrated here:

```
> obj = Mathematician.new
> obj.class_method
 => undefined method `class_method' for
#< Mathematician:0x007fdd8384d1c8 (NoMethodError)
```

Now, keeping in mind that Mathematician is also a Ruby object, recall the following definition:

> A Ruby class is a Ruby object that also contains method definitions, attribute names, a superclass pointer, and a constants table.

We assume that Ruby should save methods for Mathematician just as it saves them for any object: in the method table for the object's class. In other words, Ruby should get Mathematician's class using the klass pointer and save the method in the method table in that RClass structure, as shown in Figure 5-22.

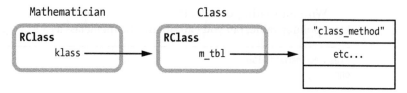

Mathematician   Class

```
RClass          RClass
      klass →          m_tbl →
```

```
"class_method"
   etc...
```

Figure 5-22: Shouldn't Ruby save class methods in the method table for the class's class?

But Ruby doesn't actually do this, as you can discover by creating another class and trying to call the new method:

```
> class AnotherClass; end
> AnotherClass.class_method
 => undefined method `class_method' for AnotherClass:Class (NoMethodError)
```

If Ruby had added the class method to the method table in the Class class, all classes in your application would have the method. Obviously this isn't what we intended by writing a class method, and thankfully Ruby doesn't implement class methods this way.

Then where do the class methods go? For a clue, use the method ObjectSpace.count_objects, shown in Listing 5-20:

```
$ irb
❶ > ObjectSpace.count_objects[:T_CLASS]
❷  => 859
 > class Mathematician; end
  => nil
 > ObjectSpace.count_objects[:T_CLASS]
❸  => 861
```

Listing 5-20: Using ObjectSpace.count_objects with :T_CLASS

ObjectSpace.count_objects at ❶ returns the number of objects of a given type that exist. In this test, I'm passing the :T_CLASS symbol to get the count of class objects that exist in my IRB session. Before I create Mathematician, there are 859 classes at ❷. After I declare Mathematician, there are 861 at ❸—two more. That's odd. I declared one new class, but Ruby actually created two! What is the second one for and where is it?

It turns out that whenever you create a new class, internally Ruby creates two classes! The first class is your new class: Ruby creates a new RClass structure to represent your class, as described above. But internally Ruby also creates a second, hidden class called the *metaclass*. Why? To save any class methods that you might later create for your new class. In fact, Ruby sets the metaclass to be the class of your new class: It sets the klass pointer of your new RClass structure to point to the metaclass.

Without writing C code, there's no easy way to see the metaclass or the klass pointer value, but you can obtain the metaclass as a Ruby object like this:

```
class Mathematician
end

p Mathematician
 => Mathematician

p Mathematician.singleton_class
 => #<Class:Mathematician>
```

The first print statement displays the object's class, while the second displays the object's metaclass. The odd #<Class:Mathematician> syntax indicates that the second class is the metaclass for Mathematician. This is the second RClass structure that Ruby automatically created for me when I declared the Mathematician class. And this second RClass structure is where Ruby saves my class method, as shown in Figure 5-23.

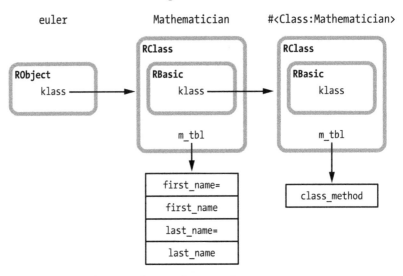

Figure 5-23: An object, its class, and its metaclass

If we now display the methods for the metaclass, we'll see all the methods of the Class class, along with the new class method for Mathematician:

```
p obj.singleton_class.methods
 => [ ... :class_method, ... ]
```

Summary

In this chapter we've seen how Ruby represents objects and classes internally: Ruby uses the RObject structure to represent instances of any custom classes you define in your code and of some classes predefined by Ruby itself. The RObject structure is remarkably simple, containing just a pointer to the object's class and a table of instance variable values, along with a count of the variables. The simplicity of its structure leads us to a very simple definition of a Ruby object:

> Every Ruby object is the combination of a class pointer and an array of instance variables.

This definition is powerful and useful because everything in Ruby is an object: Whenever you use a value in your Ruby program, regardless of what it is, remember that it will be an object and will therefore have a class pointer and instance variables.

We also saw that Ruby uses special C structures to represent instances of many commonly used, built-in Ruby classes called "generic" objects. For example, Ruby uses the RString structure to represent an instance of the String class, RArray for an instance of the Array class, or RRegexp for an instance of the Regexp class. While these structures are different, Ruby also saves a class pointer and an array of instance variables for each of these generic objects. Finally, we saw that Ruby saves some simple values, such as small integers and symbols, without using a C structure at all. Ruby saves these values right inside the VALUE pointers that otherwise would point to the structure holding the value.

While Ruby objects are simple, we learned in this chapter that Ruby classes aren't quite so simple. The RClass structure working with the rb_classext_struct structure saves a large set of information. Learning this forced us to write a more complex definition for Ruby classes:

> A Ruby class is a Ruby object that also contains method definitions, attribute names, a superclass pointer, and a constants table.

Looking inside RClass and rb_classext_struct, we saw that Ruby classes are also Ruby objects, which therefore also contain instance variables and a class pointer. We looked at the difference between a class's instance variables and class variables and learned that Ruby saves both of these variable types in the same hash table. We discovered how classes also contain a series of hash tables that store their methods, the names of the object-level instance variables, and constants defined within the class. Finally, we saw how each Ruby class records its superclass using the super pointer.

Inside of Ruby,
modules are classes.

6

METHOD LOOKUP AND CONSTANT LOOKUP

As we saw in Chapter 5, classes play an important role in Ruby, holding method definitions and constant values, among other things. We also learned how Ruby implements inheritance using the super pointer in each RClass structure.

In fact, as your program grows, you might imagine it organized by class and superclass, creating a kind of giant tree structure. At the base is the Object class (or, actually, the internal BasicObject class). This class is Ruby's default superclass, and all of your classes appear somewhere higher up in the tree, branching out in different directions. In this chapter we'll study how Ruby uses this superclass tree to look up methods. When you write code that calls a method, Ruby looks through this tree in a very precise manner. We'll step through a concrete example to see the method lookup process in action.

Later in this chapter we'll learn another way to visualize your Ruby code. Every time you create a new class or module, Ruby adds a new scope to a different tree, a tree based on the syntactical structure of your program. The trunk of this tree is the top-level scope, or the beginning of your Ruby code file where you start typing. As you define more and more highly nested modules and classes, this tree would grow higher and higher as well. We'll learn how this syntax, or namespace, tree allows Ruby to find constant definitions, just as the superclass tree allows Ruby to find methods.

But before we get to method and constant lookup, let's get started with a look at Ruby modules. What are modules? How are they different from classes? What happens when you include a module into a class?

How Ruby Implements Modules

As you may know, modules are very similar to classes in Ruby. You can create a module just as you create a class—by typing the module keyword followed by a series of method definitions. But while modules are similar to classes, they are handled differently by Ruby in three important ways:

- Ruby doesn't allow you to create objects directly from modules. In practice this means that you can't call the new method on a module because new is a method of Class, not of Module.
- Ruby doesn't allow you to specify a superclass for a module.
- In addition, you can include a module into a class using the include keyword.

But what are modules exactly? How does Ruby represent them internally? Does it use an RModule structure? And what does it mean to "include" a module into a class?

Modules Are Classes

As it turns out, internally Ruby implements modules as classes. When you create a module, Ruby creates another RClass/rb_classext_struct structure pair, just as it would for a new class. For example, suppose we define a new module like this.

```
module Professor
end
```

Internally, Ruby would create a class, not a module! Figure 6-1 shows how Ruby represents a module internally.

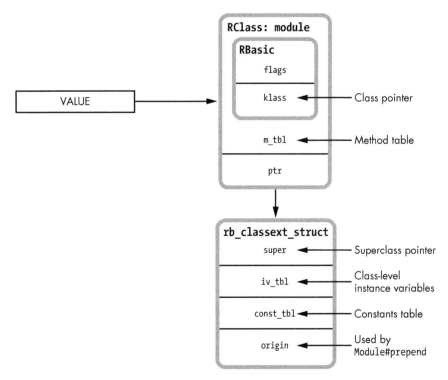

Figure 6-1: The portion of Ruby's class structures that's used for modules

In this figure I show Ruby's `RClass` structure again. However, I've removed some of the values from the diagram because modules don't use all of them. Most importantly, I removed `iv_index_tbl` because you can't create object instances of a module—in other words, you can't call the `new` method on a module. This means there are no object-level attributes to keep track of. I also removed the `refined_class` and `allocator` values because modules don't use them either. I've left the super pointer because modules do have superclasses internally even though you aren't allowed to specify them yourself.

A technical definition of a Ruby module (ignoring the `origin` value for now) might look like this:

> A Ruby module is a Ruby object that also contains method definitions, a superclass pointer, and a constants table.

Including a Module into a Class

The real magic behind modules happens when you include a module into a class, as shown in Listing 6-1.

```
module Professor
end
```

```
class Mathematician < Person
  include Professor
end
```

Listing 6-1: Including a module into a class

When we run Listing 6-1, Ruby creates a copy of the RClass structure for the Professor module and uses it as the new superclass for Mathematician. Ruby's C source code refers to this copy of the module as an *included class*. The superclass of the new copy of Professor is set to the original superclass of Mathematician, which preserves the superclass, or ancestor chain. Figure 6-2 summarizes this somewhat confusing state of affairs.

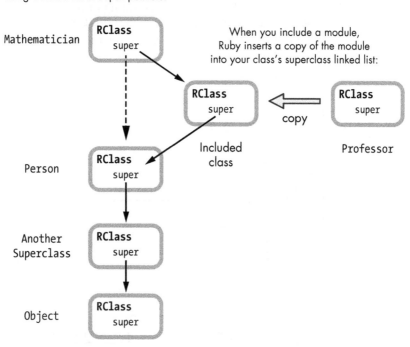

Figure 6-2: Including a module into a class

You can see the Mathematician class at the top-left corner of Figure 6-2. Below it and along the left side, you see its superclass chain: Mathematician's superclass is Person, whose superclass is Another Superclass, and so on. The super pointer in each RClass structure (actually, each rb_classext_struct structure) points down to the next superclass.

Now to the Professor module on the right side of Figure 6-2. When we include this module into the Mathematician class, Ruby changes the super pointer of Mathematician to point to a copy of Professor and the super pointer of this copy of Professor to point to Person, the original superclass of Mathematician.

Ruby implements extend *in exactly the same way, except the included class becomes the superclass of the target class's class, or metaclass. Thus,* extend *allows you to add class methods to a class.*

Ruby's Method Lookup Algorithm

Whenever you call a method, whenever you "send a message to a receiver" to use object-oriented programming jargon, Ruby needs to determine which class implements that method. Sometimes this is obvious: The receiver's class might implement the target method. However, this isn't often the case. It might be that some other module or class in your system implements the method. Ruby uses a very precise algorithm to search through the modules and classes in your program in a particular order to find the target method. An understanding of this process is essential for every Ruby developer, so let's take a close look at it.

The flowchart in Figure 6-3 gives you a graphical picture of Ruby's method lookup algorithm.

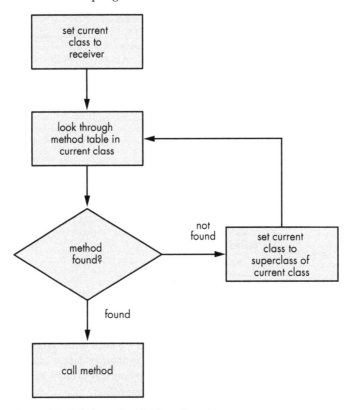

Figure 6-3: Ruby's method lookup algorithm

This algorithm is remarkably simple, isn't it? As you can see, Ruby simply follows the super pointers until it finds the class or module that contains the target method. You might imagine that Ruby would have to distinguish between modules and classes using some special logic—that it would have to handle the case where there are multiple included modules, for example. But no, it's just a simple loop on the super pointer linked list.

A Method Lookup Example

In a moment we'll walk through this algorithm to be sure we understand it thoroughly. But first, let's set up an example we can use that has a class, a superclass, and a module. This will allow us to see how classes and modules work together inside of Ruby.

Listing 6-2 shows the Mathematician class with the accessor methods first_name and last_name.

```
class Mathematician
  attr_accessor :first_name
  attr_accessor :last_name
end
```

Listing 6-2: A simple Ruby class, repeated from Listing 5-1

Now let's introduce a superclass. In Listing 6-3, at ❶ we set Person as the superclass of Mathematician.

```
class Person
end

❶ class Mathematician < Person
  attr_accessor :first_name
  attr_accessor :last_name
end
```

Listing 6-3: Person is the superclass of Mathematician.

We'll move the name attributes to the Person superclass because not only mathematicians have names. We end up with the code shown in Listing 6-4.

```
class Person
  attr_accessor :first_name
  attr_accessor :last_name
end

class Mathematician < Person
end
```

Listing 6-4: Now the name attributes are in the Person superclass.

Finally, we'll include the Professor module into the Mathematician class at ❶. Listing 6-5 shows the completed example.

```
class Person
  attr_accessor :first_name
  attr_accessor :last_name
end

module Professor
  def lectures; end
end

class Mathematician < Person
❶  include Professor
end
```

Listing 6-5: Now we have a class that includes a module and has a superclass.

The Method Lookup Algorithm in Action

Now that we have our example set up, we're ready to see how Ruby finds a method we call. Every time you call any method in one of your programs, Ruby follows the same process we're about to see here.

To kick things off, let's call a method. Using this code, we create a new mathematician object and set its first name:

```
ramanujan = Mathematician.new
ramanujan.first_name = "Srinivasa"
```

To execute this code, Ruby needs to find the first_name= method. Where is this method? How does Ruby find it exactly?

First, Ruby gets the class from the ramanujan object via the klass pointer, as shown in Figure 6-4.

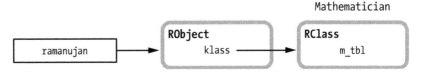

Figure 6-4: Ruby first looks for the first_name= method in the object's class.

Next, Ruby checks to see whether Mathematician implements first_name= directly by looking through its method table, as shown in Figure 6-5.

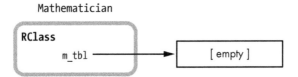

Figure 6-5: Ruby first looks for first_name= in the class's method table.

Because we've moved all of the methods down into the Person super-class, the first_name= method is no longer there. Ruby continues through the algorithm and gets the superclass of Mathematician using the super pointer, as shown in Figure 6-6.

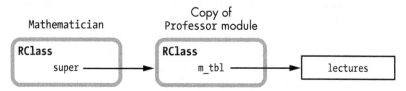

Figure 6-6: The superclass of Mathematician is the copy of the Professor module.

Remember, this is not the Person class; it's the *included* class, which is a copy of the Professor module. This copy refers to the same method table as the original module, which Ruby now searches. Recall from Listing 6-5 that Professor contains only the single method lectures. Ruby won't find the first_name= method.

NOTE   *Notice that because Ruby inserts modules above the original superclass in the super-class chain, methods in an included module override methods present in a superclass. In this case, if Professor also had a first_name= method, Ruby would call it and not the method in Person.*

Because Ruby doesn't find first_name= in Professor, it continues to iterate over the super pointers, but this time it uses the super pointer in Professor, as shown in Figure 6-7.

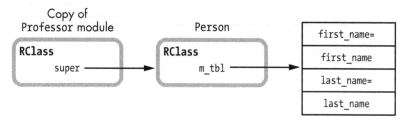

Figure 6-7: The Person class is the superclass of the included copy of the Professor module.

Note that the superclass of the Professor module—or more precisely, the superclass of the included copy of the Professor module—is the Person class. This was the original superclass of Mathematician. Finally, Ruby sees the first_name= method in the method table for Person. Because it has identified which class implements first_name=, Ruby can now call the method using the method dispatch process we learned about in Chapter 4.

Multiple Inheritance in Ruby

What is most interesting here is that internally, Ruby implements module inclusion using class inheritance. Essentially, there is no difference between including a module and specifying a superclass. Both procedures make new methods available to the target class, and both use the class's super pointer internally. Including multiple modules into a Ruby class is equivalent to specifying multiple superclasses.

Still, Ruby keeps things simple by enforcing a single list of ancestors. While including multiple modules does create multiple superclasses internally, Ruby maintains them in a single list. The result? As a Ruby developer, you get the benefits of multiple inheritance (adding new behavior to a class from as many different modules as you would like) while keeping the simplicity of the single inheritance model.

Ruby benefits from this simplicity as well! By enforcing this single list of superclass ancestors, its method lookup algorithm can be very simple. Whenever you call a method on an object, Ruby simply has to iterate through the superclass linked list until it finds the class or module that contains the target method.

The Global Method Cache

Depending on the number of superclasses in the chain, method lookup can be time consuming. To alleviate this, Ruby caches the result of a lookup for later use. It records which class or module implemented the method that your code called in two caches: a global method cache and an inline method cache.

Let's learn about the global method cache first. Ruby uses the *global method cache* to save a mapping between the receiver and implementer classes, as shown in Table 6-1.

Table 6-1: An Example of What the Global Method Cache Might Contain

klass	defined_class
Fixnum#times	Integer#times
Object#puts	BasicObject#puts
etc...	etc...

The left column in Table 6-1, klass, shows the receiver class; this is the class of the object you call a method on. The right column, defined_class, records the result of the method lookup. This is the implementer class, or the class that implements the method Ruby was looking for.

Let's take the first row of Table 6-1 as an example; it reads Fixnum#times and Integer#times. In the global method cache, this information means that Ruby's method lookup algorithm started to look for the times method in the Fixnum class but actually found it in the Integer class. In a similar way, the second row of Table 6-1 means that Ruby started to look for the puts method in the Object class but actually found it in the BasicObject class.

The global method cache allows Ruby to skip the method lookup process the next time your code calls a method listed in the first column of the global cache. After your code has called Fixnum#times once, Ruby knows that it can execute the Integer#times method, regardless of from where in your program you call times.

The Inline Method Cache

Ruby uses another type of cache, called an *inline method cache*, to speed up method lookup even more. The inline cache saves information alongside the compiled YARV instructions that Ruby executes (see Figure 6-8).

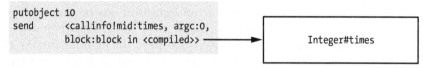

Figure 6-8: The YARV instructions on the left should call the implementation of Integer#times on the right.

On the left side of this figure, we see the compiled YARV instructions that correspond to the code 10.times do... end. First, putobject 10 pushes the Fixnum object 10 onto YARV's internal stack. This is the receiver of the times method call. Next, send calls the times method, as indicated by the text between the angle brackets.

The rectangle on the right side of the figure represents the Integer#times method, which Ruby found using its method lookup algorithm (after looking up the times method among the Fixnum class and its superclasses). Ruby's inline cache enables it to save the mapping between the times method call and the Integer#times implementation right in the YARV instructions. Figure 6-9 shows how the inline cache might look.

Figure 6-9: The inline cache saves the result of method lookup next to the send instruction that needs to call the method.

If Ruby executes this line of code again, it will immediately execute Integer#times without having to call the method lookup algorithm.

Clearing Ruby's Method Caches

Because Ruby is a dynamic language, you can define new methods when you like. In order for you to be able to do so, Ruby must clear the global and inline method caches, because the results of method lookups might change. For example, if we add a new definition of the times method to the Fixnum or Integer classes, Ruby would need to call the new times method, not the Integer#times method that it was previously using.

In effect, whenever you create or remove (*undefine*) a method, include a module into a class, or perform a similar action, Ruby clears the global and inline method caches, forcing a new call to the method lookup code. Ruby also clears the cache when you use refinements or employ other types of metaprogramming. In fact, clearing the cache happens quite frequently in Ruby. The global and inline method caches might remain valid for only a short time.

Including Two Modules into One Class

While Ruby's method lookup algorithm may be simple, the code that it uses to include modules is not. As we saw above, when you include a module into a class, Ruby inserts a copy of the module into the class's ancestor chain. This means that if you include two modules, one after the other, the second module appears first in the ancestor chain and is found first by Ruby's method lookup logic.

For example, suppose we include two modules into Mathematician, as shown in Listing 6-6.

```
class Mathematician < Person
  include Professor
  include Employee
end
```

Listing 6-6: Including two modules into one class

Now Mathematician objects have methods from the Professor module, the Employee module, and the Person class. But which methods does Ruby find first and which methods override which?

Figures 6-10 and 6-11 show the order of precedence. Because we include the Professor module first, Ruby inserts the included class corresponding to the Professor module as a superclass first.

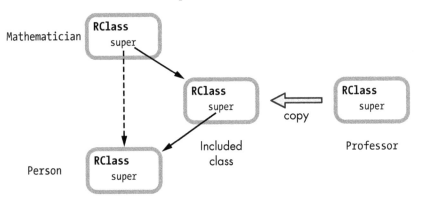

Figure 6-10: In Listing 6-6 we include the Professor module first.

Now, when we include the Employee module, the included class for the Employee module is inserted above the included class for the Professor module, as shown in Figure 6-11.

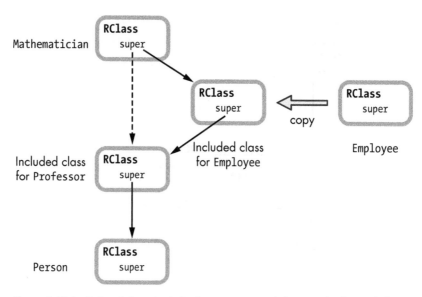

Figure 6-11: In Listing 6-6 we include the Employee *module second, after including* Professor.

Because Employee appears above Professor in the superclass chain, as shown along the left side of Figure 6-11, methods from Employee override methods from Professor, which in turn override methods from Person, the actual superclass.

Including One Module into Another

Modules don't allow you to specify superclasses. For example, we can't write the following:

```
module Professor < Employee
end
```

But we can include one module into another, as shown in Listing 6-7.

```
module Professor
  include Employee
end
```

Listing 6-7: One module including another module

What if we include Professor, a module with other modules included into it, into Mathematician? Which methods will Ruby find first? As shown in Figure 6-12, when we include Employee into Professor, Ruby creates a copy of Employee and sets it as the superclass of Professor.

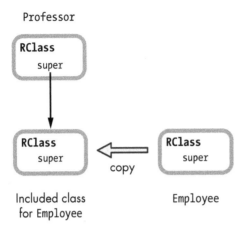

Professor

Figure 6-12: When you include one module into another, Ruby sets it as the superclass of the target module.

Modules can't have a superclass in your code, but they can inside Ruby because Ruby represents modules with classes internally!

Finally, when we include Professor into Mathematician, Ruby iterates over the two modules and inserts them both as superclasses of Mathematician, as shown in Figure 6-13.

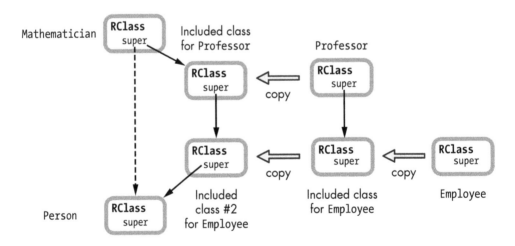

Figure 6-13: Including two modules into a class at the same time

Now Ruby will find the methods in Professor first and Employee second.

A Module#prepend Example

In Figure 6-2 we saw how Ruby includes a module into a class. Specifically, we saw how Ruby inserts a copy of the module's RClass structure into the superclass chain for the target class, between the class and its superclass.

Beginning with version 2.0, Ruby now allows you to "prepend" a module into a class. We'll use the Mathematician class to explain, as shown in Listing 6-8.

```
class Mathematician
❶   attr_accessor :name
end

poincaré = Mathematician.new
poincaré.name = "Henri Poincaré"
❷ p poincaré.name
   => "Henri Poincaré"
```

Listing 6-8: A simple Ruby class with a name attribute

First, we define the Mathematician class with just the single attribute name at ❶. Then, we create an instance of Mathematician, set its name, and display it at ❷.

Now suppose we make all of our mathematicians professors by including the Professor module into the Mathematician class again, as shown at ❶ in Listing 6-9.

```
module Professor
end

class Mathematician
   attr_accessor :name
❶   include Professor
end
```

Listing 6-9: Including the Professor module into the Mathematician class

Figure 6-14 shows the superclass chain for Mathematician and Professor.

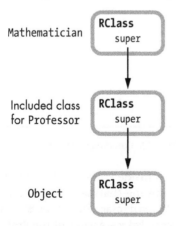

Figure 6-14: Professor is a superclass of Mathematician.

If we decide to display the title `Prof.` in front of each mathematician's name, we can just add that behavior to the `Mathematician` class, as shown in Listing 6-10.

```
module Professor
end

class Mathematician
  attr_writer :name
  include Professor
❶ def name
    "Prof. #{@name}"
  end
end
```

Listing 6-10: An ugly way to display the `Prof.` title before each mathematician's name

But this is a very ugly solution: The `Mathematician` class has to do the work of displaying the professor title at ❶. What if other classes include `Professor`? Shouldn't they display the `Prof.` title also? If `Mathematician` contains the code for showing `Prof.`, then any other classes that include `Professor` would be missing this code.

It makes more sense to include the code for displaying the title in the `Professor` module, as shown in Listing 6-11. This way every class that includes `Professor` will be able to display the title `Prof.` along with its class name.

```
module Professor
❶ def name
    "Prof. #{super}"
  end
end

class Mathematician
  attr_accessor :name
❷ include Professor
end

poincaré = Mathematician.new
poincaré.name = "Henri Poincaré"
❸ p poincaré.name
  => "Henri Poincaré"
```

Listing 6-11: How can we get Ruby to call the module's `name` method?

At ❶ we define a `name` method inside `Professor` that will display the `Prof.` title before the actual name (assuming that `name` is defined in a superclass). At ❷ we include `Professor` into `Mathematician`. Finally, at ❸ we call the `name` method, but we get the name `Henri Poincaré` without the `Prof.` title. What went wrong?

The problem, as shown in Figure 6-14, is that `Professor` is a super-class of `Mathematician`, not the other way around. This means when I call poincaré.name at ❸ in Listing 6-11, Ruby finds the `name` method from `Mathematician`, not from `Professor`. Figure 6-15 shows visually what Ruby's method lookup algorithm finds when I call poincaré.name.

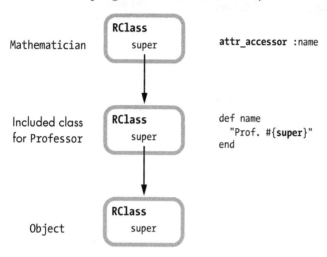

Figure 6-15: Ruby calls the `attr_accessor` method before finding the `name` method from Professor.

When we call `name` at ❸ in Listing 6-11, Ruby finds the first `name` method that it sees in the superclass chain starting from the top and moving down. As you can see in Figure 6-15, the first `name` method is the simple `attr_accessor` method in `Mathematician`.

However, if we prepend `Professor` instead of including it, we get the behavior we were hoping for, as shown in Listing 6-12.

```
module Professor
  def name
    "Prof. #{super}"
  end
end

class Mathematician
  attr_accessor :name
❶ prepend Professor
end

poincaré = Mathematician.new
poincaré.name = "Henri Poincaré"
❷ p poincaré.name
  => "Prof. Henri Poincaré"
```

Listing 6-12: Using prepend, Ruby finds the module's name method first.

The only difference here is the use of prepend at ❶.

How Ruby Implements Module#prepend

When you prepend a module to a class, Ruby places it before the class in the superclass chain, as shown in Figure 6-16.

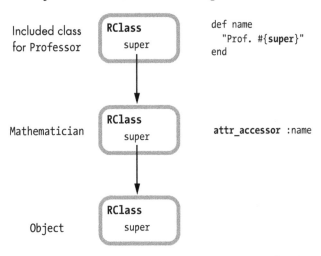

Included class
for Professor

```
def name
  "Prof. #{super}"
end
```

Mathematician

`attr_accessor :name`

Object

Figure 6-16: Using prepend, Ruby places the module before the target class in the superclass chain.

But there is something odd here. When we call `name` on a mathematician object, how does Ruby find the module's method? That is, at ❷ in Listing 6-12, we're calling `name` on the `Mathematician` class, not on the `Professor` module. Ruby should find the simple `attr_accessor` method, not the version from the module, but that's not the case. Does Ruby look backward up the superclass chain to find the module? If so, how does it do this when the super pointers point down?

The secret is that internally Ruby uses a trick to make it seem as if `Mathematician` is the superclass of `Professor` when it's not, as shown in Figure 6-17. Prepending a module is like including a module. `Mathematician` is at the top of the superclass chain, and moving down the chain, we see that Ruby still sets the included class for `Professor` to be the superclass of `Mathematician`.

But below `Professor` in Figure 6-17 we see something new, the *origin class* for `Mathematician`. This is a new copy of `Mathematician` that Ruby creates to make prepend work.

When you prepend a module, Ruby creates a copy of the target class (called the *origin class* internally) and sets it as the superclass of the prepended module. Ruby uses the origin pointer that we saw in the `rb_classext_struct` structure in Figures 6-1 and 6-2 to track this new origin copy of the class. In addition, Ruby moves all of the methods from the original class to the origin class, which means that those methods may now be overridden by methods with the same name in the prepended module. In Figure 6-17 you can see that Ruby moved the `attr_accessor` method down from `Mathematician` to the origin class.

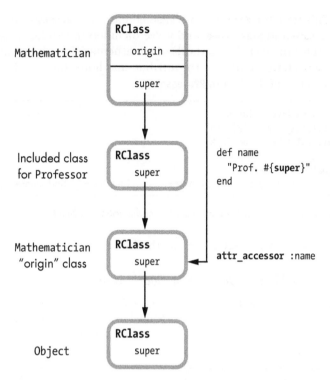

Figure 6-17: Ruby creates a copy of the target class and sets it as the superclass of the prepended module.

Experiment 6-1: Modifying a Module After Including It

Following a suggestion by Xavier Noria, this experiment will explore what happens when you modify a module once it's been included into a class. We'll use the same Mathematician class and the Professor module but with different methods, as shown in Listing 6-13.

```
module Professor
  def lectures; end
end

class Mathematician
❶  attr_accessor :first_name
   attr_accessor :last_name
❷  include Professor
end
```

Listing 6-13: Another example of including a module into a class

This time the `Mathematician` class contains the accessor methods at ❶ for `@first_name` and `@last_name`, and we've included the `Professor` module again at ❷. If we inspect the methods of a mathematician object, as shown in Listing 6-14, we should see the attribute methods, such as `first_name=` and the `lectures` method from `Professor`.

```
fermat = Mathematician.new
fermat.first_name = 'Pierre'
fermat.last_name = 'de Fermat'

p fermat.methods.sort
 => [ ... :first_name, :first_name=, ... :last_name, :last_name=, :lectures ... ]
```

Listing 6-14: Inspecting the methods of a mathematician object

No surprise; we see all the methods.

Classes See Methods Added to a Module Later

Now let's add some new methods to the `Professor` module after including it into the `Mathematician` class. Does Ruby know that the new methods should be added to `Mathematician` as well? Let's find out by running Listing 6-15 right after Listing 6-14 finishes.

```
module Professor
  def primary_classroom; end
end

p fermat.methods.sort
❶ => [ ... :first_name, :first_name=, ... :last_name, :last_name=, :lectures,
... :primary_classroom, ... ]
```

Listing 6-15: Adding a new method to `Professor` after including it into `Mathematician`

As you can see, at ❶ we get all the methods, including the new `primary_classroom` method that was added to `Professor` after it was included into `Mathematician`. No surprise here either. Ruby is one step ahead of us.

Classes Don't See Submodules Included Later

Now for one more test. What if we reopen the `Professor` module and include yet another module into it using Listing 6-16?

```
module Employee
  def hire_date; end
end

module Professor
  include Employee
end
```

Listing 6-16: Including a new module into `Professor` after it was included into `Mathematician`

This is getting confusing, so let's review what we did in Listings 6-13 and 6-16:

- In Listing 6-13 we included the Professor module into the Mathematician class.

- Then, in Listing 6-16 we included the Employee module into the Professor module. Therefore, the methods of the Employee module should now be available on a mathematician object.

Let's see whether Ruby works as expected:

```
p fermat.methods.sort
=> [ ... :first_name, :first_name=, ... :last_name, :last_name=, :lectures ... ]
```

It didn't work! The hire_date method is *not* available in the fermat object. Including a module into a module already included into a class *does not* affect that class.

As we've learned how Ruby implements modules, this fact shouldn't be too hard to understand. Including Employee into Professor changes the Professor module, not the copy of Professor that Ruby created when we included it into Mathematician, as shown in Figure 6-18.

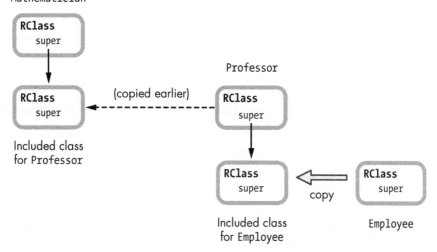

Figure 6-18: The Employee module is included into the original Professor module, not the included copy used by Mathematician.

Included Classes Share the Method Table with the Original Module

But what about the primary_classroom method we added in Listing 6-15? How was Ruby able to include the primary_classroom method into Mathematician even though we added it to Professor after we included Professor into Mathematician? Figure 6-18 shows that Ruby created a copy of the Professor module before we added the new method to it. But how does the fermat object get the new method?

As it turns out, when you include a module, Ruby copies the RClass structure, not the underlying method table, as shown in Figure 6-19.

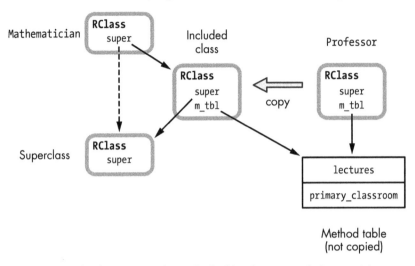

Figure 6-19: Ruby doesn't copy the method table when you include a module.

Ruby doesn't copy the method table for Professor. Instead, it simply sets m_tbl in the new copy of Professor, the "included class," to point to the same method table. This means that modifying the method table by reopening the module and adding new methods will change both the module and any classes into which it was already included.

A CLOSE LOOK AT HOW RUBY COPIES MODULES

By looking at Ruby's C source code directly, you'll gain a precise understanding of how Ruby copies modules when you include them and why Ruby behaves as you'll see in this experiment. You'll find the C function that Ruby uses to make a copy of a module in the *class.c* file. Listing 6-17 shows a portion of the function rb_include_class_new.

```
  VALUE
❶ rb_include_class_new(VALUE module, VALUE super)
  {
❷     VALUE klass = class_alloc(T_ICLASS, rb_cClass);
      --snip--
❸     RCLASS_IV_TBL(klass) = RCLASS_IV_TBL(module);
      RCLASS_CONST_TBL(klass) = RCLASS_CONST_TBL(module);
❹     RCLASS_M_TBL(klass) = RCLASS_M_TBL(RCLASS_ORIGIN(module));
❺     RCLASS_SUPER(klass) = super;
      --snip--
      return (VALUE)klass;
  }
```

Listing 6-17: A portion of the rb_include_class_new C function, from class.c

---

At ❶ Ruby passes in module (the target module to copy) and super (the super-class to use for the new copy of module). By specifying a particular superclass, Ruby inserts the new copy into the superclass chain at a particular place. If you search *class.c* for rb_include_class_new, you'll find that Ruby calls it from another C function, include_modules_at, which handles the complex internal logic that Ruby uses to include modules.

At ❷ Ruby calls class_alloc to create a new RClass structure and saves a reference to it in klass. Notice the first parameter to class_alloc is the value T_ICLASS, which identifies the new class as an included class. Ruby uses T_ICLASS throughout its C source code when dealing with included classes.

At ❸ Ruby copies a series of pointers from the original module's RClass structure over to the new copy using three C macros that operate on RClass.

- RCLASS_IV_TBL gets or sets a pointer to the instance variable table.

- RCLASS_CONST_TBL gets or sets a pointer to the constant variable table.

- RCLASS_M_TBL gets or sets a pointer to the method table.

For example, RCLASS_IV_TBL(klass) = RCLASS_IV_TBL(module) sets the instance variable table pointer in klass (the new copy) to the instance variable pointer from module (the target module to copy). Now klass and module use the same instance variables. In the same way, klass shares constant and method tables with module. Because they share the same method table, adding a new method to module also adds it to klass. This explains the behavior we saw in Experiment 6-1: Adding a method to a module also adds it to each class that includes that module.

Also note at ❹ Ruby uses RCLASS_ORIGIN(module), not module. Normally RCLASS_ORIGIN(module) is the same as module; however, if you have earlier used prepend in module, then RCLASS_ORIGIN(module) instead returns the origin class for module. Recall that when you call Module#prepend, Ruby makes a copy (the origin class) of the target module and inserts the copy into the superclass chain. By using RCLASS_ORIGIN(module), Ruby gets the original module's method table, even if you prepended it with a different module.

Finally, at ❺ Ruby sets the superclass pointer of klass to the specified superclass and returns it.

Constant Lookup

We've learned about Ruby's method lookup algorithm and how it searches through the superclass chain to find the right method to call. Now we'll turn our attention to a related process: Ruby's constant lookup algorithm, or the process Ruby uses to find a constant value that you refer to in your code.

Clearly method lookup is central to the language, but why study constant lookup? As Ruby developers, we don't use constants very often in our code—certainly not as often as we use classes, modules, variables, and blocks.

One reason is that constants, like modules and classes, are central to the way Ruby works internally and to the way we use Ruby. Whenever you define a module or class, you also define a constant. And whenever you refer to or use a module or class, Ruby has to look up the corresponding constant.

The second reason has to do with the way Ruby finds a constant that you refer to in your code. As you may know, Ruby finds constants defined in a superclass, but it also finds constants in the surrounding namespace or syntactical scope of your program. Studying how Ruby handles syntactical scope leads us to some important discoveries about how Ruby works internally.

Let's begin by reviewing how constants work in Ruby.

Finding a Constant in a Superclass

One way that Ruby searches for the definition of a constant you refer to is by using the superclass chain just as it would look for a method definition. Listing 6-18 shows an example of one class finding a constant in its superclass.

```
  class MyClass
❶   SOME_CONSTANT = "Some value..."
  end

❷ class Subclass < MyClass
    p SOME_CONSTANT
  end
```

Listing 6-18: Ruby finds constants you define in a superclass.

In Listing 6-18 we define MyClass with a single constant, SOME_CONSTANT at ❶. Then we create Subclass and set MyClass as a superclass at ❷. When we print the value of SOME_CONSTANT, Ruby uses the same algorithm it uses to find a method, as shown in Figure 6-20.

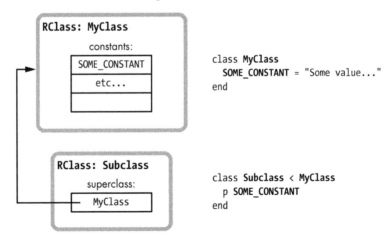

Figure 6-20: Ruby searches for constants using the superclass chain, just as it does with methods.

Here, on the right, you see the code from Listing 6-18 and, on the left, the RClass structures that correspond to each of the two classes we created. At the top left of the figure, you see MyClass, which contains the value of SOME_CONSTANT in its constants table. Below that is Subclass. When we refer to SOME_CONSTANT from inside Subclass, Ruby uses the super pointer to find MyClass and the value of SOME_CONSTANT.

How Does Ruby Find a Constant in the Parent Namespace?

Listing 6-19 shows another way to define a constant.

```
❶ module Namespace
❷   SOME_CONSTANT = "Some value..."
❸   class Subclass
❹     p SOME_CONSTANT
    end
  end
```

Listing 6-19: Using a constant defined in the surrounding namespace

Using idiomatic Ruby style, we create a module called Namespace at ❶. Then, inside this module, we declare the same SOME_CONSTANT value at ❷. Next, we declare Subclass inside Namespace at ❸, and we're able to refer to and print the value of SOME_CONSTANT, just as in Listing 6-18.

But how does Ruby find SOME_CONSTANT in Listing 6-19 when we display it at ❹? Figure 6-21 shows the problem.

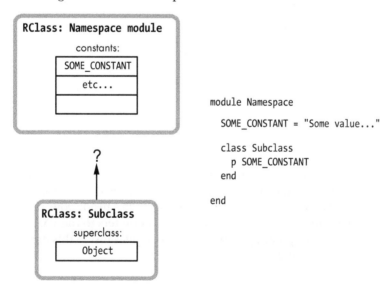

Figure 6-21: How does Ruby find constants in the surrounding namespace?

On the left side of this figure are two RClass structures, one for the Namespace module and one for Subclass. Notice that Namespace is not a super-class of Subclass; the super pointer in Subclass refers to the Object class, Ruby's default superclass. Then how does Ruby find SOME_CONSTANT when we refer to it inside of Subclass? Somehow Ruby allows you to search up the "namespace chain" to find constants. This behavior is called using lexical scope to find a constant.

Lexical Scope in Ruby

Lexical scope refers to a section of code within the syntactical structure of your program, rather than within the superclass hierarchy or some other scheme. For example, suppose we use the class keyword to define MyClass, as shown in Listing 6-20.

```
class MyClass
  SOME_CONSTANT = "Some value..."
end
```

Listing 6-20: Defining a class with the class keyword

This code tells Ruby to create a new copy of the RClass structure, but it also defines a new scope or syntactical section of your program. This is the area between the class and end keywords, as shown with shading in Figure 6-22.

```
class MyClass

  SOME_CONSTANT = "Some value..."

end
```

Figure 6-22: The class keyword creates a class and a new lexical scope.

Think of your Ruby program as a series of scopes, one for each module or class that you create and another for the default, top-level lexical scope. To keep track of where this new scope lies inside your program's lexical structure, Ruby attaches a couple of pointers to the YARV instruction snippet corresponding to the code it compiles inside this new scope, as shown in Figure 6-23.

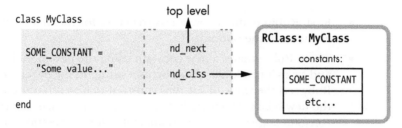

Figure 6-23: For each snippet of compiled code, Ruby uses pointers to track the parent lexical scope and the current class or module.

This figure shows the lexical scope information attached to the right side of the Ruby code. There are two important values here:

- First, the nd_next pointer is set to the parent or surrounding lexical scope—the default or top-level scope in this case.
- Next, the nd_clss pointer indicates which Ruby class or module corresponds to this scope. In this example, because we just defined MyClass using the class keyword, Ruby sets the nd_clss pointer to the RClass structure corresponding to MyClass.

Creating a Constant for a New Class or Module

Whenever you create a class or module, Ruby automatically creates a corresponding constant and saves it in the class or module for the parent lexical scope.

Let's return to the "namespace" example from Listing 6-19. Figure 6-24 shows what Ruby does internally when you create MyClass inside Namespace.

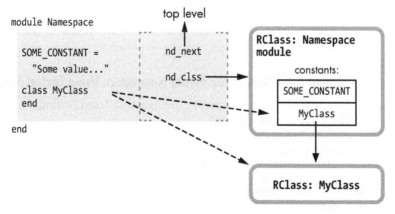

Figure 6-24: When you declare a new class, Ruby creates a new RClass structure and defines a new constant set to the new class's name.

The dashed arrows in this figure show what actions Ruby takes when you create a new class or module:

- First, Ruby creates a new RClass structure for the new module or class, as shown at the bottom.
- Then, Ruby creates a new constant using the new module or class name and saves it inside the class corresponding to the parent lexical scope. Ruby sets the value of the new constant to be a reference or pointer to the new RClass structure. In Figure 6-24 you can see that the MyClass constant appears in the constants table for the Namespace module.

The new class also gets its own new lexical scope, as shown in Figure 6-25.

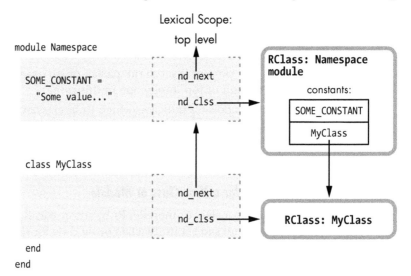

Figure 6-25: A new class also gets its own lexical scope, shown here as the second shaded rectangle.

This figure shows a new shaded rectangle for the new scope. Its nd_clss pointer is set to the new RClass structure for MyClass, and its nd_next pointer is set to the parent scope that corresponds to the Namespace module.

Finding a Constant in the Parent Namespace Using Lexical Scope

In Listing 6-21 let's return to the example from Listing 6-19, which prints the value of SOME_CONSTANT.

```
module Namespace
  SOME_CONSTANT = "Some value..."
  class Subclass
❶   p SOME_CONSTANT
  end
end
```

Listing 6-21: Finding a constant in the parent lexical scope (repeated from Listing 6-19)

In Figure 6-20 we saw how Ruby iterates over super pointers to find a constant from a superclass. But in Figure 6-21 we saw that Ruby couldn't use super pointers to find SOME_CONSTANT in this example because Namespace is not a superclass of MyClass. Instead, as Figure 6-26 shows, Ruby can use the nd_next pointers to iterate up through your program's lexical scopes in search of constant values.

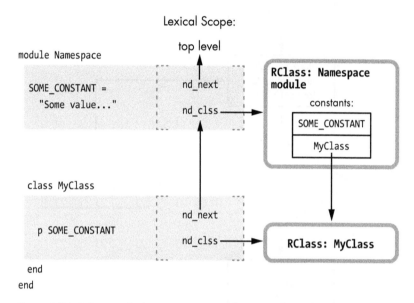

Figure 6-26: Ruby can find SOME_CONSTANT in the parent lexical scope using the nd_next and nd_clss pointers.

By following the arrows in this figure, you can see how the p SOME_CONSTANT command at ❶ in Listing 6-21 works:

- First, Ruby looks for the value of SOME_CONSTANT in the current scope's class, MyClass. In Figure 6-26 the current scope contains the p SOME_CONSTANT code. You can see how Ruby finds the current scope's class on the right using the nd_clss pointer. Here, MyClass has no constants table.
- Next, Ruby finds the parent lexical scope using the nd_next pointer, moving up Figure 6-26.
- Ruby repeats the process, searching the current scope's class using the nd_clss pointer. This time the current scope's class is the Namespace module, at the top right of Figure 6-26. Now Ruby finds SOME_CONSTANT in Namespace's constants table.

Ruby's Constant Lookup Algorithm

The flowchart in Figure 6-27 summarizes how Ruby iterates over the lexical scope chain while looking for constants.

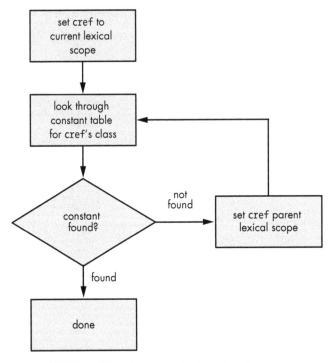

Figure 6-27: Part of Ruby's constant lookup algorithm

Notice that this figure is very similar to Figure 6-3. Ruby iterates over the linked list formed by the nd_next pointers in each lexical scope while looking for a constant, just as it iterates over the super pointers while looking for a method. Ruby uses superclasses to find methods and parent lexical scopes to find constants.

However, this is just part of Ruby's constant lookup algorithm. As we saw earlier in Figure 6-20, Ruby also looks through superclasses for constants.

Experiment 6-2: Which Constant Will Ruby Find First?

We've just learned that Ruby iterates over a linked list of lexical scopes in order to look up constant values. However, we saw earlier in Figure 6-20 that Ruby also uses the superclass chain to look up constants. Let's use Listing 6-22 to see how this works in more detail.

```
class Superclass
❶  FIND_ME = "Found in Superclass"
end
```

```
   module ParentLexicalScope
❷  FIND_ME = "Found in ParentLexicalScope"

   module ChildLexicalScope

    class Subclass < Superclass
      p FIND_ME
    end

   end
end
```

Listing 6-22: Does Ruby search the lexical scope chain first? Or does it search the super-class chain first? (find-constant.rb)

Notice here that I've defined the constant `FIND_ME` twice—at ❶ and at ❷. Which constant will Ruby find first? Will Ruby first iterate over the lexical scope chain and find the constant at ❷? Or will it iterate over the superclass chain and find the constant value at ❶?

Let's find out! When we run Listing 6-22, we get the following:

```
$ ruby find-constant.rb
"Found in ParentLexicalScope"
```

You can see that Ruby looks through the lexical scope chain first.

Now let's comment out the second definition at ❷ in Listing 6-22 and try the experiment again:

```
   module ParentLexicalScope
❷  #FIND_ME = "Found in ParentLexicalScope"
```

When we run the modified Listing 6-22, we get the following:

```
$ ruby find-constant.rb
"Found in Superclass"
```

Because now there is only one definition of `FIND_ME`, Ruby finds it by iterating over the superclass chain.

Ruby's Actual Constant Lookup Algorithm

Unfortunately, things aren't quite so simple; there are some other quirks in Ruby's behavior with regard to constants. Figure 6-28 is a simplified flow-chart showing Ruby's entire constant lookup algorithm.

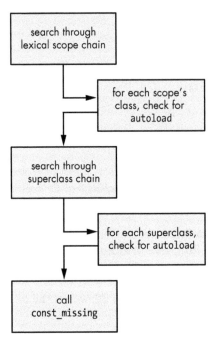

Figure 6-28: A high-level summary of Ruby's constant lookup algorithm

At the top, you can see that Ruby begins by iterating up the lexical scope chain, as we saw in Listing 6-22. Ruby always finds constants, including classes or modules, that are defined in a parent lexical scope. However, as Ruby iterates up the scope chain, it looks to see whether you used the autoload keyword, which instructs it to open and read in a new code file if a given constant is undefined. (The Rails framework uses autoload to allow you to load models, controllers, and other Rails objects without having to use require explicitly.)

If Ruby loops through the entire lexical scope chain without finding the given constant or a corresponding autoload keyword, it then iterates up the superclass chain, as we saw in Listing 6-18. This allows you to load constants defined in a superclass. Ruby once again honors any autoload keyword that might exist in any of those superclasses, loading an additional file if necessary.

Finally, if all else fails and the constant still isn't found, Ruby calls the const_missing method on your module if you provided one.

Summary

In this chapter we've learned two very different ways to look at your Ruby program. On the one hand, you can organize your code by class and superclass, and on the other, you can organize it by lexical scope. We saw how internally Ruby uses different sets of C pointers to keep track of these two trees as it executes your program. The super pointers found in the RClass structures form the superclass tree, while the nd_next pointers from the lexical scope structures form the namespace or lexical scope tree.

We studied two important algorithms that use these trees: how Ruby looks up methods and constants. Ruby uses the class tree to find the methods that your code (and Ruby's own internal code) calls. Similarly, Ruby uses both the lexical scope tree and the superclass hierarchy to find constants that your code refers to. Understanding the method and constant lookup algorithms is essential. They allow you to design your program and organize your code using these two trees in a way that is appropriate for the problem you are trying to solve.

At first glance, these two organizational schemes seem completely orthogonal, but in fact they are closely related by the way Ruby's classes behave. When you create a class or module, you add both to the superclass and lexical scope hierarchy, and when you refer to a class or superclass, you instruct Ruby to look up a particular constant using the lexical scope tree.

Ruby stores much of its own internal data in hash tables.

7

THE HASH TABLE: THE WORKHORSE OF RUBY INTERNALS

Experiment 5-1 showed us how in Ruby 1.9 and 2.0 the `ivptr` member of the `RObject` structure pointed to a simple array of instance variable values. We learned that adding a new value was usually very fast but that Ruby was somewhat slower while saving every third or fourth instance variable because it had to allocate a larger array.

Taking a broader look across Ruby's C source code base, we find that this technique is unusual. Instead, Ruby often uses a data structure called a *hash table*. Unlike the simple array we saw in Experiment 5-1, hash tables can automatically expand to accommodate more values; the client of a hash table doesn't need to worry about how much space is available or about allocating more memory for it.

Among other things, Ruby uses a hash table to hold the data you save in the hash objects you create in your Ruby script. Ruby also saves much of its internal data in hash tables. Every time you create a method or a constant, Ruby inserts a new value in a hash table, and Ruby saves many of the special variables we saw in Experiment 3-2 in hash tables. Additionally, Ruby saves instance variables for generic objects, such as integers or symbols, in hash tables. Thus, the hash table is the workhorse of Ruby internals.

In this chapter I'll begin by explaining how hash tables work: what happens inside the table when you save a new value with a key and what happens when you later retrieve that value using the same key. I'll also explain how hash tables automatically expand to accommodate more values. Finally, we'll look at how hash functions work in Ruby.

Hash Tables in Ruby

Hash tables are a commonly used, well-known, age-old concept in computer science. They organize values into groups, or *bins*, based on an integer value calculated from each value—a *hash*. When you need to find a value, you can figure out which bin it's in by recalculating its hash value, thus speeding up the search.

Every time you write a method, Ruby creates an entry in a hash table.

Saving a Value in a Hash Table

Figure 7-1 shows a single hash object and its hash table.

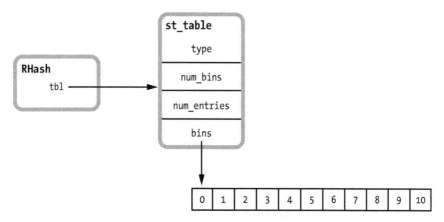

Figure 7-1: A Ruby hash object with an empty hash table

On the left is the RHash (short for *Ruby hash*) structure. On the right, you see the hash table used by this hash, represented by the st_table structure. This C structure contains the basic information about the hash table, including the number of entries saved in the table, the number of bins, and a pointer to the bins. Each RHash structure contains a pointer to a corresponding st_table structure. The empty bins on the lower right are there because Ruby 1.8 and 1.9 initially create 11 bins for a new, empty hash. (Ruby 2.0 and later work somewhat differently; see "Hash Optimization in Ruby 2.x" on page 187.)

The best way to understand how a hash table works is by stepping through an example. Suppose I add a new key/value to a hash called my_hash:

```
my_hash[:key] = "value"
```

While executing this line of code, Ruby creates a new structure called an st_table_entry that it will save into the hash table for my_hash, as shown in Figure 7-2.

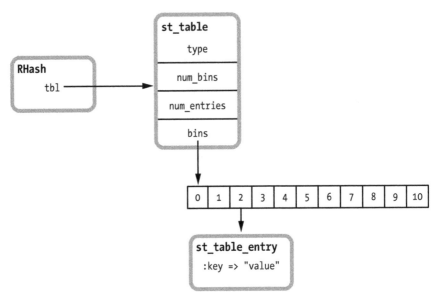

Figure 7-2: A Ruby hash object containing a single value

Here you can see Ruby saved the new key/value pair under the third bucket, number 2. Ruby did this by taking the given key—in this example, the symbol :key—and passing it to an internal hash function that returns a pseudorandom integer:

```
some_value = internal_hash_function(:key)
```

Next, Ruby takes the hash value—in this example, some_value—and calculates the modulus by the number of bins, which is the remainder after dividing by the number of bins.

```
some_value % 11 = 2
```

NOTE   *In Figure 7-2, I assume that the actual hash value for :key divided by 11 leaves a remainder of 2. Later in this chapter, I'll explore in more detail the hash functions that Ruby actually uses.*

Now let's add a second element to the hash:

```
my_hash[:key2] = "value2"
```

This time let's imagine that the hash value of :key2 divided by 11 yields a remainder of 5.

```
internal_hash_function(:key2) % 11 = 5
```

Figure 7-3 shows that Ruby places a second st_table_entry structure under bin number 5, the sixth bin.

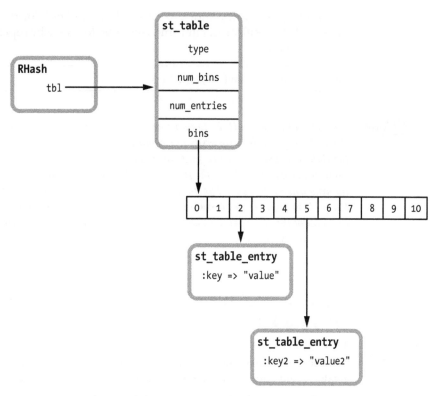

Figure 7-3: A Ruby hash object containing two values

Retrieving a Value from a Hash Table

The benefit of using a hash table becomes clear when you ask Ruby to retrieve the value for a given key. For example:

```
p my_hash[:key]
 => "value"
```

If Ruby had saved all of the keys and values in an array or linked list, it would have to iterate over all the elements in that array or list, looking for :key. This might take a very long time, depending on the number of elements. But using a hash table, Ruby can jump straight to the key it needs to find by recalculating the hash value for that key.

To recalculate the hash value for a particular key, Ruby simply calls the hash function again:

```
some_value = internal_hash_function(:key)
```

Then, it redivides the hash value by the number of bins to get the remainder, or the modulus.

```
some_value % 11 = 2
```

At this point, Ruby knows to look in bin number 2 for the entry with the key of :key. Ruby can later find the value for :key2 by repeating the same hash calculation.

```
internal_hash_function(:key2) % 11 = 5
```

NOTE   *The C library used by Ruby to implement hash tables was written in the 1980s by Peter Moore from the University of California, Berkeley. Later, it was modified by the Ruby core team. You can find Moore's hash table code in the C code files st.c and include/ruby/st.h. All of the function and structure names in that code use the naming convention st_. The definition of the RHash structure that represents every Ruby Hash object is in the include/ruby/ruby.h file. Along with RHash, this file contains all of the other primary object structures used in the Ruby source code: RString, RArray, and so on.*

Experiment 7-1: Retrieving a Value from Hashes of Varying Sizes

This experiment will create hashes of wildly different sizes, from 1 to 1 million elements, and then measure how long it takes to find and return a value from each of these hashes. Listing 7-1 shows the experiment code.

```
require 'benchmark'

❶ 21.times do |exponent|

    target_key = nil

❷   size = 2**exponent
    hash = {}
❸   (1..size).each do |n|
      index = rand
❹     target_key = index if n > size/2 && target_key.nil?
❺     hash[index] = rand
    end

    GC.disable

    Benchmark.bm do |bench|
      bench.report("retrieving an element
                  from a hash with #{size} elements 10000 times") do
        10000.times do
❻         val = hash[target_key]
        end
      end
    end
```

```
    GC.enable
end
```

Listing 7-1: Measuring how long it takes to retrieve an element from hashes of wildly different sizes

At ❶ the outer loop iterates over powers of two, calculating different values for size at ❷. These sizes will vary from 1 to about 1 million. Next, the inner loop at ❸ inserts that number of elements into a new empty hash at ❺.

After disabling garbage collection to avoid skewing the results, Experiment 7-1 uses the benchmark library to measure how long it takes to retrieve a value 10,000 times from each hash at ❻. The line of code at ❹ saves one of the random key values to use below at ❻ as target_key.

The results in Figure 7-4 show that Ruby can find and return a value from a hash containing over 1 million elements just as fast as it can return one from a small hash.

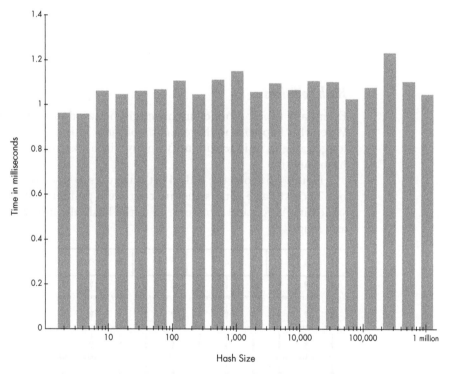

Figure 7-4: Time to retrieve 10,000 values (ms) vs. hash size for Ruby 2.0

Clearly Ruby's hash function is very fast, and once Ruby identifies the bin containing the target key, it can very quickly find the corresponding value and return it. What's remarkable here is that the chart is more or less flat.

How Hash Tables Expand to Accommodate More Values

If there are millions of st_table_entry structures, why does distributing them among 11 bins help Ruby search quickly? Because even if the hash function is fast, and even if Ruby distributes the values evenly among the 11 bins in the hash table, Ruby still has to search among almost 100,000 elements in each bin to find the target key if there are 1 million elements overall.

Something else must be going on here. It seems that Ruby must add more bins to the hash table as more and more elements are added. Let's look again at how Ruby's internal hash table code works. Continuing with the example from Figures 7-1 through 7-3, suppose I keep adding more and more elements to my hash.

```
my_hash[:key3] = "value3"
my_hash[:key4] = "value4"
my_hash[:key5] = "value5"
my_hash[:key6] = "value6"
```

As we add more elements, Ruby continues to create more st_table_entry structures and add them to different bins.

Hash Collisions

Eventually two or more elements might be saved into the same bin. When this happens, we have a *hash collision*. This means that Ruby is no longer able to uniquely identify and retrieve a key based solely on the hash function.

Figure 7-5 shows the linked list Ruby uses to track the entries in each bin. Each st_table_entry structure contains a pointer to the next entry in the same bin. As you add more entries to the hash, the linked lists get longer and longer.

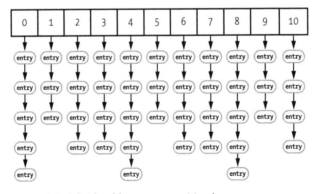

Figure 7-5: A hash table containing 44 values

To retrieve a value, Ruby needs to iterate over the linked list and compare each key with the target. This isn't a serious problem as long as the number of entries in a single bin doesn't grow too large. For integers or symbols, which are typically used as hash keys, this is a simple numerical comparison. However, if you use a more complex data type, such as a custom object, Ruby calls the eql? method on the keys to check whether each key in the list is the target. As you might guess, eql? returns *true* if two values are equal and *false* if they are not.

Rehashing Entries

To keep these linked lists from growing out of control, Ruby measures the *density*, or average number of entries per bin. In Figure 7-5 you can see that the average number of entries per bin is about 4. This means that the hash value modulus 11 has started to return repeated values for different keys and hash values; thus, there have been some hash collisions.

Once the density exceeds 5, a constant value in Ruby's C source code, Ruby allocates more bins and then *rehashes*, or redistributes, the existing entries across the new bin set. If we keep adding more key/value pairs, for example, Ruby eventually discards the array of 11 bins and allocates an array of 19 bins, as shown in Figure 7-6.

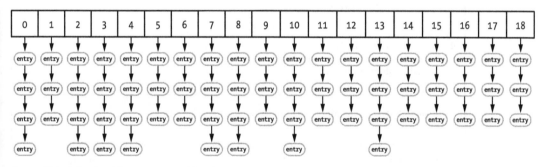

Figure 7-6: A hash table containing 65 values

In this figure the bin density has dropped to about 3.

By monitoring bin density, Ruby guarantees that the linked lists remain short and that retrieving a hash element is always fast. After calculating the hash value, Ruby just needs to step through one or two elements to find the target key.

HOW DOES RUBY REHASH ENTRIES IN A HASH TABLE?

You can find the rehash function (the code that loops through the st_table_entry structures and recalculates which bin to put the entry into) in the *st.c* source file. To keep things simple, Listing 7-2 shows the version of rehash from Ruby 1.8.7. While Ruby 1.9 and 2.0 work largely the same way, their C rehash code is somewhat more complex.

```
static void
rehash(table)
    register st_table *table;
{
    register st_table_entry *ptr, *next, **new_bins;
    int i, old_num_bins = table->num_bins, new_num_bins;
    unsigned int hash_val;
❶  new_num_bins = new_size(old_num_bins+1);
    new_bins = (st_table_entry**)Calloc(new_num_bins,
                                    sizeof(st_table_entry*));
❷  for(i = 0; i < old_num_bins; i++) {
        ptr = table->bins[i];
        while (ptr != 0) {
            next = ptr->next;
❸          hash_val = ptr->hash % new_num_bins;
❹          ptr->next = new_bins[hash_val];
            new_bins[hash_val] = ptr;
            ptr = next;
        }
    }
❺  free(table->bins);
    table->num_bins = new_num_bins;
    table->bins = new_bins;
}
```

Listing 7-2: The C code inside Ruby 1.8.7 that rehashes a hash table

In this listing, the new_size method call at ❶ returns the new bin count. Once Ruby has the new bin count, it allocates the new bins and then iterates over all the existing st_table_entry structures (all the key/value pairs in the hash) beginning at ❷. For each st_table_entry Ruby recalculates the bin position using the same modulus formula at ❸: hash_val = ptr->hash % new_num_bins. Then, Ruby saves each entry in the linked list for that new bin at ❹. Finally, Ruby updates the st_table structure and frees the old bins at ❺.

Experiment 7-2: Inserting One New Element into Hashes of Varying Sizes

One way to test whether this rehashing, or redistribution, of entries really occurs is to measure the amount of time Ruby takes to save one new element into existing hashes of different sizes. As we add more elements to the same hash, we should eventually see evidence that Ruby is taking extra time to rehash the elements.

The code for this experiment is shown in Listing 7-3.

```
require 'benchmark'

❶ 100.times do |size|

  hashes = []
❷ 10000.times do
    hash = {}
    (1..size).each do
      hash[rand] = rand
    end
    hashes << hash
  end

  GC.disable

  Benchmark.bm do |bench|
    bench.report("adding element number #{size+1}") do
      10000.times do |n|
❸       hashes[n][size] = rand
      end
    end
  end

  GC.enable
end
```

Listing 7-3: Adding one more element to hashes of different sizes

At ❶ the outer loop iterates over hash sizes from 0 to 100, and at ❷ the inner loop creates 10,000 hashes of the given size. After disabling garbage collection, this experiment uses the benchmark library to measure how long it takes Ruby to insert a single new value at ❸ into all 10,000 hashes of the given size.

The results are surprising! Figure 7-7 shows the results for Ruby 1.8.

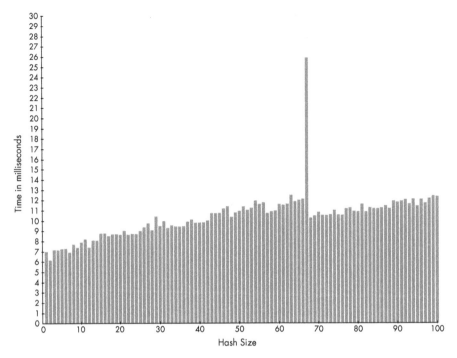

Figure 7-7: Time to add 10,000 key/value pairs vs. hash size (Ruby 1.8)

Interpreting these data values from left to right, we see the following:

- It takes about 7 ms to insert the first element into an empty hash (10,000 times).

- As the hash size increases from 2 to 3 and then up to about 60 or 65, the amount of time required to insert a new element slowly increases.

- It takes around 11 to 12 ms to insert each new key/value pair into a hash that contains 64, 65, or 66 elements (10,000 times).

- A huge spike! Inserting the 67th key/value pair takes over twice as much time: about 26 ms instead of 11 ms for 10,000 hashes!

- After inserting the 67th element, the time required to insert additional elements drops to about 10 ms or 11 ms and then slowly increases again from there.

What's going on here? Well, Ruby spends the extra time required to insert that 67th key/value pair reallocating the bin array from 11 to 19 bins and then reassigning the st_table_entry structures to the new bin array.

Figure 7-8 shows the same graph for Ruby 2.0. This time the bin density threshold is different. Instead of taking extra time to reallocate the elements into bins on the 67th insert, Ruby 2.0 does it when the 57th element is inserted. Later Ruby 2.0 performs another reallocation after the 97th element is inserted.

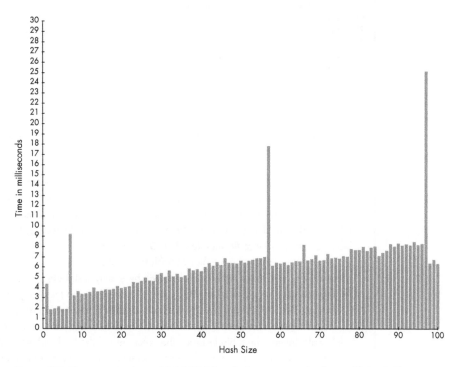

Figure 7-8: Time required to add 10,000 key/value pairs vs. hash size (Ruby 2.0)

The two smaller spikes on the 1st and 7th insert in this figure are curious. While not as pronounced as the spikes at the 57th and 97th elements, these smaller spikes are nonetheless noticeable. As it turns out, Ruby 2.0 contains another optimization that speeds up hash access even more for small hashes that contain less than 7 elements. I'll discuss this further in "Hash Optimization in Ruby 2.x" on page 187.

WHERE DO THE MAGIC NUMBERS 57 AND 67 COME FROM?

To see where these magic numbers come from (57, 67, and so on), look at the top of the *st.c* code file for your version of Ruby. You should find a list of prime numbers like the ones shown in Listing 7-4.

```
/*
Table of prime numbers 2^n+a, 2<=n<=30.
*/
static const unsigned int primes[] = {
❶    8 + 3,
❷    16 + 3,
❸    32 + 5,
     64 + 3,
     128 + 3,
     256 + 27,
     512 + 9,
--snip--
```

Listing 7-4: Ruby uses an algorithm based on prime numbers to determine the number of buckets required in each hash table.

This C array lists some prime numbers that occur near powers of 2. Peter Moore's hash table code uses this table to decide how many bins to use in the hash table. For example, the first prime number in the list above is 11 at ❶, which is why Ruby hash tables start with 11 bins. Later, as the number of elements increases, the number of bins increases to 19 at ❷, then to 37 at ❸, and so on.

Ruby always sets the number of hash table bins to a prime number in order to make it more likely that the hash values will be evenly distributed among the bins. Mathematically, prime numbers help here because they are less likely to share a common factor with the hash values, should a poor hash function return not entirely random values. Remember Ruby divides the hash values by the number of bins while calculating which bin to place the value into. If the hash values and bin count shared a factor, or even worse if the hash values were multiples of the bin count, the bin number (modulus) might always be the same. This would lead to the table entries being unevenly distributed among the bins.

Elsewhere in the *st.c* file, you should see this C constant:

```
#define ST_DEFAULT_MAX_DENSITY 5
```

This constant defines the maximum allowed density, or the average number of elements per bin.

Finally, you should see the code that decides when to perform a bin reallocation by finding where the constant ST_DEFAULT_MAX_DENSITY is used in *st.c*. For Ruby 1.8, you'll find this code:

```
if (table->num_entries/(table->num_bins) > ST_DEFAULT_MAX_DENSITY) {
  rehash(table);
}
```

Ruby 1.8 rehashes from 11 to 19 bins when the value num_entries/11 is greater than 5—that is, when it equals 66. As this check is performed before a new element is added, the condition becomes true when you add the 67th element because num_entries would then be 66.

For Ruby 1.9 and Ruby 2.0, you'll find this code instead:

```
if ((table)->num_entries >
    ST_DEFAULT_MAX_DENSITY * (table)->num_bins) {
  rehash(table);
```

You can see that Ruby 2.0 rehashes for the first time when num_entries is greater than 5*11, or when you insert the 57th element.

How Ruby Implements Hash Functions

Now for a closer look at the actual hash function Ruby uses to assign keys and values to bins in hash tables. This function is central to the way the hash object is implemented—if it works well, Ruby hashes are fast, but a poor hash function can cause severe performance problems. Furthermore, Ruby uses hash tables internally to store its own information, in addition to the data values you save in hash objects. Clearly having a good hash function is very important!

Hash functions allow Ruby to find which bin contains a given key and value.

Let's review how Ruby uses hash values. Remember that when you save a new element in a hash—a new key/value pair—Ruby assigns that element to a bin inside the internal hash table used by that hash object, as shown in Figure 7-9.

Ruby calculates the modulus of the key's hash value based on the number of bins.

```
bin_index = internal_hash_function(key) % bin_count
```

Using the same example values we used earlier, this formula becomes:

```
2 = hash(:key) % 11
```

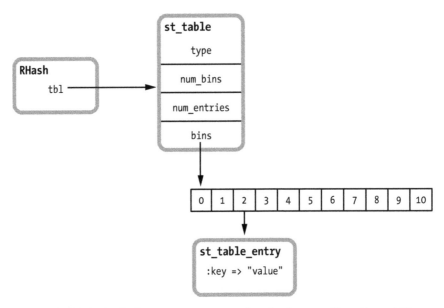

Figure 7-9: A Ruby hash object containing a single value (repeated from Figure 7-2)

This formula works well because Ruby's hash values are basically random integers for any given input data. To get a feel for how Ruby's hash function works, call the hash method, as shown in Listing 7-5.

```
$ irb
> "abc".hash
 => 3277525029751053763
> "abd".hash
 => 234577060685640459
> 1.hash
 => -3466223919964109258
> 2.hash
 => -2297524640777648528
```

Listing 7-5: Displaying the hash value for different Ruby objects

Here, even similar values have very different hash values. And if we call hash again, we always get the same integer value for the same input data.

```
> "abc".hash
 => 3277525029751053763
> "abd".hash
 => 234577060685640459
```

Here's how Ruby's hash function actually works for most Ruby objects:

- When you call hash, Ruby finds the default implementation in the Object class. You can override this if you want to.

- The C code used by the Object class's implementation of the hash method gets the C pointer value for the target object—that is, the actual memory address of that object's RValue structure. This is essentially a unique ID for that object.

- Ruby passes the pointer value through a complex C function (the hash function), which scrambles the bits in the value, producing a pseudo-random integer in a repeatable way.

In the case of strings and arrays, Ruby actually iterates through all of the characters in the string or the elements in the array and calculates a cumulative hash value. This guarantees that the hash will always be the same for any instance of a string or array and that it will change if any of the values in the string or array change. Integers and symbols are another special case. Ruby just passes their values right to the hash function.

To calculate hashes from values, Ruby 1.9 and 2.0 use a hash function called *MurmurHash*, which was invented by Austin Appleby in 2008. The name *Murmur* comes from the machine language operations used in the algorithm: *multiply* and *rotate*. (To learn how the Murmur algorithm actually works, read its C code in the *st.c* Ruby source code file. Or read Austin's web page on Murmur: *http://sites.google.com/site/murmurhash/.*)

Ruby 1.9 and 2.0 initialize MurmurHash using a random seed value that is reinitialized each time you restart Ruby. This means that if you stop and restart Ruby, you'll get different hash values for the same input data. It also means that if you try this yourself, you'll get different values than those above, but the hash values will always be the same within the same Ruby process.

Experiment 7-3: Using Objects as Keys in a Hash

Because hash values are evenly distributed, once Ruby divides them by the bin count, say 11, the remaining values (the modulus values) are random numbers between 0 and 10. This means that the st_table_entry structures are evenly distributed over the available bins as they are saved in the hash table, which ensures that Ruby will be able to quickly find any given key. The number of entries per bin will always be small.

But what if Ruby's hash function didn't return random integers but rather returned the same integer for every input data value? What would happen?

In that case, every time you added a key/value to a hash, it would always be assigned to the same bin. Ruby would end up with all of the entries in a single long list under that one bin, with no entries in any other bin, as shown in Figure 7-10.

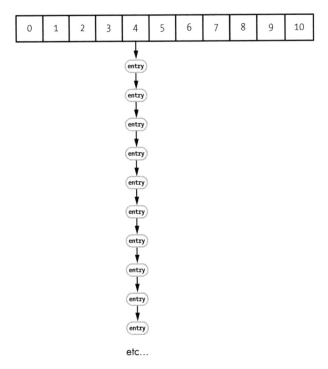

Figure 7-10: A hash table created with a very poor hash function

If you tried to retrieve a value from this hash, Ruby would have to look through this long list, one element at a time, to find the requested key. In this scenario, loading a value from the hash would be very, very slow.

To prove this is the case—and to illustrate just how important Ruby's hash function really is—we'll use objects with poor hash functions as keys in a hash. We'll repeat Experiment 7-1 here, but we'll use instances of a class I defined as the key values instead of random numbers. Listing 7-6 shows the code from Experiment 7-1, updated in two places.

```
require 'benchmark'

❶ class KeyObject
    def eql?(other)
      super
    end
  end

  21.times do |exponent|

    target_key = nil

    size = 2**exponent
    hash = {}
    (1..size).each do |n|
❷     index = KeyObject.new
      target_key = index if n > size/2 && target_key.nil?
```

```
    hash[index] = rand
  end

GC.disable

Benchmark.bm do |bench|
  bench.report("retrieving an element
               from a hash with #{size} elements 10000 times") do
    10000.times do
      val = hash[target_key]
    end
  end
end

GC.enable

end
```

Listing 7-6: Measuring how long it takes to retrieve an element from hashes of wildly different sizes. This is the same as Listing 7-1, but using instances of KeyObject as keys.

At ❶ we define an empty class called KeyObject. Note that I implemented the eql? method; this allows Ruby to search for the target key properly when I retrieve a value. However, in this example, I don't have any interesting data in KeyObject, so I simply call super and use the default implementation of eql? in the Object class.

Then, at ❷ we use new instances of KeyObject as the keys for my hash values. Figure 7-11 shows the results of this test.

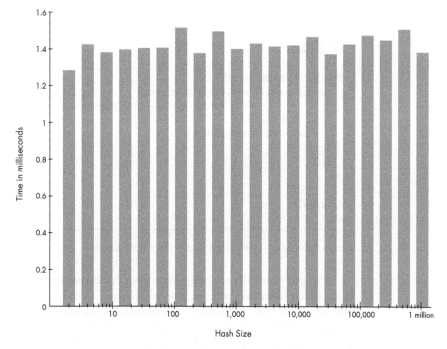

Figure 7-11: Time to retrieve 10,000 values vs. hash size, using objects as keys (Ruby 2.0)

As you can see, the results are very similar to those in Figure 7-4. The chart is more or less flat. It takes about the same amount of time to retrieve a value from a hash with 1 million elements as it does for a hash with just 1 element. No surprise there; using objects as keys hasn't slowed down Ruby at all.

Now let's change the KeyObject class and try again. Listing 7-7 shows the same code with a new hash function added at ❶.

```
require 'benchmark'

class KeyObject
  def hash
❶   4
  end
  def eql?(other)
    super
  end
end

21.times do |exponent|

  target_key = nil

  size = 2**exponent
  hash = {}
  (1..size).each do |n|
    index = KeyObject.new
    target_key = index if n > size/2 && target_key.nil?
    hash[index] = rand
  end

  GC.disable

  Benchmark.bm do |bench|
    bench.report("retrieving an element
                  from a hash with #{size} elements 10000 times") do
      10000.times do
        val = hash[target_key]
      end
    end
  end

  GC.enable
end
```

Listing 7-7: KeyObject now has a very poor hash function.

I've purposefully written a very poor hash function. Instead of returning a pseudorandom integer, the hash function in Listing 7-7 always returns the integer 4 at ❶, regardless of which KeyObject object instance you call it on. Now Ruby will always get 4 when it calculates the hash value. It will have to assign all of the hash elements to bin number 4 in the internal hash table, as in Figure 7-10.

Let's try this to see what happens! Figure 7-12 shows the results of running the code from Listing 7-7.

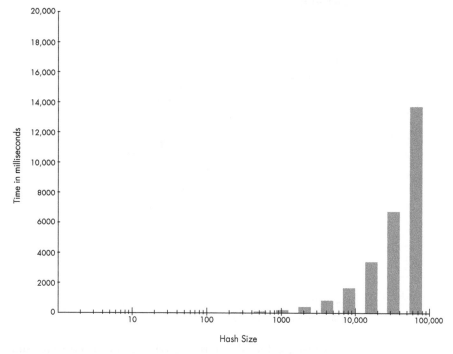

Figure 7-12: Time to retrieve 10,000 values vs. hash size, using a poor hash function (Ruby 2.0)

Figure 7-12 is very different from Figure 7-11! Notice the scale of the graph. The y-axis shows milliseconds, and the x-axis shows the number of elements in the hash on a logarithmic scale. But this time, notice that we have thousands of milliseconds—which means actual seconds—on the y-axis!

With one or a few elements, we can retrieve the 10,000 values very quickly—so quickly that the time is too small to appear on this graph. In fact, it takes about the same 1.5 ms. However, when the number of elements increases past 100 and especially 1,000, the time required to load the 10,000 values increases linearly with the hash size. For a hash containing about 10,000 elements, it takes over 1.6 full seconds to load the 10,000 values. If we continued the test with larger hashes, it would take minutes or even hours to load the values.

What's happening here is that all of the hash elements are saved into the same bin, forcing Ruby to search through the list one key at a time.

Hash Optimization in Ruby 2.x

Starting with version 2.0, Ruby introduced a new optimization to make hashes work even faster. For hashes that contain 6 or fewer elements, Ruby now avoids calculating the hash value entirely and simply saves the hash data in an array. These are known as *packed hashes*. Figure 7-13 shows a packed hash.

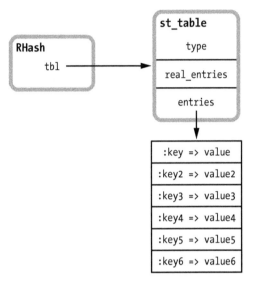

Figure 7-13: Internally, Ruby 2.x saves small hashes with 6 or fewer elements as arrays.

Ruby 2.x doesn't use the st_table_entry structure for small hashes, nor does it create a table of bins. Instead, it creates an array and saves the key/value pairs directly into this array. The array is large enough to fit 6 key/value pairs; once you insert a 7th key and value, Ruby discards the array, creates the bin array, and moves all 7 elements into st_table_entry structures as usual by calculating hash values. This explains the small spike we saw inserting the 7th element in Figure 7-8 (page 179). real_entries saves the number of values saved in the array between 0 and 6.

In a packed hash, there are only 6 or fewer elements; thus, it's faster for Ruby to iterate over the key values looking for a target value than it would be to calculate a hash value and use a bin array. Figure 7-14 shows how Ruby 2.x retrieves an element from a packed hash.

To find the value for a given key of target, Ruby iterates through the array and calls the eql? method on each key value if the values are objects. For simple values, such as integers or symbols, Ruby just uses a numerical comparison. Ruby 2.x never calls the hash function at all for packed hashes.

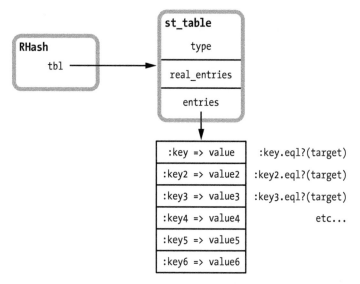

Figure 7-14: For small hashes, Ruby 2.x iterates over the array to find a given key.

Summary

Understanding hash tables is key to understanding how Ruby works internally because the speed and flexibility of hash tables allow Ruby to use them in many ways.

At the beginning of this chapter, we learned how hash tables are able to return values quickly, regardless of how many elements are in the table. Next, we learned how Ruby automatically increases the size of a hash table as you add more and more elements to it. The user of the hash table doesn't need to worry about how fast or large the table is. Hash tables will always be fast and will automatically expand as necessary.

Finally, we looked at the importance of Ruby's hash function. The hash table's algorithm depends on the underlying hash function. With an effective hash function, values are evenly distributed across the bins in the hash table with few collisions, allowing them to be saved and retrieved quickly. However, with a poor hash function, values would be saved in the same bin, leading to poor performance.

*Blocks are Ruby's
implementation of
closures.*

8

HOW RUBY BORROWED A DECADES-OLD IDEA FROM LISP

Blocks are one of the most commonly used and powerful features of Ruby because they allow you to pass a code snippet to Enumerable methods, such as each, detect, or inject. Using the yield keyword, you can also write your own custom iterators or functions that call blocks for other reasons. Ruby code containing blocks is often more succinct, elegant, and expressive than equivalent code in older languages, such as C.

But don't jump to the conclusion that blocks are a new idea! In fact, blocks are not new to Ruby at all. The computer science concept behind blocks, called *closures*, was first invented by Peter J. Landin in 1964, a few years after the original version of Lisp was created by John McCarthy in 1958. Closures were later adopted by Lisp, or—more precisely—a dialect of Lisp called *Scheme*, which was invented by Gerald Sussman and Guy Steele in 1975. Sussman and Steele's use of closures in Scheme brought the idea to many programmers for the first time.

But what does the word *closure* actually mean in this context? In other words, exactly what are Ruby blocks? Are they just the snippet of Ruby code that appears between the do and end keywords? In this chapter I'll review how Ruby implements blocks internally and demonstrate how they meet the definition of *closure* used by Sussman and Steele back in 1975. I'll also show how blocks, lambdas, and procs are all different ways of looking at closures.

Blocks: Closures in Ruby

Internally, Ruby represents each block using a C structure called rb_block_t, shown in Figure 8-1. By learning what Ruby stores in rb_block_t, we can find out exactly what a block is.

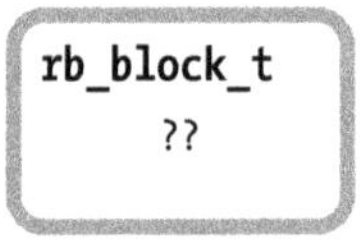

```
rb_block_t
    ??
```

Figure 8-1: What's inside the rb_block_t C structure?

As we did in Chapter 5 with the RClass structure, let's deduce the contents of the rb_block_t structure based on what we know blocks can do in Ruby. We'll begin with the most obvious attribute of blocks. We know that each block must consist of a piece of Ruby code, or internally a set of compiled YARV bytecode instructions. For example, suppose we call a method and pass a block as a parameter, as shown in Listing 8-1.

```
10.times do
  str = "The quick brown fox jumps over the lazy dog."
  puts str
end
```

Listing 8-1: Superficially, a block is just a snippet of Ruby code.

When executing the 10.times call, Ruby needs to know what code to iterate over. Therefore, the rb_block_t structure must contain a pointer to that code, as shown in Figure 8-2.

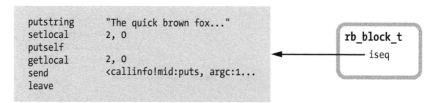

Figure 8-2: The rb_block_t structure contains a pointer to a snippet of YARV instructions.

The value iseq is a pointer to the YARV instructions for the Ruby code in the block.

Another obvious but often overlooked behavior of blocks is that they can access variables in the surrounding or parent Ruby scope, as shown in Listing 8-2.

```
❶ str = "The quick brown fox"
❷ 10.times do
❸   str2 = "jumps over the lazy dog."
❹   puts "#{str} #{str2}"
  end
```

Listing 8-2: The code inside the block accesses the variable str from the surrounding code.

Here the puts function call at ❹ refers equally to the str2 variable inside the block and the str variable defined in the surrounding code at ❶. Obviously blocks can access values from the code surrounding them. This ability is one of the things that makes blocks useful.

Blocks have in some sense a dual personality. On the one hand, they behave like separate methods: You can call them and pass them arguments just as you would any method. On the other hand, they're part of the surrounding function or method.

Stepping Through How Ruby Calls a Block

How does this work internally? Does Ruby implement blocks as separate methods or as part of the surrounding method? Let's step through Listing 8-2 to see what happens inside Ruby when you call a block.

When Ruby executes the first line of code from Listing 8-2 at ❶, str = "The quick brown fox", YARV stores the local variable str on its internal stack. YARV tracks the location of str using the EP, or environment pointer, located in the current rb_control_frame_t structure, as shown in Figure 8-3.[1]

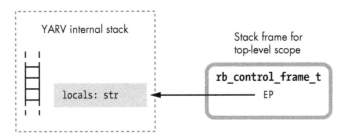

Figure 8-3: Ruby saves the local variable str on the stack.

Next, Ruby reaches the 10.times do call at ❷ in Listing 8-2. Before executing the actual iteration—that is, before calling the times method—Ruby creates and initializes a new rb_block_t structure to represent the block. Ruby needs to create the block structure now because the block is really just another argument to the times method. Figure 8-4 shows this new rb_block_t structure.

When creating the new block structure, Ruby copies the current value of the EP into the new block. In other words, Ruby saves the location of the current stack frame in the new block.

---

1. If the outer code was located inside a function or method, then the EP would point to the stack frame as shown. But if the outer code was located in the top-level scope of your Ruby program, then Ruby would use dynamic access to save the variable in the TOPLEVEL_BINDING environment instead. Regardless, the EP will always indicate the location of the str variable.

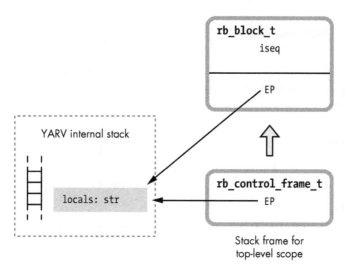

Figure 8-4: Ruby creates a new *rb_block_t* structure before calling
the method and passing the block to it.

Next, Ruby calls the times method on the object 10, an instance of the
Fixnum class. While doing this, YARV creates a new frame on its internal
stack. Now we have two stack frames: above, a new stack frame for the
Fixnum.times method, and below, the original stack frame used by the top-
level function (see Figure 8-5).

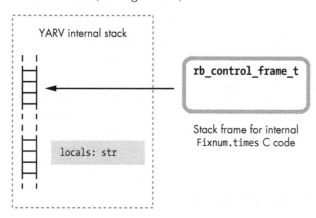

Figure 8-5: Ruby creates a new stack frame when it executes
the 10.times call.

Ruby implements the times method internally using its own C code.
Although this is a built-in method, Ruby implements it just as you probably
would. Ruby starts to iterate over the numbers 0, 1, 2, and so on, up to 9,
and then it calls yield, calling the block once for each of these integers.
Finally, the code that implements yield internally calls the block each time
it moves through the loop, pushing a third frame onto the top of the stack
for the code inside the block to use. Figure 8-6 shows this third stack frame.

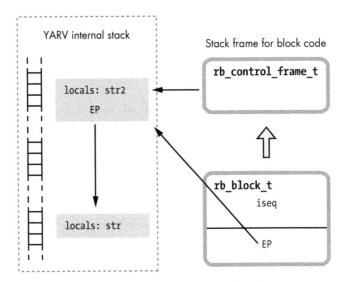

Figure 8-6: Ruby creates a third stack frame when the `10.times`
method yields to the block.

On the left side of the figure, we now have three stack frames:

- On the top is the new stack frame for the block, containing the str2
  variable defined at ❸ in Listing 8-2.
- In the middle is the stack frame used by the internal C code that implements the Fixnum#times method.
- And at the bottom is the original function's stack frame, containing the
  str variable defined at ❶ in Listing 8-2.

While creating the new stack frame, Ruby's internal yield code copies the
EP from the block into the new stack frame. Now the code inside the block
can access both its local variables, directly via the rb_control_frame_t structure,
and the variables from the parent scope, indirectly via the EP pointer using
dynamic variable access. Specifically, this allows the puts statement at ❹ in
Listing 8-2 to access the str2 variable from the parent scope.

Borrowing an Idea from 1975

So far we've seen that Ruby's rb_block_t structure contains two important
values:

- A pointer to a snippet of YARV code instructions—the iseq pointer
- A pointer to a location on YARV's internal stack, the location that was
  at the top of the stack when the block was created—the EP pointer

Figure 8-7 shows these two values in the rb_block_t structure.

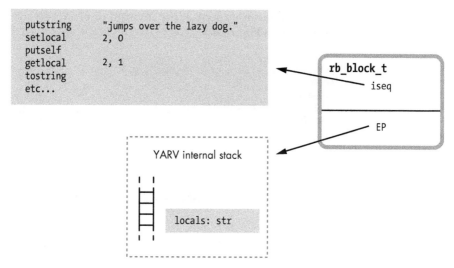

```
putstring     "jumps over the lazy dog."
setlocal      2, 0
putself
getlocal      2, 1
tostring
etc...
```

rb_block_t

iseq

EP

YARV internal stack

locals: str

Figure 8-7: So far we've seen that Ruby blocks contain a pointer to a YARV instruction snippet and a location on the YARV stack.

We also saw that Ruby uses the EP when a block accesses values from the surrounding code. At first, this seems like a very technical, unimportant detail. This is obviously a behavior we expect Ruby blocks to exhibit, and the EP seems to be a minor, uninteresting part of Ruby's internal implementation of blocks. Or is it?

The EP is actually a profoundly important part of Ruby internals. It's the basis for Ruby's implementation of *closures*, the computer science concept introduced in Lisp long before Ruby was created in the 1990s. Here's how Sussman and Steele defined the term *closure* in 1975:

The IBM 704, above, was the first computer to run Lisp, in the early 1960s. (Credit: NASA)

> In order to solve this problem we introduce the notion of a closure [11, 14] which is a data structure containing a lambda expression, and an environment to be used when that lambda expression is applied to arguments.[2]

They define a closure to be the combination of the following:

- A "lambda expression"—that is, a function that takes a set of arguments
- An environment to be used when calling that lambda or function

---

2. Gerald J. Sussman and Guy L. Steele, Jr., "Scheme: An Interpreter for Extended Lambda Calculus" (MIT Artificial Intelligence Laboratory, AI Memo No. 349, December 1975).

Let's take another look at the internal rb_block_t structure, repeated for convenience in Figure 8-8.

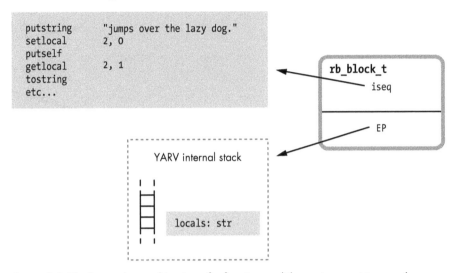

Figure 8-8: Blocks are the combination of a function and the environment to use when calling that function.

This structure meets Sussman and Steele's definition of a closure:

- iseq is a pointer to a lambda expression—a function or code snippet.
- EP is a pointer to the environment to be used when calling that lambda or function—that is, a pointer to the surrounding stack frame.

Following this train of thought, we can see that blocks are Ruby's implementation of closures. Ironically, blocks—one of the features that makes Ruby so elegant and modern—are based on research and work done at least 20 years before the birth of Ruby!

THE RB_BLOCK_T AND RB_CONTROL_FRAME_T STRUCTURES

In Ruby 1.9 and later, you'll find the definition of the rb_block_t structure in the *vm_core.h* file, as shown in Listing 8-3.

```
typedef struct rb_block_struct {
❶    VALUE self;
❷    VALUE klass;
❸    VALUE *ep;
❹    rb_iseq_t *iseq;
❺    VALUE proc;
} rb_block_t;
```

Listing 8-3: The definition of rb_block_t from vm_core.h

You can see the `iseq` ❹ and `ep` ❸ values described above, along with a few other values:

- `self` ❶: The value the `self` pointer had when the block was first referred to is also an important part of the closure's environment. Ruby executes block code inside the same object context that the code had outside the block.

- `klass` ❷: Along with `self`, Ruby also keeps track of the class of the current object using this pointer.

- `proc` ❺: Ruby uses this value when it creates a proc object from a block. As we'll see in the next section, procs and blocks are closely related.

Right above the definition of `rb_block_t` in *vm_core.h*, we see the definition of the `rb_control_frame_t` structure, as shown in Listing 8-4.

```
   typedef struct rb_control_frame_struct {
       VALUE *pc;                    /* cfp[0] */
       VALUE *sp;                    /* cfp[1] */
       rb_iseq_t *iseq;              /* cfp[2] */
       VALUE flag;                   /* cfp[3] */
❶     VALUE self;                   /* cfp[4] / block[0] */
       VALUE klass;                  /* cfp[5] / block[1] */
       VALUE *ep;                    /* cfp[6] / block[2] */
       rb_iseq_t *block_iseq;        /* cfp[7] / block[3] */
❷     VALUE proc;                   /* cfp[8] / block[4] */
       const rb_method_entry_t *me;/* cfp[9] */

   #if VM_DEBUG_BP_CHECK
       VALUE *bp_check;              /* cfp[10] */
   #endif
   } rb_control_frame_t;
```

Listing 8-4: The definition of `rb_control_frame_t` from vm_core.h

Notice that this C structure also contains the same values as the `rb_block_t` structure: everything from `self` at ❶ to `proc` at ❷. The fact that these two structures share the same values is one of the interesting, but confusing, optimizations Ruby uses internally to speed things up. Whenever you first refer to a block by passing it into a method call, Ruby needs to create a new `rb_block_t` structure and copy values such as the EP from the current `rb_control_frame_t` structure into it. However, because these two structures contain the same values in the same order (`rb_block_t` is a subset of `rb_control_frame_t`), Ruby can avoid creating a new `rb_block_t` structure and instead set the new block pointer to the common portion of the `rb_control_frame_t` structure. In other words, instead of allocating new memory to hold the new `rb_block_t` structure, Ruby simply passes a pointer to the middle of the `rb_control_frame_t` structure. By doing so, Ruby avoids unnecessary calls to `malloc` and speeds up the process of creating blocks.

Experiment 8-1: Which Is Faster: A while Loop or Passing a Block to each?

Ruby code containing blocks is often more elegant and succinct than the equivalent code in older languages, such as C. For example, in C we would write the simple while loop shown in Listing 8-5 to add up the numbers 1 through 10.

```
#include <stdio.h>
main()
{
  int i, sum;
  i = 1;
  sum = 0;
  while (i <= 10) {
    sum = sum + i;
    i++;
  }
  printf("Sum: %d\n", sum);
}
```

Listing 8-5: Adding up 1 through 10 in C using a while loop

Listing 8-6 shows the same while loop in Ruby.

```
sum = 0
i = 1
while i <= 10
  sum += i
  i += 1
end
puts "Sum: #{sum}"
```

Listing 8-6: Adding up 1 through 10 in Ruby using a while loop

However, most Rubyists would write this code using a range object with a block, as shown in Listing 8-7.

```
sum = 0
(1..10).each do |i|
  sum += i
end
puts "Sum: #{sum}"
```

Listing 8-7: Adding up 1 through 10 in Ruby using a range object and a block

Aesthetics aside, is there any performance penalty for using a block here? Does Ruby slow down significantly in order to create the new rb_block_t structure, copy the EP value, and create new stack frames?

Well, I won't benchmark the C code because clearly it will be faster than either option using Ruby. Instead, let's measure how long it takes Ruby, using a simple while loop, to add up the integers 1 through 10 to obtain 55, as shown in Listing 8-8.

```ruby
require 'benchmark'
ITERATIONS = 1000000
Benchmark.bm do |bench|
  bench.report("iterating from 1 to 10, one million times") do
    ITERATIONS.times do
      sum = 0
      i = 1
      while i <= 10
        sum += i
        i += 1
      end
    end
  end
end
```

Listing 8-8: Benchmarking the while loop (while.rb)

Here, I'm using the benchmark library to measure the time required to run the while loop one million times. Admittedly, I'm using a block to control the million iterations (ITERATIONS.times do), but I'll use the same block in the next test as well. Using Ruby 2.0 on my laptop, I can run through this code in just under a half second:

```
$ ruby while.rb
      user     system      total        real
iterating from 1 to 10, one million times  0.440000   0.000000
                                           0.440000 (  0.445757)
```

Now let's measure the time required to run the code shown in Listing 8-9, which uses each with a block.

```ruby
require 'benchmark'
ITERATIONS = 1000000
Benchmark.bm do |bench|
  bench.report("iterating from 1 to 10, one million times") do
    ITERATIONS.times do
      sum = 0
      (1..10).each do |i|
        sum += i
      end
    end
  end
end
```

Listing 8-9: Benchmarking a call to a block (each.rb)

This time it takes somewhat longer to run through the loop a million times, about 0.75 seconds:

```
$ ruby each.rb
      user     system       total         real
      iterating from 1 to 10, one million times  0.760000   0.000000
                                                 0.760000 (  0.765740)
```

Ruby requires about 71 percent more time to call the block 10 times, compared to iterating through the simple while loop 10 times (see Figure 8-9).

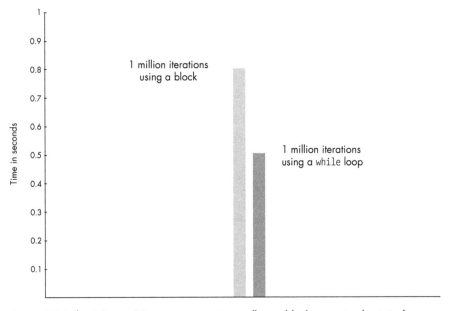

Figure 8-9: Ruby 2.0 uses 71 percent more time calling a block vs. a simple while loop. The graph shows the time for one million iterations (in seconds).

Using each is slower because internally the Range#each method has to call or yield to the block each time around the loop. This involves a fairly large amount of work. In order to yield to a block, Ruby first has to create a new rb_block_t structure for that block, setting the EP in the new block to the referencing environment and passing the block into the call to each. Then each time around the loop Ruby has to create a new stack frame on YARV's internal stack, call the block's code, and finally copy the EP from the block to the new stack frame. Running a simple while loop is faster because Ruby needs only to reset the PC, or program counter, each time around the loop. It never calls a method or creates a new stack frame or a new rb_block_t structure.

Seventy-one percent more time seems like a large performance penalty, and, depending on your work and the context of this while loop, it may or may not be important. If this loop were part of a time-sensitive, critical operation that your end users were waiting for, and if there weren't other expensive operations inside the loop, it might be worth writing the iteration using an old-fashioned C-style while loop. However, the performance of most Ruby applications, and certainly Ruby on Rails websites, is usually limited by database queries, network connections, and other factors, not by Ruby execution speed. It's rare that Ruby's execution speed has an immediate, direct impact on your application's overall performance. (Of course, if you're using a large framework, such as Ruby on Rails, then your Ruby code is a very small piece of a very large system. I imagine that Rails uses blocks and iterators many, many times while processing a simple HTTP request, apart from the Ruby code you write yourself.)

Lambdas and Procs: Treating a Function as a First-Class Citizen

Now to look at a more convoluted way of printing the "quick brown fox" string to the console. Listing 8-10 shows an example of using `lambda`.

```
❶ def message_function
❷   str = "The quick brown fox"
❸   lambda do |animal|
❹     puts "#{str} jumps over the lazy #{animal}."
    end
  end
❺ function_value = message_function
❻ function_value.call('dog')
```

Listing 8-10: Using lambda in Ruby

Let's step through this code carefully. First, at ❶ we define a method called `message_function`. Inside `message_function`, we create a local variable at ❷ called `str`. Next, at ❸ we call `lambda`, and pass it a block. Inside this block, at ❹, we print the "quick brown fox" string again. However, `message_function` won't immediately display the string because it doesn't actually call the block at ❸. Instead, `lambda` returns the block we give it as a data value, which in turn is returned by `message_function`.

This is an example of "treating a function as a first-class citizen," to paraphrase a commonly used computer science expression. Once the block is returned from `message_function`, we save it in the local variable `function_value` at ❺ and then call it explicitly, using the `call` method at ❻. With the `lambda` keyword—or the equivalent `proc` keyword—Ruby allows you to convert a block into a data value in this way.

I have lots of questions about Listing 8-10. What happens when we call `lambda`? How does Ruby convert the block into a data value, and what does it mean to treat this block as a first-class citizen? Does `message_function` return an `rb_block_t` structure directly, or does it return an `rb_lambda_t` structure? And what information would `rb_lambda_t` contain (see Figure 8-10)?

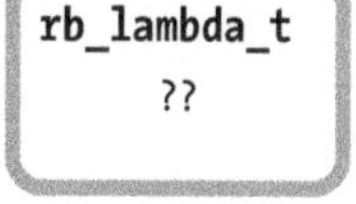

```
rb_lambda_t
    ??
```

Figure 8-10: Does Ruby use an rb_lambda_t C structure? And if so, what would it contain?

Stack vs. Heap Memory

Before we can answer these questions, we need to take a closer look at how Ruby saves your data. Internally, Ruby saves your data in two places: on the *stack* or in the *heap*.

We've seen the *stack* before. This is where Ruby saves local variables, return values, and arguments for each of the methods in your program. Values on the stack are valid only for as long as that method is running. When a method returns, YARV deletes its stack frame and all the values inside it.

Ruby uses the *heap* to save information that you might need for a while, even after a particular method returns. Each value in the heap remains valid for as long as there is a reference to it. Once a value is no longer referred to by any variable or object in your program, Ruby's garbage collection system deletes it, freeing its memory for other uses.

This scheme is not unique to Ruby. In fact, it's used by many other programming languages, including Lisp and C. And remember, Ruby itself is a C program. YARV's stack design is based on the way C programs use the stack, and Ruby's heap uses the underlying C heap implementation.

The stack and heap differ in one other important aspect. Ruby saves only references to data on the stack—that is, the VALUE pointers. For simple integer values, symbols, and constants such as nil, true, or false, the reference is the actual value. However, for all other data types, the VALUE is a pointer to a C structure containing the actual data, such as RObject. If only the VALUE references go on the stack, where does Ruby save the structures? In the heap. Let's look at an example to understand this better.

A Closer Look at How Ruby Saves a String Value

Let's look in detail at how Ruby handles the string value str from Listing 8-10. First, imagine YARV has a stack frame for the outer scope but has yet to call message_function. Figure 8-11 shows this initial stack frame.

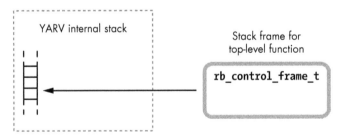

Figure 8-11: To execute the code in Listing 8-11, Ruby starts with an initial stack frame.

In this figure you can see YARV's internal stack on the left and the rb_control_frame_t structure on the right. Now suppose Ruby executes the message_function function call shown at ❺ in Listing 8-10. Figure 8-12 shows what happens next.

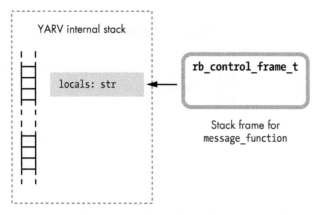

Figure 8-12: Ruby creates a second stack frame when calling
message_function.

Ruby saves the str local variable in the new stack frame used by
message_function. Let's take a closer look at that str variable and how
Ruby stores the "quick brown fox" string into it. Ruby stores each of your
objects in a C structure called RObject, each of your arrays in a structure
called RArray, each of your strings in a structure called RString, and so on.
Figure 8-13 shows the "quick brown fox" string saved with RString.

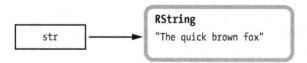

Figure 8-13: Ruby uses the RString C structure to save
string values.

The actual string structure is shown on the right side of the figure, and
a reference, or pointer, to the string is shown on the left. When Ruby saves a
string value (or any object) onto the YARV stack, it actually places only the
reference to the string on the stack. The actual string structure is saved in
the heap instead, as shown in Figure 8-14 on the next page.

Once there are no longer any pointers referencing a particular object
or value in the heap, Ruby frees that object or value during the next run of
the garbage collection system. To demonstrate, suppose that my example
code didn't call lambda at all but rather immediately returned nil after saving the str variable, as shown in Listing 8-11.

```
def message_function
  str = "The quick brown fox"
  nil
end
```

Listing 8-11: This code doesn't call lambda.

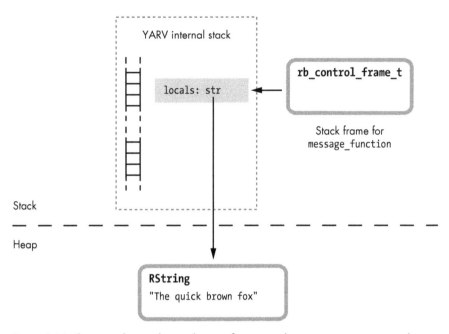

Figure 8-14: The str value on the stack is a reference to the RString structure saved in the heap.

Once this call to message_function finishes, YARV simply pops the str value off the stack (as well as any other temporary values saved there) and returns to the original stack frame, as shown in Figure 8-15.

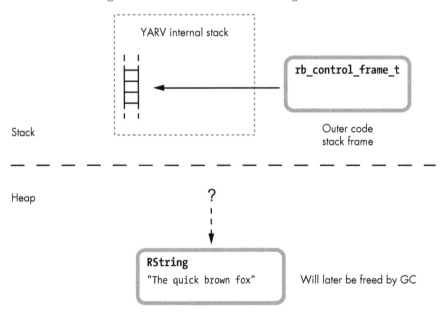

Figure 8-15: Now there is no longer a reference to the RString structure.

As you can see in the figure, there is no longer a reference to the RString structure containing the "quick brown fox" string. Ruby's garbage collection system is designed to identify values in the heap that don't have any references to them, like the "quick brown fox" string here. After it identifies them, the GC system will free those orphaned values, returning that memory to the heap.

How Ruby Creates a Lambda

Now that we understand a bit more about the heap and how Ruby uses it, we're ready to learn more about lambdas. Earlier when I used the phrase "treating a function as a first-class citizen," I meant that Ruby allows you to treat functions or code as a data value, saving them into variables, passing them as arguments, and so on. Ruby implements this idea using blocks.

The lambda (or proc) keyword converts a block into a data value. But remember, blocks are Ruby's implementation of closures. This means the new data value must somehow contain both the block's code and referencing environment.

To see what I mean, let's return to Listing 8-10, repeated here in Listing 8-12 with an eye toward its use of lambda.

```
    def message_function
❶     str = "The quick brown fox"
❷     lambda do |animal|
❸       puts "#{str} jumps over the lazy #{animal}."
      end
    end
    function_value = message_function
❹   function_value.call('dog')
```

Listing 8-12: Using lambda in Ruby (repeated from Listing 8-10)

Notice at ❹ that when we call the lambda (the block), the puts statement inside the block at ❸ can access the str string variable defined at ❶ inside message_function. How can this be? We've just seen how the str reference to the RString structure is popped off the stack when message_function returns! Obviously, after calling lambda, the value of str lives on so that the block can access it later.

When you call lambda, Ruby copies the entire contents of the current YARV stack frame into the heap, where the RString structure is located. For example, Figure 8-16 shows how the YARV stack looks just after the message_function starts at ❶ in Listing 8-12. (To keep things simple, I'm not showing the RString structure, but remember that the RString structure will also be saved in the heap.)

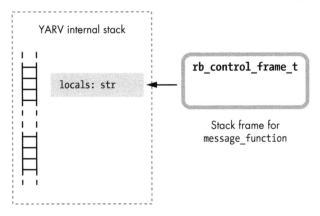

Figure 8-16: Ruby creates a second stack frame when calling
message_function.

Next, Listing 8-12 calls lambda at ❷. Figure 8-17 shows what happens in
Ruby when you call lambda.

The horizontal stack icon below the dotted line shows that Ruby creates
a new copy of the stack frame for message_function in the heap. Now there
is a second reference to the str RString structure, which means that Ruby
won't free it when message_function returns.

In fact, along with the copy of the stack frame, Ruby creates two other
new objects in the heap:

- An internal environment object, represented by the rb_env_t C structure
  at the lower left of the figure. It's essentially a wrapper for the heap copy
  of the stack. As we'll see in Chapter 9, you can access this environment
  object indirectly in your programs using the Binding class.

- A Ruby proc object, represented by the rb_proc_t structure. This
  is the actual return value from the lambda keyword; it's what the
  message_function function returns.

Note that the new proc object, the rb_proc_t structure, contains an
rb_block_t structure, including the iseq and EP pointers. Think of a proc as
a kind of Ruby object that wraps up a block. As with a normal block, these
keep track of the block's code and the referencing environment for its
closure. Ruby sets the EP in this block to point to the new heap copy of the
stack frame.

Also, notice that the proc object contains an internal value called
is_lambda. This is set to true for this example because we used the lambda
keyword to create the proc. If I had instead created the proc using the
proc keyword, or simply by calling Proc.new, then is_lambda would have been
set to false. Ruby uses this flag to produce the slight behavior differences
between procs and lambdas, though it's best to think of procs and lambdas
as essentially the same.

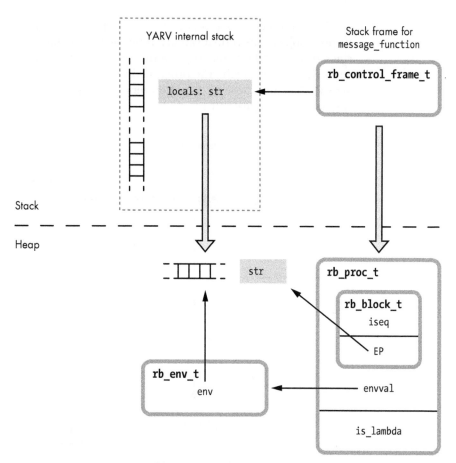

Figure 8-17: When you call `lambda`, Ruby copies the current stack frame to the heap.

How Ruby Calls a Lambda

Let's go back to our lambda example in Listing 8-13.

```
def message_function
  str = "The quick brown fox"
  lambda do |animal|
    puts "#{str} jumps over the lazy #{animal}."
  end
end
❶ function_value = message_function
❷ function_value.call('dog')
```

Listing 8-13: Using `lambda` in Ruby (repeated again from Listing 8-10)

What happens when `message_function` returns at ❶? Because the lambda or proc object is its return value, a reference to the lambda is saved in the stack frame for the outer scope in the `function_value` local variable. This prevents Ruby from freeing the proc, the internal environment object, and the `str` variable, and there are now pointers referring to all of these values in the heap (see Figure 8-18).

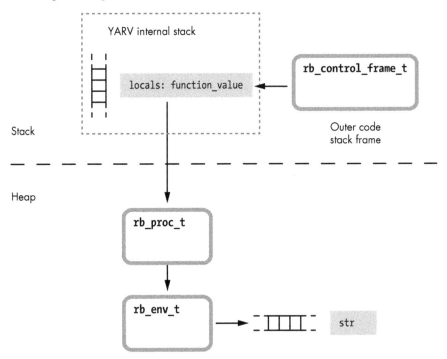

Figure 8-18: Once `message_function` returns, the surrounding code holds a reference to the proc object.

When Ruby executes the `call` method on the proc object at ❷, it executes its block as well. Figure 8-19 shows what happens in Ruby when you use the `call` method on a lambda or proc.

As with any block, when Ruby calls the block inside a proc object it creates a new stack frame and sets the EP to the block's referencing environment. However, that environment is a copy of a stack frame previously copied into the heap; the new stack frame contains an EP that points to the heap. This EP allows the block's call to `puts` to access the `str` value defined in `message_function`. Figure 8-19 shows the argument to the proc, `animal`, saved in the new stack frame, like any other method or block argument.

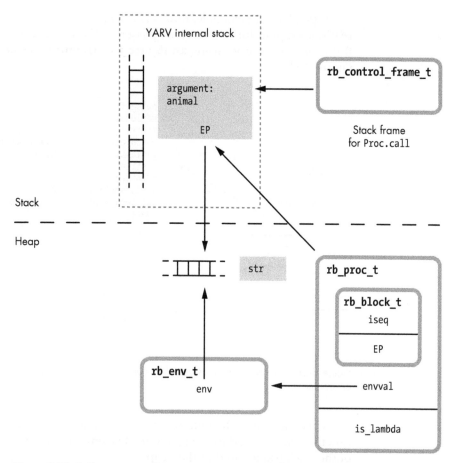

Figure 8-19: Calling a proc object creates a new stack frame as usual and sets the EP to point to the heap's referencing environment.

The Proc Object

We've seen that Ruby really has no structure called `rb_lambda_t`. In other words, the structure shown in Figure 8-20 doesn't actually exist.

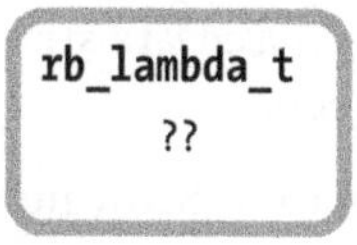

Figure 8-20: Ruby doesn't actually use a structure called `rb_lambda_t`.

Instead, in this example, Ruby's `lambda` keyword created a proc object—really, a wrapper for the block we passed to the `lambda` or `proc` keyword. Ruby represents procs using an `rb_proc_t` C structure, as you can see in Figure 8-21.

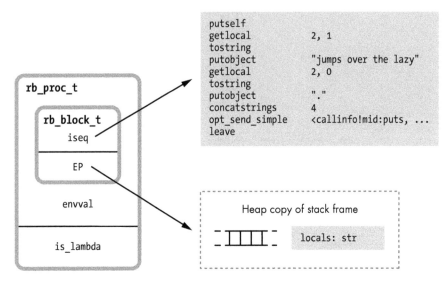

Figure 8-21: Ruby procs are closures; they contain pointers to a function and a referencing environment.

This is a closure: It contains a function along with the environment that function was referred to or created in. The environment is a persistent copy of the stack frame saved in the heap.

A proc is a Ruby object. It contains the same information as other objects, including the `RBasic` structure. To save its object-related information, Ruby uses a structure called `RTypedData`, along with `rb_proc_t`, to represent instances of the proc object. Figure 8-22 shows how these structures work together.

You might think of `RTypedData` as a kind of trick that Ruby's C code uses to create a Ruby object wrapper around a C data structure. In this case, Ruby uses `RTypedData` to create an instance of the `Proc` Ruby class that represents a single copy of the `rb_proc_t` structure. The `RTypedData` structure contains the same `RBasic` information as all Ruby objects:

flags Certain internal technical information Ruby needs to track

klass A pointer to the Ruby class that the object is an instance of; the `Proc` class in this example

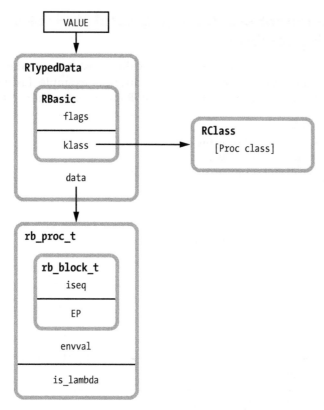

Figure 8-22: Ruby saves the object-related information about proc objects in the RTypedData structure.

Figure 8-23 takes another look at how Ruby represents a proc object. The proc object is on the right next to an RString structure.

Notice that Ruby handles the string value and the proc similarly. As with strings, procs can be saved into variables or passed as arguments to a function call. Ruby uses the VALUE pointer to the proc whenever you refer to one or save one into a variable.

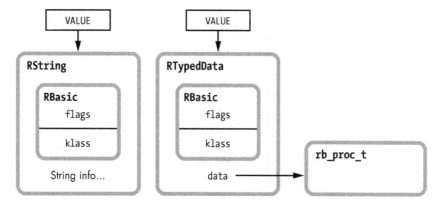

Figure 8-23: Comparing a Ruby string with a proc

Experiment 8-2: Changing Local Variables After Calling lambda

Listings 8-10 through 8-13 show how calling lambda copies the current stack frame in the heap. Now for a slightly different example. Listing 8-14 is basically the same, except that the line at ❷ changes str after calling lambda.

```ruby
def message_function
  str = "The quick brown fox"
❶  func = lambda do |animal|
    puts "#{str} jumps over the lazy #{animal}."
  end
❷  str = "The sly brown fox"
  func
end
function_value = message_function
❸ function_value.call('dog')
```

Listing 8-14: Which version of str will lambda copy to the heap (modify_after_lambda.rb)?

Because we call lambda at ❶ before changing str to The sly brown fox at ❷, Ruby should have copied the stack frame to the heap, including the original value of str. That means that when we call the lambda at ❸, we should see the original "quick brown fox" string. However, running the code, we get the following:

```
$ ruby modify_after_lambda.rb
The sly brown fox jumps over the lazy dog.
```

What happened? Ruby somehow copied the new value of str, The sly brown fox, to the heap so we could access it when we called the lambda at ❸.

To find out how Ruby did this, let's look more closely at what happens when you call lambda. Figure 8-24 shows how Ruby copies the stack frame to the heap, including the value str from Listing 8-14.

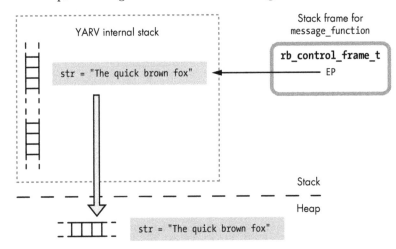

Figure 8-24: When you call lambda, Ruby copies the stack frame to the heap.

Once this copy is made, the code at ❷ in Listing 8-14 changes str to the "sly fox" string:

```
str = "The sly brown fox"
```

Because Ruby copied the stack frame when we called lambda, we should be modifying the original copy of str, not the new lambda copy (see Figure 8-25).

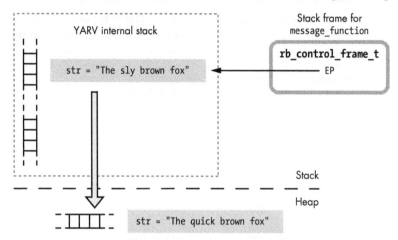

Figure 8-25: Does Ruby continue to use the original stack frame after making a heap copy?

The new heap copy of the string should have remained unmodified, and calling the lambda later should have given the original "quick fox" string, not the modified "sly fox" one. How does Ruby allow us to modify the new persistent copy of the stack once it's been created by lambda?

As it turns out, once Ruby creates the new heap copy of the stack (the new rb_env_t structure or internal environment object), it resets the EP in the rb_control_frame_t structure to point to the copy. Figure 8-26 shows how Ruby resets the EP after creating a persistent heap copy of a stack frame.

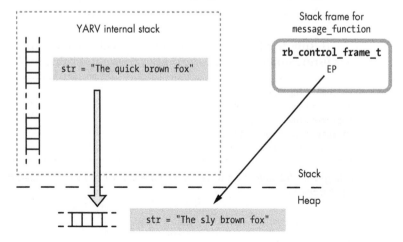

Figure 8-26: Ruby resets the EP after creating a persistent heap copy of a stack frame.

The difference here is that the EP now points down to the heap. Now when we call str = "The sly brown fox" at ❷ in Listing 8-14, Ruby will use the new EP and access the value in the heap, not the original value on the stack. Notice The sly brown fox appears in the heap at the bottom of Figure 8-26.

Calling lambda More Than Once in the Same Scope

Another interesting behavior of the lambda keyword is that Ruby avoids making copies of the stack frame more than once, as you can see in Listing 8-15.

```
i = 0
increment_function = lambda do
  puts "Incrementing from #{i} to #{i+1}"
  i += 1
end
decrement_function = lambda do
  i -= 1
  puts "Decrementing from #{i+1} to #{i}"
end
```

Listing 8-15: Calling lambda *twice in the same scope*

This code expects both lambda functions to operate on the local variable i in the main scope.

But if Ruby made a separate copy of the stack frame for each call to lambda, each function would operate on a separate copy of i. Look at the following example in Listing 8-16.

```
increment_function.call
decrement_function.call
increment_function.call
increment_function.call
decrement_function.call
```

Listing 8-16: Calling the lambdas created in Listing 8-15

If Ruby used a separate copy of i for each lambda function, the previous listing would generate the output shown in Listing 8-17.

```
Incrementing from 0 to 1
Decrementing from 0 to -1
Incrementing from 1 to 2
Incrementing from 2 to 3
Decrementing from -1 to -2
```

Listing 8-17: The output we would expect if each call to lambda *created its own copy of the stack frame*

But we actually see the output shown in Listing 8-18.

```
Incrementing from 0 to 1
Decrementing from 1 to 0
Incrementing from 0 to 1
Incrementing from 1 to 2
Decrementing from 2 to 1
```

Listing 8-18: Because the lambda functions share the same heap copy of the stack, running Listing 8-16 generates this output.

Usually this is what you expect: Each block you pass to the lambdas accesses the same variable in the parent scope. Ruby achieves this by checking whether the EP already points to the heap. If so, as with the second call to lambda in Listing 8-15, Ruby won't create a second copy; it will simply reuse the same rb_env_t structure in the second rb_proc_t structure. Ultimately, both lambdas use the same heap copy of the stack.

Summary

In Chapter 3 we saw how YARV creates a new stack frame whenever you call a block, just as it does when you call a method. At first glance, Ruby blocks appear to be a special kind of method that you can call and pass arguments to. However, as we've seen in this chapter, there's more to blocks than meets the eye.

Looking closely at the rb_block_t structure, we saw how blocks implement the computer science concept of *closure* in Ruby. Blocks are the combination of a function and an environment to use when calling that function. We learned that blocks have a curious dual personality in Ruby: They are similar to methods, but they also become part of the method that you call them from. The simplicity with which Ruby's syntax allows for this dual role is one of the language's most beautiful and elegant features.

Later we saw how Ruby allows you to treat functions or code as first-class citizens using the lambda keyword, which converts a block into a data value that you can pass, save, and reuse. After reviewing the differences between stack and heap memory, we explored the way that Ruby implements lambdas and procs, and we saw that Ruby copies the stack frame to the heap when you call lambda or proc and reuses it when you call the lambda's block. Finally, we saw how the proc object represents code as a data object in Ruby.

Metaprogramming becomes much easier to understand once you learn how Ruby implements it internally.

9

METAPROGRAMMING

One of the most confusing and daunting subjects Ruby developers face is *metaprogramming*. Metaprogramming, as indicated by the prefix *meta*, literally means to program at a different or higher level of abstraction. Ruby provides many different ways for you to do this, allowing your program to inspect and change itself dynamically. In Ruby, your program can change itself!

Some of Ruby's metaprogramming features allow your program to query for information about itself—for example, information about methods, instance variables, and superclasses. Other metaprogramming features allow you to perform normal tasks, such as defining a method or a constant, in an alternative and more flexible manner. Finally, methods such as eval allow your program to write new Ruby code from scratch, calling the parser and compiler at run time.

In this chapter, we'll focus on two important aspects of metaprogramming. First, we'll look at how you can alter the standard method definition process, the most common and practical use for metaprogramming. We'll learn what Ruby normally does to assign a method to a class and how this is related to lexical scope. Then, we'll look at alternative ways to define methods using metaclasses and singleton classes. We'll also learn how Ruby implements the new, experimental refinements feature, allowing you to define methods and activate them later if you wish.

In the second half of this chapter, we'll see how you can write code that writes code with the eval method: metaprogramming in its purest form. We'll also see how metaprogramming and closures are related. Like blocks, lambdas, and procs, eval and its related metaprogramming methods create a closure when you call them. In fact, we'll learn how you can use the same mental model we developed in Chapter 8 for blocks to understand many of Ruby's metaprogramming features.

Alternative Ways to Define Methods

Normally we define methods in Ruby using the def keyword. After def, we specify a name for the new method followed by the method body. By using some of Ruby's metaprogramming features, however, we can define methods in alternative ways. We can create class methods instead of normal methods; we can create methods for a single object instance; and, as we'll see in Experiment 9-2, we can create methods that can access the surrounding environment using a closure.

Next, we'll look at what happens inside Ruby when you define a method in each of these ways using metaprogramming. In each case, studying what Ruby does internally will make Ruby's metaprogramming syntax easier to understand. But before we tackle metaprogramming, let's learn more about how Ruby normally defines a method. This knowledge will serve as a foundation when we learn alternative ways to define a method.

Ruby's Normal Method Definition Process

Listing 9-1 shows a very simple Ruby class containing a single method.

```
class Quote
  def display
    puts "The quick brown fox jumped over the lazy dog."
  end
end
```

Listing 9-1: Adding a method to a class using the def keyword

How does Ruby execute this small program? And how does it know to assign the display method to the Quote class?

When Ruby executes the class keyword, it creates a new lexical scope for the new Quote class (see Figure 9-1). Ruby sets the nd_clss pointer in the lexical scope to point to an RClass structure for the new Quote class. Because it's a new class, the RClass structure initially has an empty method table, as shown on the right side of the figure.

Next, Ruby executes the def keyword, which is used to define the display method. But how does Ruby create normal methods? What happens internally when you call def?

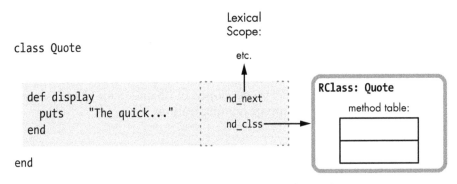

```
class Quote

  def display
    puts    "The quick..."
  end

end
```

Lexical
Scope:

etc.

nd_next

nd_clss

RClass: Quote

method table:

Figure 9-1: Ruby creates a new lexical scope when you define a class.

By default, when you use def, you provide just the name of the new method. (We'll see in the next section that you can also specify an object prefix along with the new method name.) Providing just the name of the new method with def instructs Ruby to use the current lexical scope to find the target class, as shown in Figure 9-2.

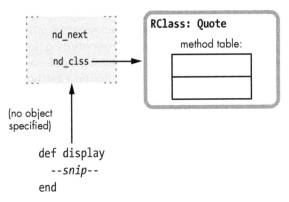

nd_next

nd_clss

RClass: Quote

method table:

(no object specified)

```
def display
    --snip--
end
```

Figure 9-2: By default, Ruby uses the current lexical scope to find the target class for a new method.

When Ruby initially compiles Listing 9-1, it creates a separate snippet of YARV code for the display method. Later, when executing the def keyword, Ruby assigns this code to the target class, Quote, saving the given method name in the method table (see Figure 9-3).

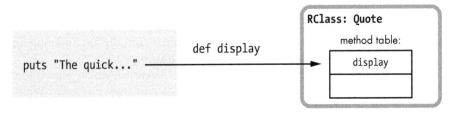

RClass: Quote

method table:

def display

puts "The quick..."

display

Figure 9-3: Ruby adds new methods to the method table for the target class.

When we execute this method, Ruby looks up the method as described in "Ruby's Method Lookup Algorithm" on page 138. Because display now appears in the method table for Quote, Ruby can find the method and execute it.

In sum, to define new methods in your program using the def keyword, Ruby follows this three-step process:

1. It compiles each method's body into a distinct snippet of YARV instructions. (This occurs when Ruby parses and compiles your program.)

2. It uses the current lexical scope to obtain a pointer to a class or module. (This occurs when Ruby encounters a def keyword while executing your program.)

3. It saves the new method's name—actually, an integer ID value that maps to the name—in the method table for that class.

Defining Class Methods Using an Object Prefix

Now that we understand how Ruby's method definition process normally works, let's learn alternative ways to define methods using metaprogramming. As we saw in Figure 9-2, Ruby normally assigns new methods to the class that corresponds to the current lexical scope. However, sometimes you'll decide to add a method to a different class—for example, when you define a class method. (Remember that Ruby saves class methods in a class's metaclass.) Listing 9-2 shows an example of creating a class method.

```
class Quote
❶  def self.display
     puts "The quick brown fox jumped over the lazy dog."
   end
end
```

Listing 9-2: Adding a class method using def self

At ❶ we use def to define the new method, but this time we use a self prefix. This prefix tells Ruby to add the method to the class of the object you specify in the prefix rather than using the current lexical scope. Figure 9-4 shows how Ruby does this internally.

This behavior is very different from the standard method definition process! When you provide an object prefix to def, Ruby uses the following algorithm to decide where to put the new method:

1. Ruby evaluates the prefix expression. In Listing 9-2 we use the self keyword. While Ruby is executing code inside the class Quote scope, self is set to the Quote class. (We could have provided any Ruby expression here instead of self.) In Figure 9-4, the arrow extending up from self to the RClass structure indicates the value of self is Quote.

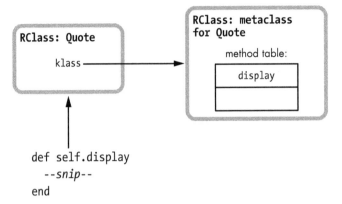

```
def self.display
  --snip--
end
```

Figure 9-4: Providing an object prefix to def instructs Ruby to add the new method to the object's class.

2. Ruby finds the class of this object. In Listing 9-2, because self is a class itself (Quote), the class of the object is actually the metaclass for Quote. Figure 9-4 indicates this with the arrow extending to the right from the RClass structure for Quote.

3. Ruby saves the new method in that class's method table. In this case, Ruby places the display method in the metaclass for Quote, making display a new class method.

NOTE   *If you call Quote.class, Ruby will return Class. All classes are officially instances of the Class class. Metaclasses are an internal concept, normally hidden from your Ruby program. To see the metaclass for Quote, you can call Quote.singleton_class instead, which will return #<Class:Quote>.*

Defining Class Methods Using a New Lexical Scope

Listing 9-3 shows a different way to assign display as a class method of Quote.

```
❶ class Quote
❷   class << self
      def display
        puts "The quick brown fox jumped over the lazy dog."
      end
    end
  end
```

Listing 9-3: Defining a class method using class << self

At ❷ class << self declares a new lexical scope, just as class Quote does at ❶. In "Ruby's Normal Method Definition Process" on page 221, we saw that using def in the scope created by class Quote assigns new methods to

Quote. But what class does Ruby assign methods to inside the scope created by class << self? The answer is self's class. Because at ❷ self is set to Quote, self's class is the metaclass of Quote.

Figure 9-5 shows how class << self creates a new lexical scope for the metaclass of Quote.

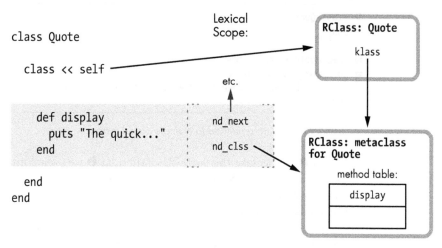

Figure 9-5: Ruby creates a new lexical scope for a class's metaclass when you use `class << self`.

In this figure, Ruby's class << metaprogramming syntax functions as follows:

1. Ruby first evaluates the expression that appears after class <<. In Listing 9-3 this is the expression self, which evaluates to the Quote class, just as it did using the object prefix syntax in Listing 9-2. The long arrow extending to the right from self to the RClass structure indicates the value of self is the Quote class.

2. Ruby finds the class for the object the expression evaluates to. In Listing 9-3 this will be the class of Quote, or Quote's metaclass, indicated by the arrow extending down from Quote to the metaclass for Quote on the right side of the figure.

3. Ruby creates a new lexical scope for this class. In this example, the lexical scope uses the metaclass of Quote, indicated by the arrow extending to the right from nd_clss in the new scope.

Now we can use the new lexical scope to define a series of class methods using def as usual. In Listing 9-3 Ruby will assign the display method directly to the metaclass of Quote. This is a different way of defining a class method for Quote. You might find class << self a bit more confusing than def self, but it is a convenient way to create a series of class methods by declaring them all inside the inner, metaclass lexical scope.

Defining Methods Using Singleton Classes

We've seen how metaprogramming allows you to declare class methods by adding methods to the class's class or metaclass. Ruby also allows you to add methods to a single object instance, as shown in Listing 9-4.

```
❶ class Quote
  end

❷ some_quote = Quote.new
❸ def some_quote.display
    puts "The quick brown fox jumped over the lazy dog."
  end
```

Listing 9-4: Adding a method to a single object instance

At ❶ we declare the Quote class; then, at ❷ we create an instance of Quote: some_quote. At ❸ this time, however, we create a new method for the some_quote instance, not the Quote class. As a result, only some_quote will have the display method; no other instances of Quote will have it.

Internally, Ruby implements this behavior using a hidden class called the *singleton class*, which is like a metaclass for a single object. Here's the difference:

- A *singleton class* is a special hidden class that Ruby creates internally to hold methods defined only for a particular object.
- A *metaclass* is a singleton class in the case when that object is itself a class.

All metaclasses are singleton classes, but not all singleton classes are metaclasses. Ruby automatically creates a metaclass for every class you create and uses it to hold class methods that you might declare later. On the other hand, Ruby creates a singleton class only when you define a method on a single object, as shown in Listing 9-4. Ruby also creates a singleton class when you use instance_eval or related methods.

NOTE   *Most Ruby developers use the terms* singleton class *and* metaclass *interchangeably, and when you call the* singleton_class *method, Ruby will return either a singleton class or a metaclass. However, internally Ruby's C source code does make a distinction between singleton classes and metaclasses.*

Figure 9-6 shows how Ruby creates a singleton class when executing Listing 9-4. Ruby evaluates the expression provided as a prefix to def: some_quote. Because some_quote is an object instance, Ruby creates a new singleton class for some_quote and then assigns the new method to this singleton class. Using the def keyword with an object prefix instructs Ruby either to use a metaclass (if the prefix is a class) or to create a singleton class (if the prefix is some other object).

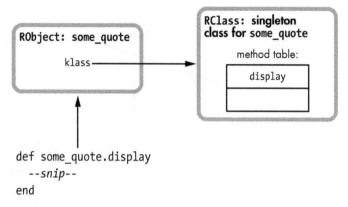

```
def some_quote.display
  --snip--
end
```

Figure 9-6: Providing an object prefix to def instructs Ruby to add the
new method to the object's singleton class.

Defining Methods Using Singleton Classes in a Lexical Scope

You can also declare a new lexical scope for adding methods to a single
object instance using the class << syntax, as shown in Listing 9-5.

```
class Quote
end

some_quote = Quote.new
❶ class << some_quote
  def display
    puts "The quick brown fox jumped over the lazy dog."
  end
end
```

Listing 9-5: Adding a singleton method using class <<

The difference between this code and that in Listing 9-4 appears at ❶,
when we use the class << syntax with the expression some_quote, which evaluates to a single object instance. As shown in Figure 9-7, class << some_quote
instructs Ruby to create a new singleton class along with a new lexical scope.

On the left side of Figure 9-7, you can see some of the code from
Listing 9-5. Ruby first evaluates the expression some_quote and finds it is an
object, not a class. Figure 9-7 indicates this with the long arrow pointing to
the RObject structure for some_quote. Because it is not a class, Ruby creates a
new singleton class for some_quote and also creates a new lexical scope. Next,
it sets the class for the new scope to be the new singleton class. If a singleton
class for some_quote already exists, Ruby will reuse it.

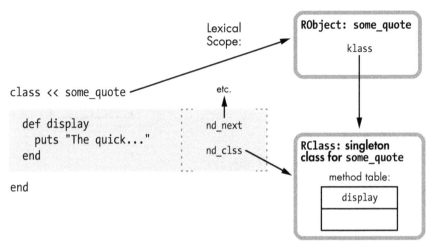

Figure 9-7: Ruby creates a new singleton class and lexical scope for some_quote.

Creating Refinements

Ruby 2.0's *refinements* feature gave us the ability to define methods and add them to a class later if we wish. To see how this works, we'll use the same Quote class and display method we used in Listing 9-1, repeated here for convenience.

```
class Quote
  def display
    puts "The quick brown fox jumped over the lazy dog."
  end
end
```

Now suppose elsewhere in our Ruby application we want to override or change what display does without changing the Quote class everywhere. Ruby provides an elegant way to do this, as shown in Listing 9-6.

```
module AllCaps
  refine Quote do
    def display
      puts "THE QUICK BROWN FOX JUMPED OVER THE LAZY DOG."
    end
  end
end
```

Listing 9-6: Refining a class inside a module

In refine Quote do, we use the refine method and pass the Quote class as a parameter. This defines new behavior for Quote that we can activate later. Figure 9-8 shows what happens internally when we call refine.

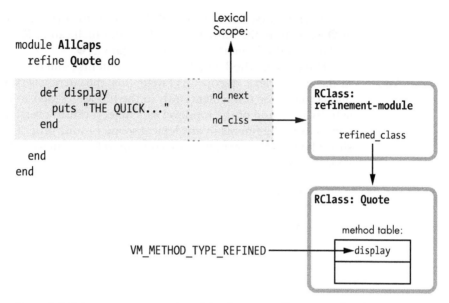

Figure 9-8: Ruby creates a special module when you call *refine* and updates the type of the target class's methods.

Working our way through Figure 9-8 from the top-left corner down, we see the following:

- The refine method creates a new lexical scope (the shaded rectangle).
- Ruby creates a new "refinement" module and uses that as the class for this new scope.
- Ruby saves a pointer to the Quote class in refined_class inside the new refinement module.

As you define new methods in the refine block, Ruby saves them in the refinement module. But it also follows the refined_class pointer and updates the same methods in the target class to use the method type VM_METHOD_TYPE_REFINED.

Using Refinements

You can decide to activate these "refined" methods in a specific part of your program with the using method, as shown in Listing 9-7.

```
❶ Quote.new.display
   => The quick brown...

❷ using AllCaps

❸ Quote.new.display
   => THE QUICK BROWN...
```

Listing 9-7: Activating a refined method

When we first call display at ❶, Ruby uses the original method. Then, at ❷ we activate the refinement with using, which causes Ruby to use the updated method when we call display again at ❸.

The using method attaches the refinements from the specified module to the current lexical scope. As I write this, the current version of Ruby, 2.0, allows you to use refinements only in the top-level scope, as in this example; using is a method of the top-level main object. (Future versions may allow you to use refinements in any lexical scope in your program.) Figure 9-9 shows how Ruby internally associates the refinement with the top-level lexical scope.

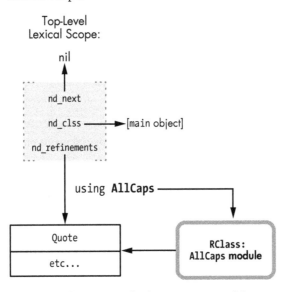

Figure 9-9: The using method associates a module's refinements with the top-level lexical scope.

Notice how each lexical scope contains an nd_refinements pointer, which tracks the refinements active in that scope. The using method sets nd_refinements, which would otherwise be nil.

And finally, Figure 9-10 shows how Ruby's method dispatch algorithm finds the updated method when I call it.

Ruby uses a complex method dispatch process when you call methods. One portion of this algorithm looks for VM_METHOD_TYPE_REFINED methods. When it encounters a refined method, Ruby looks in the current lexical scope for any active refinements. If it finds an active refinement, Ruby calls the refined method; otherwise, it calls the original method.

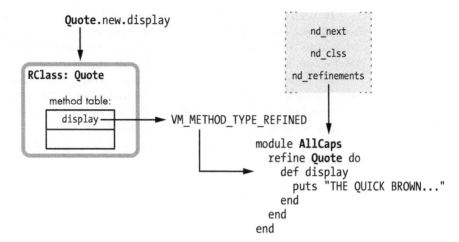

Figure 9-10: Ruby looks for a method in the refine block when the original method is marked with VM_METHOD_TYPE_REFINED.

Experiment 9-1: Who Am I? How self Changes with Lexical Scope

We've seen various ways to define methods in Ruby. We created methods in the usual way using the def keyword. Then, we looked at how to create methods on a metaclass and on a singleton class and how to use refinements.

While each technique adds the method to a different class, each also follows a simple rule: Ruby adds the new method to the class corresponding to the current lexical scope for each technique. (The def keyword, however, assigns the method to a different class when you use a prefix.) With refinements, the current scope's class is actually the special module created to hold the refined methods. In fact, this is one of the important roles lexical scope plays in Ruby: It identifies which class or module we are currently adding methods to.

We also know that the self keyword returns the current object—the receiver of the method currently being executed by Ruby. Recall that YARV saves the current value of self for each level of your Ruby call stack in the rb_control_frame_t structure. Is this object the same as the class for the current lexical scope?

self in the Top Scope

Let's see how the value of self changes as we run a simple program beginning with Listing 9-8.

```
p self
 => main
p Module.nesting
 => []
```

Listing 9-8: A simple Ruby program with only one lexical scope

To keep things simple, I've shown the output from the console inline. You can see that Ruby creates a top self object before it starts to execute your code. This object serves as the receiver for method calls in the top-level scope. Ruby represents this object with the string main.

The Module.nesting call returns an array showing the lexical scope stack—that is, which modules are "nested" until that point in the code. This array will contain an element for each lexical scope in the lexical scope stack. Because we're at the top level of the script, Ruby returns an empty array.

Figure 9-11 shows the lexical scope stack and the value self for this simple program.

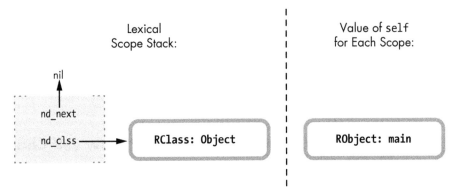

Figure 9-11: At the top level, Ruby sets self to the main object and has a single entry in the lexical scope stack.

On the right of this figure, you see the main object: the current value of self. On the left side is the lexical scope stack, which contains just a single entry for the top-level scope. Ruby sets the class of the top scope to the class of the main object, which is the Object class.

> **NOTE**   *Recall when you declare a new method using the def keyword, Ruby adds the method to the class for the current lexical scope. We've just seen the class for the top-level lexical scope is Object. Therefore, we can conclude that when you define a method at the top level of your script, outside of any class or module, Ruby adds the method to the Object class. You can call methods you define at the top level from anywhere because Object is a superclass of every other class.*

self in a Class Scope

Now let's define a new class and see what happens to the value of self and the lexical scope stack, as shown in Listing 9-9.

```
p self
p Module.nesting

class Quote
  p self
❶   => Quote
```

```
    p Module.nesting
❷      => [Quote]
    end
```

Listing 9-9: Declaring a new class changes self and creates a new entry in the lexical scope stack.

The output from the print statements is shown inline. We see at ❶ that Ruby has changed self to Quote—the new class—and we see at ❷ that there's a new level added to the lexical scope stack. Figure 9-12 shows a summary.

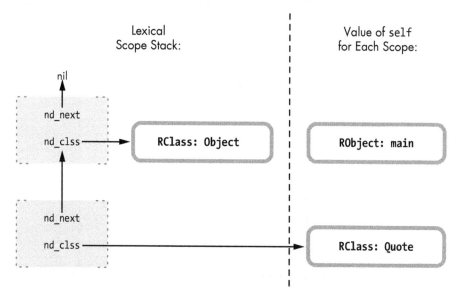

Figure 9-12: Now self is the same as the class for the current lexical scope.

On the left side of this figure, we see the lexical scope stack. The top scope is on the top left, and under it we see the new lexical scope created by the class keyword. Meanwhile, on the right side of the figure, we see how the value of self changes when we call class. On the top level, self was set to the main object, but when we call class, Ruby changes self to the new class.

self in a Metaclass Scope

Let's use the class << self syntax to create a new metaclass scope. Listing 9-10 shows the same program with a few more lines of code.

```
p self
p Module.nesting

class Quote
  p self
  p Module.nesting
```

```
      class << self
        p self
❶       => #<Class:Quote>
        p Module.nesting
❷       => [#<Class:Quote>, Quote]
      end
    end
```

Listing 9-10: Declaring a metaclass scope

At ❶ we see that Ruby has changed the value of self again. The syntax #<Class:Quote> indicates that self was set to Quote's metaclass. At ❷ we see that Ruby has also added another level to the lexical scope stack. Figure 9-13 shows the next level in the stack.

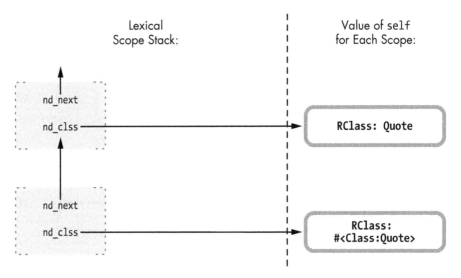

Figure 9-13: A new lexical scope is created for the metaclass.

On the left, we can see that Ruby created a new scope when it executed class << self. The right side of the figure shows the value of self in the new scope, the metaclass for Quote.

self Inside a Class Method

Now for one more test. Suppose we add a class method to the Quote class and then call it as shown in Listing 9-11. (The output is at the bottom because the p statements aren't called until we call class_method.)

```
p self
p Module.nesting

class Quote
  p self
  p Module.nesting
```

```
    class << self
      p self
      p Module.nesting

      def class_method
        p self
        p Module.nesting
      end
    end
  end

  Quote.class_method
❶ => Quote
❷ => [#<Class:Quote>, Quote]
```

Listing 9-11: Declaring and calling a class method

At ❶ we see that Ruby sets self back to the Quote class when we call class_method. This makes sense: When we call a method on a receiver, Ruby always sets self to be the receiver. Because we call a class method in this case, Ruby sets the receiver to that class.

At ❷ we see that Ruby hasn't changed the lexical scope stack. It's still set to [#<Class:Quote>, Quote], as shown in Figure 9-14.

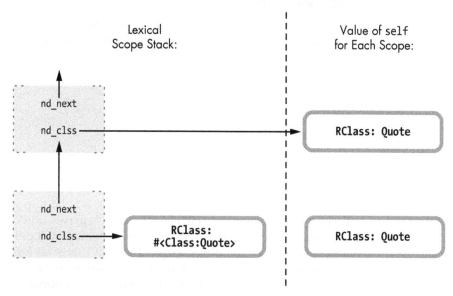

Figure 9-14: When you call a method, Ruby changes self but doesn't create a new scope.

Notice that the lexical scope hasn't changed but self has been changed to Quote, the receiver of the method call.

You can use these general rules to keep track of self and lexical scope:

- Inside a class or module scope, self will always be set to that class or module. Ruby creates a new lexical scope when you use the class or module keywords and sets the class for that scope to the new class or module.

- Inside a method (including a class method), Ruby will set self to the receiver of that method call.

Metaprogramming and Closures: eval, instance_eval, and binding

In Chapter 8 we learned that blocks are Ruby's implementation of closures, and we saw how blocks bring together a function with the environment where that function was referenced. In Ruby, metaprogramming and closures are closely related. Many of Ruby's metaprogramming constructs also act as closures, giving the code inside them access to the referencing environment. We'll learn about three important metaprogramming features and how each gives you access to the referencing environment by acting as a closure in just the way blocks do.

Code That Writes Code

In Ruby, the eval method is metaprogramming in its purest form: You pass a string to eval, and Ruby immediately parses, compiles, and executes the code, as shown in Listing 9-12.

```
str = "puts"
str += " 2"
str += " +"
str += " 2"
eval(str)
```

Listing 9-12: Parsing and compiling code using eval

We dynamically construct the string puts 2+2 and pass it to eval. Ruby then evaluates the string. That is, it tokenizes, parses, and compiles it using the same Bison grammar rules and parse engine that it did when it first processed the primary Ruby script. Once this process is finished and Ruby has another new set of YARV bytecode instructions, it executes the new code.

But one very important detail about eval isn't obvious in Listing 9-12. Specifically, Ruby evaluates the new code string in the same context from where you called eval. To see what I mean, look at Listing 9-13.

```
a = 2
b = 3
str = "puts"
str += " a"
str += " +"
```

```
  str += " b"
❶ eval(str)
```

Listing 9-13: It isn't obvious here, but eval accesses the surrounding scope via a closure, too.

You would expect the result from running this code to be 5, but notice the difference between Listings 9-12 and 9-13. Listing 9-13 refers to the local variables a and b from the surrounding scope, and Ruby can access their values. Figure 9-15 shows how YARV's internal stack looks just before calling eval at ❶.

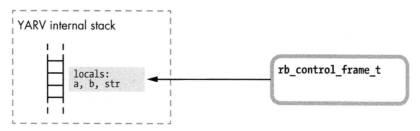

Figure 9-15: Ruby saves the local variables a, b, and str on YARV's internal stack as usual.

As expected, we see that Ruby has saved the values of a, b, and str on the stack to the left. On the right, we have the rb_control_frame_t structure, which represents the outer, or main, scope of this script.

Figure 9-16 shows what happens when we call the eval method.

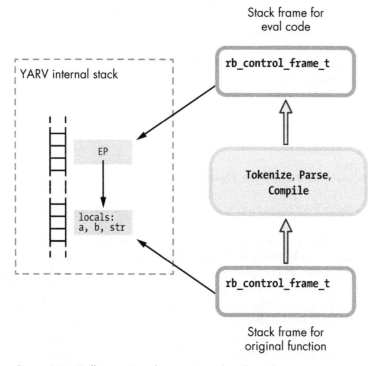

Figure 9-16: Calling eval and accessing values from the parent scope

Calling `eval` invokes the parser and compiler on the text we pass it. When the compiler finishes, Ruby creates a new stack frame (`rb_control_frame_t`) for use in running the new compiled code (as shown at the top). Notice, however, that Ruby sets the EP in this new stack frame to point to the lower stack frame where the variables a and b are. This pointer allows the code passed to eval to access these values.

Ruby's use of EP here should look familiar. Aside from parsing and compiling the code dynamically, eval works the same way as if we had passed a block to some function, as in Listing 9-14.

```
a = 2
b = 3
10.times do
  puts a+b
end
```

Listing 9-14: Code inside a block can access variables from the surrounding scope.

In other words, the eval method creates a closure: the combination of a function and the environment where that function was referenced. In this case, the function is the newly compiled code, and the environment is where we call eval from.

Calling eval with binding

The eval method can take a second parameter: a *binding*. A binding is a closure without a function—that is, it's just the referencing environment. Think of bindings as a pointer to a YARV stack frame. Passing a binding value to Ruby indicates that you don't want to use the current context as the closure's environment but instead want to use some other referencing environment. Listing 9-15 shows an example.

```
    def get_binding
      a = 2
      b = 3
❶    binding
    end
❷ eval("puts a+b", get_binding)
```

Listing 9-15: Using binding to access variables from some other environment

The function get_binding contains the local variables a and b, but it also returns a binding at ❶. At the bottom of the listing, we again want Ruby to dynamically compile and execute the code string and print out the result. By passing the binding returned by get_binding to eval, we tell Ruby to evaluate puts a+b in the context of the get_binding function. If we had called eval without the binding, it would have created new, empty local variables a and b.

Ruby makes a persistent copy of this environment in the heap because you might call eval long after the current frame has been popped off the stack. Even though get_binding has already returned in this example, Ruby can still access the values of a and b when it executes the code parsed and compiled by eval at ❷.

Figure 9-17 shows what happens internally when we call binding.

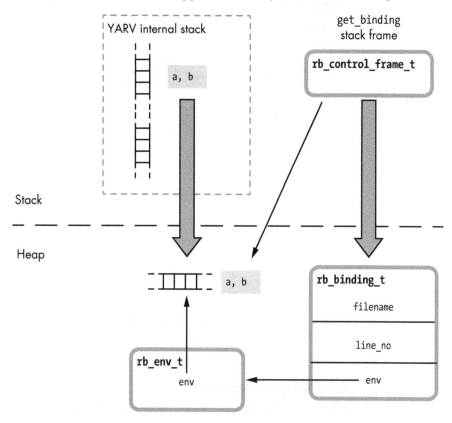

Figure 9-17: Calling binding *saves a copy of the current stack frame in the heap.*

This figure resembles what Ruby does when you call lambda (see Figure 8-18 on page 210), except that Ruby creates an rb_binding_t C structure instead of an rb_proc_t structure. The binding structure is simply a wrapper around the internal environment structure—the heap copy of the stack frame. The binding structure also contains the file name and line number of the location from where you called binding.

As with the proc object, Ruby uses the RTypedData structure to wrap a Ruby object around the rb_binding_t C structure (see Figure 9-18).

The binding object allows you to create a closure and then obtain and treat its environment as a data value. However, the closure created by the binding doesn't contain any code; it has no function. You might think of the binding object as an indirect way to access, save, and pass around Ruby's internal rb_env_t structure.

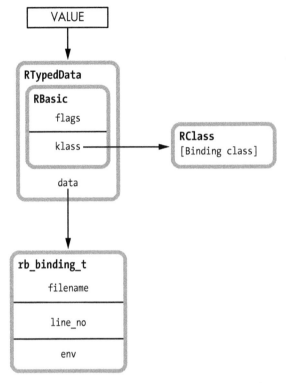

Figure 9-18: Ruby uses *RTypedData* to wrap a Ruby object around the *rb_binding_t* structure.

An instance_eval Example

Now for a variation on the eval method: instance_eval is shown in action in Listing 9-16.

```
❶ class Quote
     def initialize
❷      @str = "The quick brown fox"
     end
   end
   str2 = "jumps over the lazy dog."
❸ obj = Quote.new
❹ obj.instance_eval do
❺   puts "#{@str} #{str2}"
   end
```

Listing 9-16: The code inside *instance_eval* has access to *obj*'s instance variable.

Here's what's going on:

- At ❶ we create a Ruby class called Quote that saves the first half of the string in an instance variable in initialize at ❷.

- At ❸ we create an instance of the Quote class and then call instance_eval at ❹, passing a block. The instance_eval method is similar to eval, except that it evaluates the given string in the context of the receiver, or the object we call it on. As shown here, we can pass a block to instance_eval instead of a string if we don't want to dynamically parse and compile code.

- The block we pass to instance_eval prints out the string at ❺, accessing the first half of the string from the obj's instance variable and the second half from the surrounding scope, or environment.

How can this possibly work? It seems that the block passed to instance_eval has two environments: the quote instance and the surrounding code environment. In other words, the @str variable comes from one place and str2 from another.

Another Important Part of Ruby Closures

This example highlights another important part of closure environments in Ruby: the current value of self. Recall that the rb_control_frame_t structure for each stack frame, or level, in your Ruby call stack contains a self pointer, along with the PC, SP, and EP pointers and other values (see Figure 9-19).

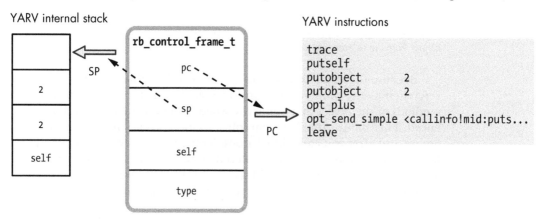

Figure 9-19: The rb_control_frame_t structure

The self pointer records the current value of self in your Ruby project; it indicates which object is the owner of the method Ruby is currently executing at that time. Each level in your Ruby call stack can contain a different value for self.

Recall that whenever you create a closure Ruby sets the EP, or environment pointer, in the rb_block_t structure to the referencing environment, giving the code inside the block access to the surrounding variables. And, as it turns out, Ruby also copies the value of self into rb_block_t. This means that the current object is also a part of closures in Ruby. Figure 9-20 looks at what closures contain in Ruby.

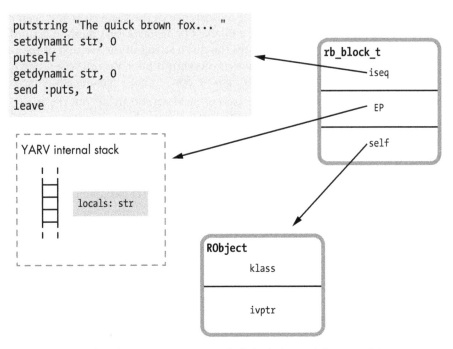

```
putstring "The quick brown fox... "
setdynamic str, 0
putself
getdynamic str, 0
send :puts, 1
leave
```

Figure 9-20: In Ruby, closure environments include both the stack frame and the current object from the referencing code.

Because the rb_block_t structure contains the value of self from the referencing environment, code inside a block can access the values and methods of the object that was active when the closure was created or referenced. This ability probably seems obvious for a block: The current object before and after you call a block doesn't change. However, if you use a lambda, proc, or binding, Ruby will remember what the current object was when you created it. And, as we'll see shortly with instance_eval, Ruby can sometimes change self when you create a closure, giving your code access to a different object's values and methods.

instance_eval Changes self to the Receiver

When you call instance_eval at ❹ in Listing 9-16, Ruby creates both a closure and a new lexical scope. For example, as you can see in Figure 9-21, the new stack frame for the code inside instance_eval uses new values for both EP and self.

On the left of the figure, we see that executing instance_eval creates a closure. This result should be no surprise. Passing a block to instance_eval at ❹ in Listing 9-16 creates a new level on the stack and sets EP to the referencing environment, giving the code inside the block access to the variables str2 and obj.

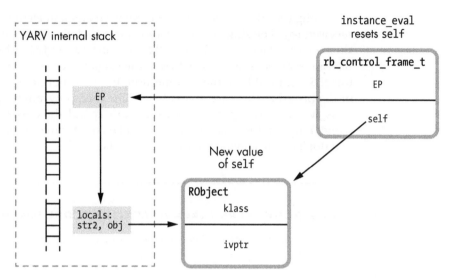

Figure 9-21: The stack frame created by running instance_eval has a new value for self.

However, as you can see on the right of the figure, instance_eval also changes the value of self in the new closure. When the code inside the instance_eval block runs, self points to the receiver of instance_eval, or obj, in Listing 9-16. This allows the code inside instance_eval to access the values inside the receiver. In Listing 9-16, the code at ❺ can access both @str from inside obj and str2 from the surrounding code.

instance_eval Creates a Singleton Class for a New Lexical Scope

The instance_eval method also creates a new singleton class and sets it as the class for a new lexical scope, as shown in Figure 9-22.

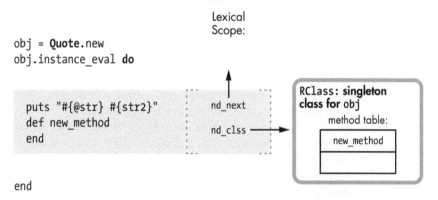

Figure 9-22: instance_eval creates a lexical scope for a new singleton class.

While executing instance_eval, Ruby creates a new lexical scope, as shown by the shaded rectangle inside the instance_eval block. If we had passed a string to instance_eval, Ruby would have parsed and compiled the string and then created a new lexical scope in the same way.

Along with the new lexical scope, Ruby creates a singleton class for the receiver, obj. The singleton class allows you to define new methods for the receiver object (see Figure 9-22): The def new_method call inside the instance_eval block adds new_method to the singleton class for obj. As a singleton class, obj will have the new method, but no other objects or classes in the program will have access to it. (The metaprogramming methods class_eval and module_eval work in a similar way and also create a new lexical scope; however, they just use the target class or module for the new scope and don't create a metaclass or singleton class.)

HOW RUBY KEEPS TRACK OF LEXICAL SCOPE FOR BLOCKS

Let's take a closer look at how Ruby represents lexical scopes internally. Figure 9-23 shows the lexical scope Ruby creates for the Quote class.

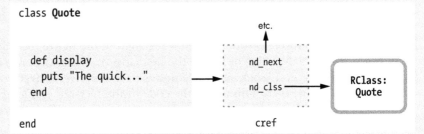

Figure 9-23: Ruby's C source code internally uses a separate structure called cref to track lexical scopes.

You can see the display method's code snippet represented as a rectangle on the left side of the figure, inside the class Quote declaration. On the right side of the rectangle, you can see a small arrow pointing to a structure labeled cref, which is the actual lexical scope. This, in turn, contains a pointer to the Quote class (nd_clss) and to the parent lexical scope (nd_next).

As indicated by the figure, Ruby's C source code internally represents lexical scopes using these cref structures. The small arrow on the left shows that each piece of code in your program refers to a cref structure with a pointer. This pointer keeps track of which lexical scope that piece of code belongs to.

Notice one important detail about Figure 9-23: Both the code snippet and lexical scope inside the class Quote declaration refer to a single RClass structure. There's a one-to-one correspondence between code, lexical scope, and class. Every time Ruby executes the code inside the class Quote declaration, it uses the same copy of the RClass structure, the one for Quote. This behavior seems obvious; the code inside a class declaration always refers to the same class.

For blocks, however, things aren't so simple. Using metaprogramming methods such as instance_eval, you can specify a different lexical scope for the same piece of code—a block, for example—to use each time it is executed. Figure 9-24 shows the problem.

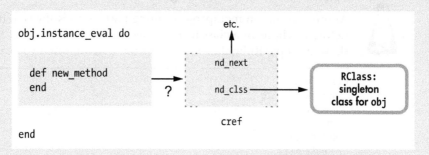

Figure 9-24: The block's code can't refer to a single lexical scope because the scope's class depends on the value of obj.

We learned in the previous section that Ruby creates a singleton class for the lexical scope created by instance_eval. However, this code might be run many times for different values of obj. In fact, your program might execute this code at the same time in different threads. This requirement means that Ruby can't keep a pointer to a single cref structure for the block as it does for a class definition. This block scope will refer to different classes at different times.

Ruby solves this problem by saving a pointer to the lexical scope used by blocks in a different place: as an entry on YARV's internal stack (see Figure 9-25).

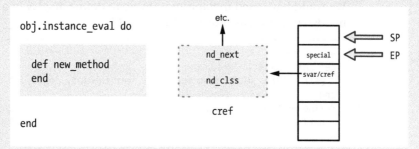

Figure 9-25: Ruby tracks lexical scope for blocks using the svar/cref *entry on the stack, not using the block's code snippet.*

On the left side of the figure, you can see the call to instance_eval and the code snippet for the block inside. In the center of the figure is the cref structure for the lexical scope. On the right side, you can see YARV saves a pointer to the scope in the second entry on its stack, labeled svar/cref.

Recall from Chapter 3 that the second entry on YARV's internal stack contains one of two values: svar or cref. As we saw in Experiment 3-2 on page 75, svar saves a pointer to a table of special variables, such as the result of the last regular expression match, while executing a method. But while executing a block, YARV saves the cref value here instead. Usually this value isn't important because blocks normally use the lexical scope of the surrounding code. But when executing instance_eval and a few other metaprogramming features, such as module_eval and instance_exec, Ruby sets cref in this way to the current lexical scope.

Experiment 9-2: Using a Closure to Define a Method

Another common metaprogramming pattern in Ruby is to dynamically define methods in a class using define_method. For example, Listing 9-17 shows a simple Ruby class that prints out a string when you call display.

```
class Quote
  def initialize
    @str = "The quick brown fox jumps over the lazy dog"
  end
  def display
    puts @str
  end
end
Quote.new.display
=> The quick brown fox jumps over the lazy dog
```

Listing 9-17: A Ruby class that displays a string from an instance variable

This code is similar to that in Listing 9-1, except that we use an instance variable @str to hold the string value.

Using define_method

We could have used metaprogramming to define display in a more verbose but dynamic way, as shown in Listing 9-18.

```
class Quote
  def initialize
    @str = "The quick brown fox jumps over the lazy dog"
  end
❶ define_method :display do
    puts @str
  end
end
```

Listing 9-18: Using define_method to create a method

We call define_method at ❶ instead of the normal def keyword. Because the name of the new method is passed as the argument :display, we can dynamically construct the method name from some data values or iterate over an array of method names, calling define_method for each one.

But there is another subtle difference between def and define_method. For define_method we provide the body of the method as a block; that is, we use a do keyword at ❶. This syntax difference may seem minor, but remember that blocks are actually closures. Adding do introduces a closure, meaning that the code inside the new method has access to the environment outside. This is not the case with the def keyword.

There are no local variables present in Listing 9-18 when we call define_method, but suppose that another place in our application did have values that we wanted to use inside our new method. By using a closure, Ruby makes an internal copy of the surrounding environment on the heap, which the new method will be able to access.

Methods Acting as Closures

Now for another test. Listing 9-19 stores only the first half of the string in the instance variable. In a moment, we'll write a new method for the `Quote` class to access this.

```
class Quote
  def initialize
    @str = "The quick brown fox"
  end
end
```

Listing 9-19: Now @str has only the first half of the string.

Listing 9-20 shows how we can use a closure to access both the instance variable and the surrounding environment.

```
def create_method_using_a_closure
  str2 = "jumps over the lazy dog."
❶ Quote.send(:define_method, :display) do
    puts "#{@str} #{str2}"
  end
end
```

Listing 9-20: Using a closure with define_method

Because `define_method` is a private method in the `Module` class, we need to use the confusing send syntax at ❶. Earlier, at ❶ in Listing 9-18, we were able to call `define_method` directly because we used it inside the class's scope. We can't do that from other places in the application. By using `send`, the `create_method_using_a_closure` method can call a private method that it wouldn't normally have had access to.

But more importantly, notice that the `str2` variable is preserved in the heap for the new method to use even after `create_method_using_a_closure` returns:

```
create_method_using_a_closure
Quote.new.display
 => The quick brown fox jumps over the lazy dog.
```

Internally, Ruby treats this as a call to `lambda`. That is, this code functions the same way as if I had written the code in Listing 9-21.

```
class Quote
  def initialize
    @str = "The quick brown fox"
  end
```

```
  end
  def create_method_using_a_closure
    str2 = "jumps over the lazy dog."
    lambda do
      puts "#{@str} #{str2}"
    end
  end
❶ Quote.send(:define_method, :display, create_method_using_a_closure)
❷ Quote.new.display
```

Listing 9-21: Passing a proc to define_method

Listing 9-21 separates the code that creates the closure and defines the method. Because at ❶ we pass three arguments to define_method, Ruby expects the third to be a proc object. While this is an even more verbose way to write this code, it's a bit less confusing because calling lambda makes it clear that Ruby will create a closure.

Finally, when we call the new method at ❷, Ruby resets the self pointer from the closure to receiver object, similar to the way that instance_eval works. This allows the new method to access @str as you would expect.

Summary

In this chapter we've seen how the concept of closures—the idea central to the way blocks, lambdas, and procs work in Ruby—also applies to methods such as eval, instance_eval, and define_method. The same underlying concept explains how these different Ruby methods work. In a similar way, the concept of lexical scope underpins all of the ways that Ruby allows you to create a method and assign it to a class. Understanding the concept of lexical scope should make the different uses of Ruby's def keyword and class << syntax easier to understand.

While metaprogramming might seem complex at first, learning how Ruby works internally can help us understand what Ruby's metaprogramming features actually do. What seems initially like a large set of different, unrelated methods in a confusing API turn out to be related by a few important ideas. Studying Ruby internals allows us to see these concepts and to understand what they mean.

*JRuby is Ruby
implemented on the
Java platform.*

10

JRUBY: RUBY ON THE JVM

In Chapters 1 through 9 we learned how the standard
version of Ruby works internally. Because Ruby is written in C, its standard implementation is often known
as *CRuby*. It's also often referred to as *Matz's Ruby
Interpreter (MRI)*, after Yukihiro Matsumoto, who created the language in the early 1990s.

In this chapter we'll see an alternative implementation of Ruby called
JRuby. JRuby is Ruby implemented in Java instead of C. The use of Java allows
Ruby applications to run like any other Java program, using the Java Virtual
Machine (JVM). It also allows your Ruby code to interoperate with thousands
of libraries written in Java and other languages that run on the JVM. Thanks
to the JVM's sophisticated garbage collection (GC) algorithms, just-in-time
(JIT) compiler, and many other technical innovations, using the JVM means
that your Ruby code often runs faster and more reliably.

In the first half of this chapter, we'll contrast standard Ruby—that is,
MRI—with JRuby. You'll learn what happens when you run a Ruby program
using JRuby and how JRuby parses and compiles your Ruby code. In the lat-
ter half of the chapter, we'll see how JRuby and MRI save your string data
using the String class.

Running Programs with MRI and JRuby

The normal way to run a Ruby program using standard Ruby is to enter ruby followed by the name of your Ruby script, as shown in Figure 10-1.

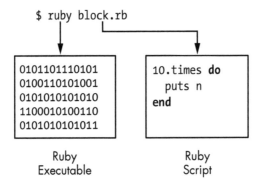

Figure 10-1: Running a script at the command line using standard Ruby

As you can see in the rectangle at the left, entering ruby at a terminal prompt launches a binary executable, the product of compiling Ruby's C source code during the Ruby build process. On the right, you see that the command line parameter to the ruby command is a text file containing your Ruby code.

To run your Ruby script using JRuby, you normally enter jruby at your terminal prompt. (Depending on how you installed JRuby, the standard ruby command might be remapped to launch JRuby.) Figure 10-2 shows how this command works at a high level.

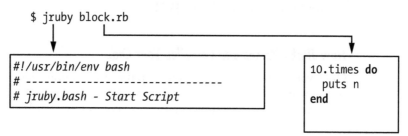

Figure 10-2: The jruby command actually maps to a shell script.

Unlike the ruby command, the jruby command doesn't map to a binary executable. It refers to a shell script that executes the java command. Figure 10-3 shows a simplified view of the command JRuby uses to launch Java.

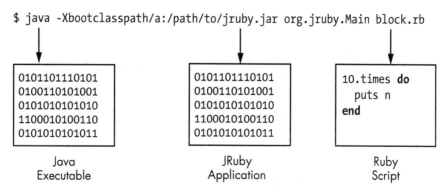

Figure 10-3: A simplified version of the command JRuby uses to launch the JVM

Notice in Figure 10-3 that JRuby executes your Ruby script using a binary executable known as the *Java Virtual Machine (JVM)*. Like the standard Ruby executable, the JVM is written in C and compiled into a binary executable. The JVM runs Java applications, while MRI runs Ruby applications.

Notice, too, that in the center of Figure 10-3 one of the parameters to the java program, *-Xbootclasspath*, specifies an additional library, or collection, of compiled Java code to make available to the new program: *jruby.jar*. The JRuby Java application is contained inside *jruby.jar*. Finally, on the right, you see the text file containing your Ruby code again.

In sum, here's what happens when standard Ruby and JRuby launch your Ruby programs:

- When you run a Ruby script using MRI, you launch a binary executable, originally written in C, that directly compiles and executes your Ruby script. This is the standard version of Ruby.
- When you run a Ruby script using JRuby, you launch a binary executable, the JVM, which executes the JRuby Java application. This Java application, in turn, parses, compiles, and executes your Ruby script while running inside the JVM.

How JRuby Parses and Compiles Your Code

Once you launch JRuby, it needs to parse and compile your code. To do this, it uses a parser generator, just as MRI does. Figure 10-4 shows a high-level overview of the JRuby parsing and compiling process.

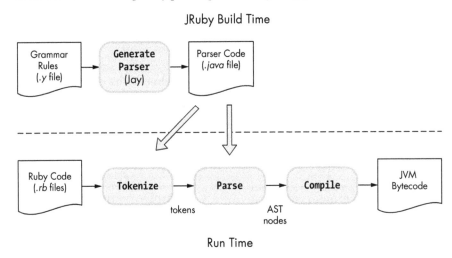

Figure 10-4: JRuby uses a parser generator called Jay.

Just as MRI uses Bison, JRuby uses a parser generator called *Jay* during the JRuby build process to create the code that will parse your Ruby code. Jay is very similar to Bison, except that it's written in Java instead of C. At run time, JRuby tokenizes and parses your Ruby code using the generated parser. As with MRI, this process produces an abstract syntax tree (AST).

Once JRuby parses your code and produces an AST, it compiles your code. However, instead of producing YARV instructions as MRI does, JRuby produces a series of instructions, known as *Java bytecode* instructions, that the JVM can execute. Figure 10-5 shows a high-level comparison of how MRI and JRuby process your Ruby code.

The left side of the figure shows how your Ruby code changes when you execute it with MRI. MRI converts your code into tokens, then into AST nodes, and finally into YARV instructions. The *Interpret* arrow indicates that the MRI executable reads the YARV instructions and interprets, or executes, them. (You don't write the C or machine language code; that work is done for you.)

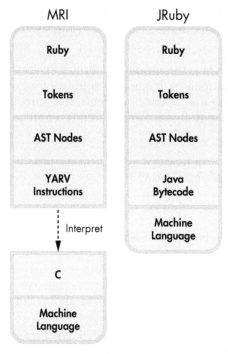

Figure 10-5: The different forms your Ruby code takes inside MRI (left) and JRuby (right)

The high-level overview at the right side of the figure shows how JRuby handles your Ruby code internally. The boxes in the one large rectangle show the different forms your code takes as JRuby executes it. You can see that, like MRI, JRuby first converts your code into tokens and later into AST nodes. But then MRI and JRuby diverge: JRuby compiles the AST nodes into Java bytecode instructions, which the JVM can execute. In addition, the JVM can convert the Java bytecode into machine language using a JIT compiler, which speeds up your program even more because executing machine language is faster than executing Java bytecode. (We'll look at the JIT compiler in more detail in Experiment 10-1.)

How JRuby Executes Your Code

We've seen that JRuby tokenizes and parses your code almost the same way that MRI does. And just as MRI Ruby 1.9 and 2.0 compile your code into YARV instructions, JRuby compiles it into Java bytecode instructions.

But that's where the similarity ends: MRI and JRuby use two very different virtual machines to execute your code. Standard Ruby uses YARV, but JRuby uses the JVM to execute your program.

The whole point of building a Ruby interpreter with Java is to be able to execute Ruby programs using the JVM. The ability to use the JVM is important for two reasons:

Environmental   The JVM allows you to use Ruby on servers, in applications, and in IT organizations where previously you could not run Ruby at all.

Technical   The JVM is the product of almost 20 years of intense research and development. It contains sophisticated solutions for many difficult computer science problems, like garbage collection and multithreading. Ruby can often run faster and more reliably on the JVM.

To get a better sense of how this works, let's see how JRuby executes the simple Ruby script *simple.rb* in Listing 10-1.

```
puts 2+2
```

Listing 10-1: A one-line Ruby program (simple.rb)

First, JRuby tokenizes and parses this Ruby code into an AST node structure. Next, it iterates through the AST nodes and converts your Ruby into Java bytecode. Use the --bytecode option, as shown in Listing 10-2, to see this bytecode for yourself.

```
$ jruby --bytecode simple.rb
```

Listing 10-2: JRuby's --bytecode option displays the Java bytecode your Ruby code is compiled into.

As the output of this command is complex, I won't dig into it here, but Figure 10-6 summarizes how JRuby compiles and executes this script.

At the left of this figure, you see the code puts 2+2. The large downward pointing arrow indicates that JRuby converts this code into a series of Java bytecode instructions that implement a Java class called simple (after the script's filename). The class simple extends AbstractScript notation is Java code; here, it declares a new Java class called simple, which uses AbstractScript as a superclass.

The simple class is a Java version of our Ruby code that adds 2 + 2 and prints the sum. The simple Java class does the same thing using Java. Inside simple, JRuby creates a Java method called __file__ that executes the 2+2 code as indicated with the inner __file__ rectangle at the bottom of the figure. The method rectangle <init> is the constructor for the simple class.

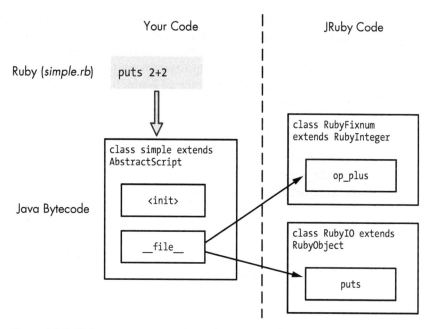

Figure 10-6: JRuby converts your Ruby code into Java classes.

At the right of Figure 10-6, you see a small part of JRuby's library of Ruby classes. These are Ruby's built-in classes, such as Fixnum, String, and Array. MRI implements these classes using C. When your code calls a method from one of these classes, the method dispatch process uses the CFUNC method type. However, JRuby implements all of the built-in Ruby classes using Java code. On the right side of Figure 10-6, you see two built-in Ruby methods that our code calls.

- First, your code adds 2 + 2, using the + method of the Ruby Fixnum class. JRuby implements the Ruby Fixnum class using a Java class called RubyFixnum. In this example, your code calls the op_plus Java method in this RubyFixnum class.

- To print the sum, the code calls the puts method of the built-in Ruby IO class (actually via the Kernel module). JRuby implements this in a similar way, using a Java class called RubyIO.

Implementing Ruby Classes with Java Classes

As you know, standard Ruby is implemented internally using C, which doesn't support the notion of object-oriented programming. C code can't use objects, classes, methods, or inheritance the way that Ruby code does.

However, JRuby is implemented in Java, an object-oriented programming language. While not as flexible and powerful as Ruby itself, Java does support writing classes, creating objects as instances of those classes, and relating one class to another through inheritance, which means that JRuby's implementation of Ruby is also object oriented.

JRuby implements Ruby objects with Java objects. To get a better idea of what this means, see Figure 10-7, which compares Ruby code with MRI C structures.

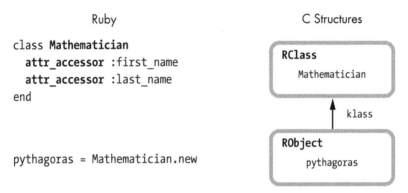

Figure 10-7: MRI implements objects and classes using C structures.

Internally Ruby creates an `RClass` C structure for each class and an `RObject` structure for each object. Ruby tracks the class for each object using the `klass` pointer in the `RObject` structure. Figure 10-7 shows one `RClass` for the `Mathematician` class and one `RObject` for `pythagoras`, an instance of `Mathematician`.

Figure 10-8 shows that the situation is very similar in JRuby, at least at first glance.

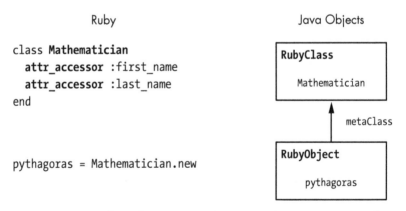

Figure 10-8: Internally, JRuby represents objects using the RubyObject Java class and classes using the RubyClass Java class.

On the left side of the figure, we see the same Ruby code. On the right are two Java objects, one an instance of the `RubyObject` Java class and the other an instance of the `RubyClass` Java class. JRuby's implementation of Ruby objects and classes closely resembles MRI's, but JRuby uses Java objects instead of using C structures. JRuby uses the names RubyObject and RubyClass because these Java objects represent your Ruby object and class.

But when we look a bit closer, things aren't so straightforward. Because RubyObject is a Java class, JRuby can use inheritance to simplify its internal implementation. In fact, the superclass of RubyObject is RubyBasicObject. This reflects how the Ruby classes are related, as we can see by calling the ancestors method on Object.

```
p Object.ancestors
 => [Object, Kernel, BasicObject]
```

Calling ancestors returns an array containing all the classes and modules in the superclass chain for the receiver. Here, we see that Object's superclass is the Kernel module and its superclass is BasicObject. JRuby uses the same pattern for its internal Java class hierarchy, as shown in Figure 10-9.

```
public class RubyBasicObject
              ↑
public class RubyObject extends RubyBasicObject
```

Figure 10-9: RubyBasicObject is the superclass of the RubyObject Java class.

The Kernel module aside, we can see that JRuby's internal Java class hierarchy reflects the Ruby class hierarchy that it implements. This similarity is made possible by Java's object-oriented design.

Now for a second example. Let's use ancestors again to show the superclasses for the Class Ruby class.

```
p Class.ancestors
 => [Class, Module, Object, Kernel, BasicObject]
```

Here, we see that the superclass of Class is Module, its superclass is Object, and so on. And as we would expect, JRuby's Java code uses the same design internally (see Figure 10-10).

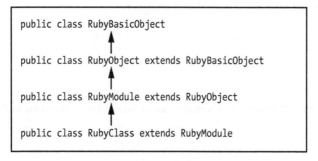

Figure 10-10: JRuby's internal Java class hierarchy for RubyClass

Experiment 10-1: Monitoring JRuby's Just-in-Time Compiler

I mentioned earlier that JRuby can speed up your Ruby code by using a JIT compiler. JRuby always translates your Ruby program into Java bytecode instructions, which the JVM can compile into machine language that your computer's microprocessor can execute directly. In this experiment we'll see when this happens and measure how much it speeds up your code.

Experiment Code

Listing 10-3 shows a Ruby program that prints out 10 random numbers between 1 and 100.

```
❶ array = (1..100).to_a
❷ 10.times do
❸   sample = array.sample
    puts sample
  end
```

Listing 10-3: A sample program for testing JRuby's JIT behavior (jit.rb)

At ❶ we create an array with 100 elements: 1 through 100. Then, at ❷ we iterate over the following block 10 times. Inside this block, we use the sample method at ❸ to pick a random value from the array and print it. When we run this code, we get the output shown in Listing 10-4.

```
$ jruby jit.rb
87
88
69
5
38
--snip--
```

Listing 10-4: The output from Listing 10-3

Now let's remove the puts statement and increase the number of iterations. (Removing the output will make the experiment more manageable.) Listing 10-5 shows the updated program.

```
  array = (1..100).to_a
  1000.times do
❶   sample = array.sample
  end
```

Listing 10-5: We remove puts and increase the number of iterations to 1,000.

Using the -J-XX:+PrintCompilation Option

Of course, if we run the program now, we won't see any output because we've removed puts. Let's run the program again—this time using a debug flag (shown in Listing 10-6) to display information about what the JVM's JIT compiler is doing.

```
$ jruby -J-XX:+PrintCompilation jit.rb
    101   1        java.lang.String::hashCode (64 bytes)
    144   2        java.util.Properties$LineReader::readLine (452 bytes)
    173   3        sun.nio.cs.UTF_8$Decoder::decodeArrayLoop (553 bytes)
    200   4        java.lang.String::charAt (33 bytes)
--snip--
```

Listing 10-6: The output generated by the -J-XX:+PrintCompilation option

Here, we use the -J option for JRuby and pass the XX:+PrintCompilation option to the underlying JVM application. PrintCompilation causes the JVM to display the information you see in Listing 10-6. The line java.lang .String::hashCode means that the JVM compiled the hashCode method of the String Java class into machine language. The other values show technical information about the JIT process (101 is a time stamp, 1 is a compilation ID, and 64 bytes is the size of the bytecode snippet that was compiled).

The goal of this experiment is to validate the hypothesis that Listing 10-5 should run faster once the JVM's JIT compiler converts it into machine language. Notice that Listing 10-5 has just one line of Ruby code inside the loop at ❶ that calls array.sample. Therefore, we should expect our Ruby program to finish noticeably faster once the JIT compiles JRuby's implementation of Array#sample into machine language because Array#sample is called so many times.

Because the output in Listing 10-6 is quite long and complex, we'll use grep to search the output for occurrences of org.jruby.RubyArray.

```
$ jruby -J-XX:+PrintCompilation jit.rb | grep org.jruby.RubyArray
```

The result is no output. None of the lines in the PrintCompilation output match the name org.jruby.RubyArray, which means the JIT compiler is not converting the Array#sample method into machine language. It doesn't do this conversion because the JVM only runs the JIT compiler to compile Java bytecode instructions that your program executes numerous times—areas of bytecode instructions known as *hot spots*. The JVM spends extra time compiling hot spots because they are called so many times. To prove this, we can increase the number of iterations to 100,000 and repeat our test, as shown in Listing 10-7.

```
array = (1..100).to_a
100000.times do
```

```
    sample = array.sample
end
```

Listing 10-7: Increasing the number of iterations should trigger the JIT compiler to convert Array#sample to machine language.

When we repeat the same jruby command again with grep, we see the output shown in Listing 10-8.

❶ $ jruby -J-XX:+PrintCompilation jit.rb | grep org.jruby.RubyArray
```
    1809 165        org.jruby.RubyArray::safeArrayRef (11 bytes)
    1810 166  !     org.jruby.RubyArray::safeArrayRef (12 bytes)
    1811 167        org.jruby.RubyArray::eltOk (16 bytes)
    1927 203        org.jruby.RubyArray$INVOKER$i$0$2$sample::call (36 bytes)
❷  1928 204  !     org.jruby.RubyArray::sample (834 bytes)
    1930 205        org.jruby.RubyArray::randomReal (10 bytes)
```

Listing 10-8: The output after running Listing 10-7 with -J-XX:+PrintCompilation piped to grep

Because we used grep org.jruby.RubyArray at ❶, we see only Java class names that match the text org.jruby.RubyArray. At ❷ we can see that the JIT compiler compiled the Array#sample method because we see the text org.jruby.RubyArray::sample.

Does JIT Speed Up Your JRuby Program?

Now to see if the JIT sped things up. Based on a command-line parameter— ARGV[0]—which I save in iterations at ❶, Listing 10-9 measures the amount of time it takes to call Array#sample a given number of times.

```
require 'benchmark'

❶ iterations = ARGV[0].to_i

Benchmark.bm do |bench|
  array = (1..100).to_a
  bench.report("#{iterations} iterations") do
    iterations.times do
      sample = array.sample
    end
  end
end
```

Listing 10-9: Sample code for benchmarking JIT performance

By running this listing as shown below, we can measure how long it takes to execute the loop 100 times, for example.

```
$ jruby jit.rb 100
```

Figure 10-11 shows the results for 100 to 100 million iterations using both JRuby and MRI.

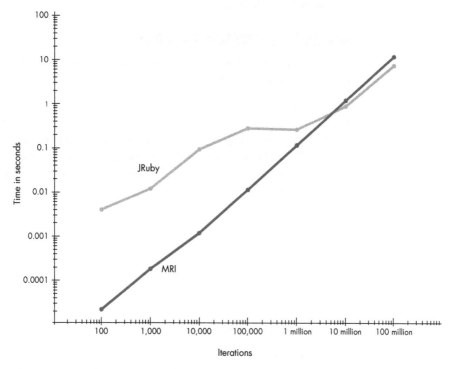

Figure 10-11: JRuby vs. MRI performance. Time is shown in seconds vs. number of iterations (using JRuby 1.7.5 and Java 1.6; MRI Ruby 2.0).

The graph for MRI is more or less a straight line moving up to the right. This means it always takes Ruby 2.0 about the same amount of time to execute the Array#sample method. The results for JRuby, however, are not so simple. At left you can see that for fewer than 100,000 iterations, JRuby takes longer to execute Listing 10-9. (The chart uses a logarithmic scale, so the absolute time differences on the left side are small.) However, once we reach about 1 million iterations, JRuby speeds up dramatically and starts to take less time to execute Array#sample.

Ultimately for many, many iterations, JRuby is faster than MRI. But what's important here is not simply that JRuby might be faster but that its performance characteristics vary. The longer your code runs, the longer the JVM has to optimize it, and the faster things will be.

Strings in JRuby and MRI

We've learned how JRuby executes bytecode instructions, passing control between your code and a library of Ruby objects implemented with Java. Now we'll take a closer look at this library, specifically at how JRuby implements the String class. How do JRuby and MRI implement strings? Where do they save the string data you use in your Ruby code, and how do their implementations compare? Let's begin to answer these questions by looking at how MRI implements strings.

How JRuby and MRI Save String Data

This code saves a famous quote from Pythagoras in a local variable. But where does this string go?

```
str = "Geometry is knowledge of the eternally existent."
```

Recall from Chapter 5 that MRI uses different C structures to implement built-in classes, such as RRegexp, RArray, and RHash, as well as RString, which saves your strings. Figure 10-12 shows how MRI represents the Geometry... string internally.

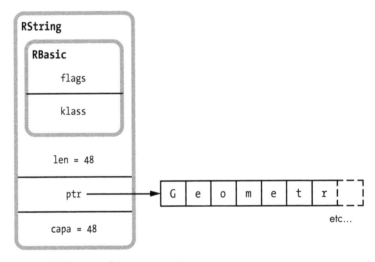

Figure 10-12: Part of the RString C structure

Notice that MRI saves the actual string data in a separate buffer, or section of memory, shown on the right. The RString structure itself contains a pointer to this buffer, ptr. Also notice that RString contains two other integer values: len, or the length of the string (48 in this example), and capa, or the capacity of the data buffer (also 48). The size of the data buffer can be longer than the string, in which case capa would be larger than len. (This would be the case if you executed code that reduced the length of the string.)

Now let's consider JRuby. Figure 10-13 shows how JRuby represents this string internally. JRuby uses the Java class RubyString to represent strings in your Ruby code, following the naming pattern we saw above with RubyObject and RubyClass. RubyString uses another class to track the actual string data: ByteList. This lower-level code tracks a separate data buffer (called bytes) similar to the way that the RString structure does so in MRI. ByteList also stores the length of the string in the realSize instance variable.

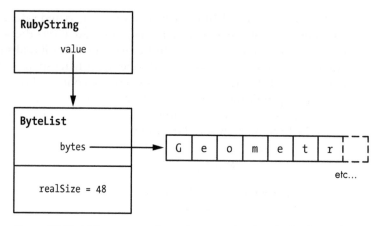

Figure 10-13: JRuby uses two Java objects and a data buffer for each string.

Copy-on-Write

Internally, both JRuby and MRI use an optimization called *copy-on-write* for strings and other data. This trick allows two identical string values to share the same data buffer, which saves both memory and time because Ruby avoids making separate copies of the same string data unnecessarily.

For example, suppose we use the dup method to copy a string.

```
str = "Geometry is knowledge of the eternally existent."
str2 = str.dup
```

Does JRuby have to copy the Geometry is... text from one string object to another? No. Figure 10-14 shows how JRuby shares the string data across two different string objects.

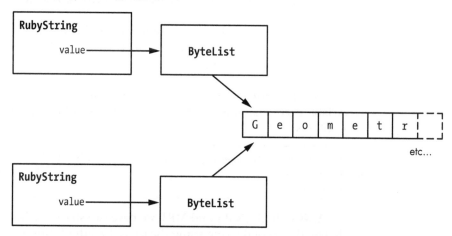

Figure 10-14: Two JRuby string objects can share the same data buffer.

When we call dup, JRuby creates new RubyString and ByteList Java objects, but it doesn't copy the actual string data. Instead, it sets the second ByteList object to point to the same data buffer used by the original string. Now we have two sets of Java objects but only one underlying string value, as shown on the right of the figure. Because strings can contain thousands of bytes or more, this optimization can often save a tremendous amount of memory.

MRI uses the same trick, although in a slightly more complex way. Figure 10-15 shows how standard Ruby shares strings.

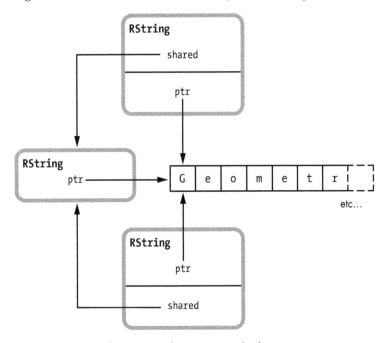

Figure 10-15: MRI shares strings by creating a third RString structure.

Like JRuby, MRI shares the underlying string data. However, when you copy a string in standard MRI Ruby, it creates a third RString structure and then sets both the original RString and new RString to refer to it using the shared pointer.

In either case, we have a problem. What if we change one of the string variables? For example, suppose we convert one of the strings to uppercase as follows:

```
  str = "Geometry is knowledge of the eternally existent."
❶ str2 = str.dup
❷ str2.upcase!
```

At ❶ in both JRuby and MRI, we have two shared strings, but at ❷ I change the second string using the upcase! method. Now the two strings differ, which means that Ruby clearly can't continue to share the underlying string buffer or upcase! would change both strings. We can see the strings are now different by displaying the string values.

```
p str
 => "Geometry is knowledge of the eternally existent."
p str2
 => "GEOMETRY IS KNOWLEDGE OF THE ETERNALLY EXISTENT."
```

At some point, Ruby must have separated these two strings, creating a
new data buffer. This is what the phrase *copy-on-write* means: Both MRI and
JRuby create a new copy of the string data buffer when you write to one of
the strings.

Experiment 10-2: Measuring Copy-on-Write Performance

In this experiment we'll collect evidence that this extra copy operation
really occurs when we write to a shared string. First, we'll create a simple,
nonshared string and write to it. Then we'll create two shared strings and
write to one of them. If copy-on-write really occurs, then writing to a shared
string should take a bit longer because Ruby has to create a new copy of
the string before writing.

Creating a Unique, Nonshared String

Let's begin by creating our example string again, str. Initially Ruby can't
possibly share str with anything else because there is only one string. We'll
use str for our baseline performance measurement.

```
str = "Geometry is knowledge of the eternally existent."
```

But as it turns out, Ruby shares str immediately! To see why, we'll examine the YARV instructions that MRI uses to execute this code, as shown in
Listing 10-10.

```
code = <<END
str = "Geometry is knowledge of the eternally existent."
END

puts RubyVM::InstructionSequence.compile(code).disasm
== disasm: <RubyVM::InstructionSequence:<compiled>@<compiled>>==========
local table (size: 2, argc: 0 [opts: 0, rest: -1, post: 0, block: -1] s1)
❶ [ 2] str
  0000 trace            1                                          (   1)
❷ 0002 putstring        "Geometry is knowledge of the eternally existent."
❸ 0004 dup
❹ 0005 setlocal_OP__WC__0 2
  0007 leave
```

*Listing 10-10: MRI Ruby uses a dup YARV instruction internally when you use a literal
string constant.*

Reading the YARV instructions above carefully, we see at ❷ that Ruby puts the string onto the stack using putstring. This YARV instruction internally copies the string argument to the stack, creating a shared copy already. At ❸ Ruby uses dup to create yet another shared copy of the string to use as an argument for setlocal. Finally, at ❹ setlocal_OP__WC__0 2 saves this string into the str variable, shown as [2] in the local table ❶.

Figure 10-16 summarizes this process.

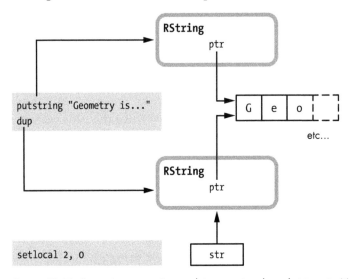

Figure 10-16: Executing putstring and dup creates shared strings in MRI.

On the left are the YARV instructions putstring, dup, and setlocal. On the right are the RString structures that these instructions create, as well as the underlying shared string data. As I just mentioned, putstring in fact copies the string constant from a third RString left off the diagram, meaning the string is actually shared a third time.

Because Ruby initially shares strings created from constant values, we need to create our string differently by concatenating two strings together as follows:

```
str = "This string is not shared" + " and so can be modified faster."
```

The result of this concatenation will be a new, unique string. Ruby will not share its string data with any other string objects.

Experiment Code

Let's take some measurements. Listing 10-11 shows the code for this experiment.

```
require 'benchmark'

ITERATIONS = 1000000

Benchmark.bm do |bench|
  bench.report("test") do
    ITERATIONS.times do
❶     str = "This string is not shared" + " and so can be modified faster."
❷     str2 = "But this string is shared" + " so Ruby will need to copy it
                before writing to it."
❸     str3 = str2.dup
❹     str3[3] = 'x'
    end
  end
end
```

Listing 10-11: Measuring a delay for copy-on-write

Before we run this test, let's walk through this code. At ❶ we create a unique, unshared string by concatenating two strings. This is str. Then at ❷ we create a second unshared string, str2. But at ❸ we use dup to create a copy of this string, str3, and now str2 and str3 share the same value.

Visualizing Copy-on-Write

At ❹ in Listing 10-11 we change the fourth character in str3 using the code str3[3] = 'x'. But here Ruby can't change the character in str3 without changing str2 as well, as shown in Figure 10-17.

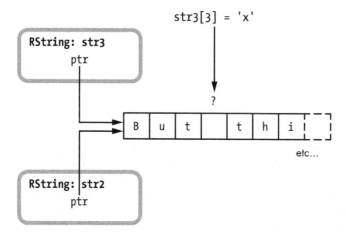

Figure 10-17: Ruby can't change str3 without also changing str2.

Ruby has to make a separate copy of str3 first, as shown in Figure 10-18.

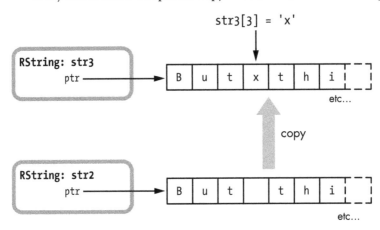

Figure 10-18: Ruby copies the string into a new buffer for str3 before writing to it.

Now Ruby can write into the new buffer for str3 without affecting str2.

Modifying a Shared String Is Slower

When we execute Listing 10-11, the benchmark library measures how long it takes to run the inner block 1 million times. This block creates str, str2, and str3 and then modifies str3. On my laptop, benchmark yields a measurement of about 1.87 seconds.

Next, let's change str3[3] = 'x' at ❹ to modify str instead.

```
#str3[3] = 'x'
str[3] = 'x'
```

Now we're modifying the unshared, unique string instead of the shared string. Running the test again yields a result of about 1.69 seconds, or about 9.5 percent less than the time benchmark reported for the shared string. As expected, it takes slightly less time to modify a unique string than it does to modify a shared one.

The graph in Figure 10-19 shows my cumulative results averaged over 10 different observations for both MRI and JRuby. On the left side of the graph are my average measurements for MRI. The bar on the far left represents the time required to modify the shared string, str3, and the right MRI bar shows how long it took to modify the unique string, str. The two bars on the right side exhibit the same pattern for JRuby, but the difference in the height of the bars is much less. Apparently, the JVM can make a new copy of the string faster than MRI.

But there's more: Notice that overall JRuby ran the experiment code in 60 percent less time. That is, it was 2.5 times faster than MRI! Just as in Experiment 10-1, we must be seeing the JVM optimizations, such as JIT compilation, speed up JRuby when compared to MRI.

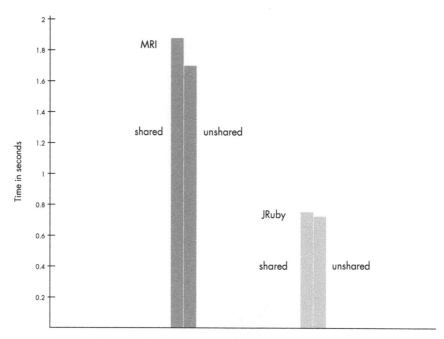

Figure 10-19: Both MRI and JRuby show a delay for copy-on-write (seconds).

Summary

In this chapter we took a look at JRuby, a version of Ruby written in Java. We saw how the jruby command launches the JVM, passing *jruby.jar* as a parameter. We explored how JRuby parses and compiles our code, and learned in Experiment 10-1 how the JVM can compile hot spots, or frequently executed snippets of Java bytecode, into machine language. Our results from Experiment 10-1 showed that compiling hot spots dramatically improves performance, allowing JRuby to run even faster than MRI in some cases.

In the second half of this chapter, we learned how MRI and JRuby represent our string data internally. We discovered that both versions of Ruby use copy-on-write optimization, sharing string data between different string objects when possible. Finally, in Experiment 10-2 we proved that copy-on-write actually occurred in both JRuby and MRI.

JRuby is a very powerful and clever implementation of Ruby: By running your Ruby code using the Java platform, you can benefit from the many years of research, development, tuning, and testing that have been invested in the JVM. The JVM is one of the most popular, mature, and powerful software platforms in use today. It's being used not only by Java and JRuby but also by many other software languages, such as Clojure, Scala, and Jython, to name a few. By using this shared platform, JRuby can take advantage of the speed, robustness, and diversity of the Java platform—and it can do this for free!

JRuby is a groundbreaking piece of technology with which every Ruby developer should be familiar.

Rubinius uses Ruby to implement Ruby.

11

RUBINIUS: RUBY IMPLEMENTED WITH RUBY

Like JRuby, Rubinius is an alternative implementation of Ruby. Much of Rubinius's internal source code is written in Ruby itself instead of in only C or Java. Rubinius implements built-in classes, such as Array, String, and Integer, just as you would—with Ruby code!

This design offers a unique opportunity for you to learn about Ruby internals. If you aren't sure how a particular Ruby feature or method works, you can read the Ruby code inside Rubinius to find out, without special knowledge of C or Java programming.

Rubinius also includes a sophisticated virtual machine written in C++. This machine executes your Ruby program and, like JRuby, supports JIT and true concurrency and uses a sophisticated garbage collection algorithm.

This chapter starts with a high-level overview of Rubinius and an example of how to use backtrace output to dig through the Rubinius source code. Later in the chapter, we'll learn how Rubinius and MRI implement the Array class, including how Ruby saves data into an array and what happens when you remove an element from an array.

The Rubinius Kernel and Virtual Machine

To run a Ruby program using Rubinius (see Figure 11-1), you typically use the ruby command (as with MRI) or rbx because the ruby command is actually a symbolic link to the executable *rbx* in Rubinius.

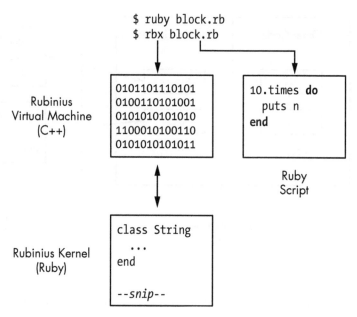

```
$ ruby block.rb
$ rbx block.rb
```

Rubinius
Virtual Machine
(C++)

```
0101101110101
0100110101001
0101010101010
1100010100110
0101010101011
```

```
10.times do
  puts n
end
```

Ruby
Script

Rubinius Kernel
(Ruby)

```
class String
  ...
end

--snip--
```

Figure 11-1: Rubinius consists of a C++ virtual machine and a Ruby kernel.

As with MRI, you launch Rubinius using an executable that reads and executes the Ruby program specified on the command line. But the Rubinius executable is completely different from the standard Ruby executable. As the preceding figure shows, Rubinius consists of two major pieces:

The Rubinius kernel   This is the part of Rubinius written in Ruby. It implements a lot of the language, including the definitions of many built-in, core classes, such as String and Array. The Rubinius kernel is compiled into bytecode instructions that are installed onto your computer.

The Rubinius virtual machine   The Rubinius virtual machine is written in C++. It executes the bytecode instructions from the Rubinius kernel and performs a range of other low-level tasks, such as garbage collection. The Rubinius executable contains a compiled, machine-language version of this virtual machine.

Figure 11-2 takes a closer look at Rubinius's virtual machine and kernel. The Rubinius kernel contains a set of Ruby classes, such as String, Array, and Object, as well as other Ruby classes that perform various tasks, such as compiling or loading code. The Rubinius virtual machine at the left of the figure is the *rbx* executable that you launch from the command line. The C++ virtual machine contains code to perform garbage collection, just-in-time compilation (and many other tasks), as well as additional code for built-in classes, such as String or Array. In fact, as indicated by the arrows, each Ruby class built into Rubinius consists of both C++ and Ruby code working together. Rubinius defines certain methods using Ruby and other methods using C++.

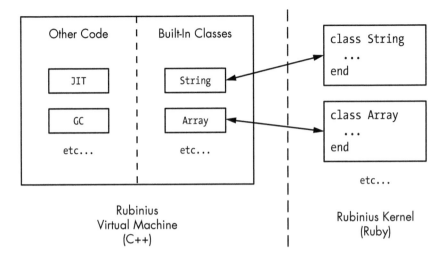

Figure 11-2: A closer view of Rubinius internals

Why implement Ruby using two languages? Because C++ speeds up Rubinius programs and allows them to interact with the operating system directly at a low level. The use of C++ instead of C also allows Rubinius to use an elegant object-oriented design internally. And the use of Ruby to implement built-in classes and other features makes it easy for Ruby developers to read and understand much of the Rubinius source code.

Tokenization and Parsing

Rubinius processes your Ruby program in much the same way that MRI does, as shown in Figure 11-3.

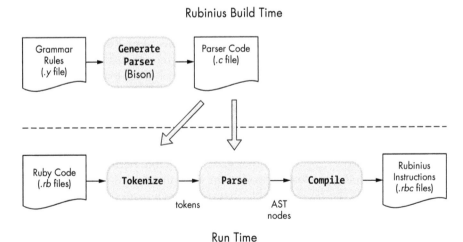

Figure 11-3: How Rubinius processes your code

Rubinius generates an LALR parser using Bison during its build process, just as MRI does. When you run your program, the parser converts your code into a token stream, an abstract syntax tree (AST) structure, and then a series of high-level virtual machine instructions called *Rubinius instructions*. Figure 11-4 compares the forms that your code takes inside MRI and Rubinius.

At first, Rubinius and MRI work similarly, but instead of interpreting your code as MRI does, Rubinius uses a compiler framework called the Low-Level Virtual Machine (LLVM) to compile your code again into lower-level instructions. LLVM, in turn, may compile these instructions all the way to machine language, using a JIT compiler.

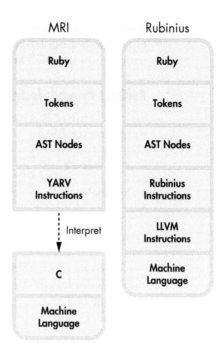

Figure 11-4: How MRI and Rubinius transform your code internally

Using Ruby to Compile Ruby

One of the most fascinating aspects of Rubinius is how it implements a Ruby compiler with a combination of Ruby and C++. When you run a program using Rubinius, your code is processed by both C++ and Ruby code, as shown in Figure 11-5.

At the top left of the diagram, Rubinius, like MRI, uses C code to parse Ruby code with a series of grammar rules. At right, Rubinius starts to process your Ruby program using Ruby code, representing each node in the AST with an instance of a Ruby class. Each Ruby AST node knows how to generate

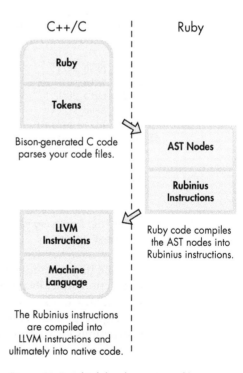

Figure 11-5: A high-level overview of how Rubinius compiles your code

Rubinius instructions for its piece of your program during compilation. Finally, at bottom left, the LLVM framework further compiles the Rubinius instructions into LLVM instructions and ultimately into machine language.

Rubinius Bytecode Instructions

To get a sense of Rubinius instructions, let's run a short program using Rubinius (see Listing 11-1).

```
$ cat simple.rb
puts 2+2
$ rbx simple.rb
4
```

Listing 11-1: Using Rubinius to calculate 2 + 2 = 4 (simple.rb)

When we rerun *simple.rb* using the rbx compile command with the -B option, Rubinius displays the bytecode instructions its compiler generates, as shown in Listing 11-2.

```
$ rbx compile simple.rb -B
============= :__script__ ==============
Arguments:   0 required, 0 post, 0 total
Arity:       0
Locals:      0
Stack size:  3
Literals:    2: :+, :puts
Lines to IP: 1: 0..12

  0000:  push_self
  0001:  meta_push_2
  0002:  meta_push_2
❶ 0003:  send_stack              :+, 1
  0006:  allow_private
❷ 0007:  send_stack              :puts, 1
  0010:  pop
  0011:  push_true
  0012:  ret
  ----------------------------------------
```

Listing 11-2: Displaying Rubinius bytecode instructions using the rbx compile command with the -B option

The instructions vaguely resemble MRI's YARV instructions. Each instruction typically pushes a value onto an internal stack, operates on stack values, or executes a method such as the + at ❶ or puts at ❷.

Figure 11-6 shows both the Ruby code and corresponding Rubinius instructions for *simple.rb* and part of the Kernel module.

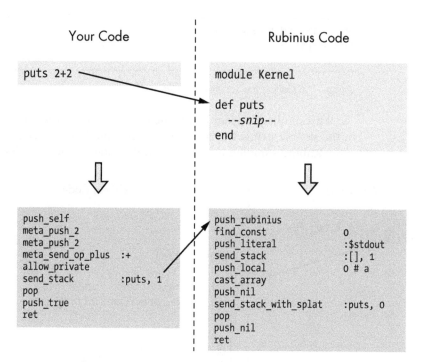

Your Code   Rubinius Code

```
puts 2+2
```

```
module Kernel

def puts
  --snip--
end
```

```
push_self
meta_push_2
meta_push_2
meta_send_op_plus    :+
allow_private
send_stack           :puts, 1
pop
push_true
ret
```

```
push_rubinius
find_const           0
push_literal         :$stdout
send_stack           :[], 1
push_local           0 # a
cast_array
push_nil
send_stack_with_splat    :puts, 0
pop
push_nil
ret
```

Figure 11-6: The puts method in Rubinius is implemented with Ruby code.

You can see Ruby code at the top of the figure: the puts 2+2 code at left and Rubinius's definition of the puts method at right. Rubinius implements built-in Ruby classes, such as the Kernel module, in Ruby; therefore, when we call the puts method, Rubinius simply passes control to the Ruby code for the Kernel#puts method contained inside the Rubinius kernel.

The lower portion of the figure shows the Rubinius instructions into which the Ruby code is compiled. At left are the instructions for puts 2+2, and at right is the compiled version of the Kernel#puts method. Rubinius compiles its built-in Ruby code and your Ruby code in the same manner (except that Rubinius compiles the built-in Ruby code during the Rubinius build process).

Ruby and C++ Working Together

In order to handle certain low-level technical details and to speed things up, Rubinius uses C++ code in its virtual machine to help implement built-in classes and modules. That is, it uses both Ruby and C++ to implement the language's core classes.

To understand how this works, let's execute this short Ruby script in Rubinius (see Listing 11-3).

```
str = "The quick brown fox..."
puts str[4]
 => q
```

Listing 11-3: Calling the String#[] method

This simple program prints the fifth character (the letter *q* at index 4) in the sample string. Because the String#[] method is part of a built-in Ruby class, Rubinius implements it using Ruby code, as shown in Figure 11-7.

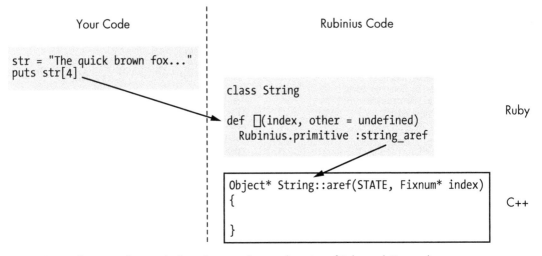

Figure 11-7: Rubinius implements built-in classes with a combination of Ruby and C++ code.

On the left of the figure is the Ruby script that prints the letter *q*. On the right is the Ruby code that Rubinius uses to implement the String#[] method, taken from a Rubinius source code file called *string.rb* (named after the String class). (We'll learn how to find Rubinius source code files in Experiment 11-1.)

Notice that the beginning of String#[] starts with the method call Rubinius.primitive. This indicates that Rubinius actually uses C++ code to implement this method; Rubinius.primitive is a directive that tells the Rubinius compiler to generate a call to the corresponding C++ code. The code that actually implements String#[] is a C++ method called String::aref, shown at the bottom right of Figure 11-7.

Implementing Ruby Objects with C++ Objects

Ruby's use of the object-oriented C++ allows its virtual machine to represent each Ruby object internally using a corresponding C++ object (see Figure 11-8).

Rubinius uses C++ objects the way that MRI uses the RClass and RObject C structures. When you define a class, Rubinius creates an instance of the Class C++ class. When you create a Ruby object, Rubinius creates an instance of the `Object` C++ class. A `klass_` pointer in the `pythagoras` object indicates it is an instance of `Mathematician`, just as the `klass` pointer in the `RObject` C structure does in MRI.

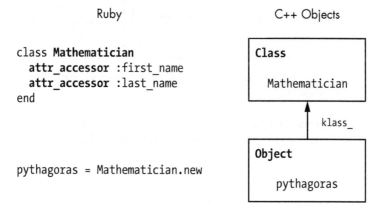

Figure 11-8: Rubinius represents classes and objects using C++ objects.

Experiment 11-1: Comparing Backtraces in MRI and Rubinius

Recall that Ruby displays a backtrace when an exception occurs in order to help you find the problem. Listing 11-4 shows a simple example.

```
10.times do |n|
  puts n
  raise "Stop Here"
end
```

Listing 11-4: A Ruby script that raises an exception

We call raise to tell Ruby to stop the first time it executes the block after displaying the value of the parameter n. Listing 11-5 shows the output from running Listing 11-4 with MRI.

```
$ ruby iterate.rb
0
iterate.rb:3:in 'block in <main>': Stop Here (RuntimeError)
    from iterate.rb:1:in 'times'
    from iterate.rb:1:in '<main>'
```

Listing 11-5: How MRI displays a backtrace for an exception

You probably see output like this many times while developing a Ruby program. However, one subtle detail is worth a closer look. Figure 11-9 shows a diagram of the MRI backtrace output.

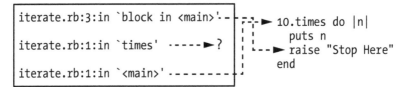

Figure 11-9: MRI displays where built-in CFUNC methods are called, not where they are defined.

Notice that line 3 of *iterate.rb*, containing the call to raise, is at the top of the call stack. At the bottom of the call stack, MRI displays iterate.rb:1, where the short script began.

Notice, too, that MRI's backtrace contains a broken link: *iterate.rb* doesn't contain a definition for the method times. Instead, MRI refers to the line of code that *calls* the times method: 10.times do. The actual times method is implemented with C code inside MRI—a CFUNC method. MRI displays the location of calls to CFUNC methods in backtraces, not the location of the actual C implementation of these methods.

Backtraces in Rubinius

Unlike MRI, Rubinius implements built-in methods using Ruby, not C. This implementation allows Rubinius to include accurate source file and line number information about built-in methods in backtraces. To demonstrate, let's run Listing 11-4 again using Rubinius. Listing 11-6 shows the result.

```
$ rbx iterate.rb
0
An exception occurred running iterate.rb
    Stop Here (RuntimeError)

Backtrace:
            { } in Object#__script__ at iterate.rb:3
                Integer(Fixnum)#times at kernel/common/integer.rb:83
                  Object#__script__ at iterate.rb:1
  Rubinius::CodeLoader#load_script at kernel/delta/codeloader.rb:68
  Rubinius::CodeLoader.load_script at kernel/delta/codeloader.rb:119
           Rubinius::Loader#script at kernel/loader.rb:645
             Rubinius::Loader#main at kernel/loader.rb:844
```

Listing 11-6: How Rubinius displays a backtrace for an exception

Rubinius displays much more information! To understand this output a bit better, see Figures 11-10 and 11-11.

At left in Figure 11-10 is a simplified version of the backtrace information Rubinius displayed while running *iterate.rb*. Rubinius displays the two lines in the backtrace corresponding to *iterate.rb* just as MRI does. But Rubinius also includes new entries in the Ruby call stack that correspond to Ruby source code files inside the Rubinius kernel. We can guess that the *loader.rb* and *codeloader.rb* files contain code that load and execute our script.

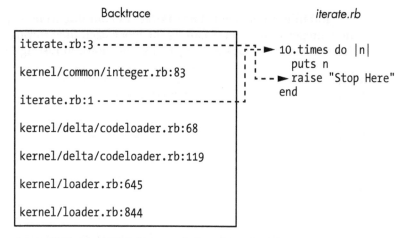

Figure 11-10: Like MRI, Rubinius includes information about your program in backtraces.

But the most interesting entry in the call stack is kernel/common/integer .rb:83. This entry tells us where the Integer#times method is implemented inside the Rubinius kernel, as shown in Figure 11-11.

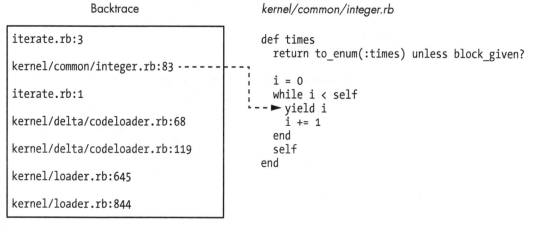

Figure 11-11: Rubinius includes information about its kernel in backtraces.

The backtrace information on the left of the figure is the same as that in Figure 11-10. The arrow points from the second level of the Ruby call stack to the code that calls the puts n block—the yield instruction in the Integer#times method.

Using Rubinius, *iterate.rb* becomes part of a larger Ruby program: the Rubinius kernel. When we call 10.times, Rubinius calls the Ruby code shown at the right, which then executes our block using the yield keyword on line 83.

The path kernel/common/integer.rb *refers to a location in the Rubinius source code tree. If you installed Rubinius using a binary installer, you'll need to download the source code from* http://rubini.us/ *or GitHub in order to read it.*

Rubinius implements `Integer#times` by counting from 0 up to the specified integer (minus one), calling the block each time through the loop. Let's take a closer look at `Integer#times`, as shown in Listing 11-7.

```
❶ def times
❷   return to_enum(:times) unless block_given?

❸   i = 0
❹   while i < self
❺     yield i
      i += 1
    end
❻   self
  end
```

Listing 11-7: The Rubinius implementation of Integer#times, *from* kernel/common/integer.rb

The definition of the `times` method starts at ❶. At ❷ Rubinius returns the result of `to_enum` if a block is not provided, as shown below. (The `to_enum` method returns a new enumerator object, which allows you to perform the enumeration later if you prefer.)

```
p 10.times
=> #<Enumerable::Enumerator:0x120 @generator=nil @args=[] @lookahead=[]
     @object=10 @iter=:times>
```

Rubinius continues to execute the rest of the method if you provide a block. At ❸ Rubinius creates a counter `i` and initializes it to 0. Next, it uses a while loop at ❹ to perform the iteration. Notice that the while loop condition `i < self` refers to the value of `self`. Inside `Integer#times`, `self` is set to the current integer object, or 10 in our script. At ❺ Rubinius yields to (calls) the given block, passing in the current value of `i`. This calls our `puts n` block. Finally, at ❻ Rubinius returns `self`, which means the return value of `10.times` will be 10.

Arrays in Rubinius and MRI

Arrays are so ubiquitous in Ruby that it's easy to take them for granted. But how do they work inside Ruby? Where does Ruby save objects that you place into an array, and how does it represent array objects internally? In the following sections, we'll look at the internal data structures that Rubinius and MRI use to hold values in an array.

Arrays Inside of MRI

Suppose you put the first six numbers from the Fibonacci sequence into an array.

```
fibonacci_sequence = [1, 1, 2, 3, 5, 8]
```

As Figure 11-12 illustrates, MRI creates a C structure for the array but saves its elements elsewhere.

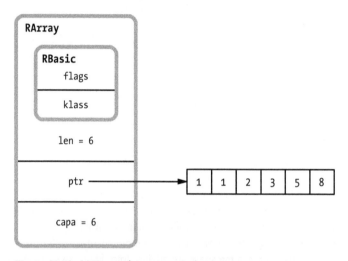

Figure 11-12: MRI uses the RArray C structure to represent arrays.

MRI uses one `RArray` structure to represent each array you create. Like `RString`, `RObject`, and other C structures, `RArray` uses the inner `RBasic` structure to hold the `klass` pointer and other technical information. (In this case, the `klass` pointer points to the `RClass` structure for the `Array` class.)

Below `RBasic` are a few additional values specific to arrays—`ptr`, `len`, and `capa`:

- `ptr` is a pointer to a memory segment Ruby allocates separately to store the array elements. The Fibonacci numbers appear in this memory segment at the right side of Figure 11-12.
- `len` is the length of the array—that is, the number of values saved in the separate memory segment.
- `capa` tracks the capacity of the memory segment. This number is often larger than `len`. MRI avoids continually resizing the memory segment each time you change the size of the array; instead, as you add array elements, it occasionally increases the size of the separate memory segment, each time allocating more memory than the new elements require.

Each value in the separate memory segment is actually a `VALUE` pointer to a Ruby object. In this case, the Fibonacci numbers would be saved directly inside the `VALUE` pointers because they are simple integers.

THE RARRAY C STRUCTURE DEFINITION

Listing 11-8 shows the definition of RArray from the MRI C source code.

```
#define RARRAY_EMBED_LEN_MAX 3
struct RArray {
  struct RBasic basic;
❶ union {
    struct {
❷     long len;
      union {
❸       long capa;
❹       VALUE shared;
      } aux;
❺     VALUE *ptr;
    } heap;
❻   VALUE ary[RARRAY_EMBED_LEN_MAX];
  } as;
};
```

Listing 11-8: The definition of RArray (from include/ruby/ruby.h)

This definition shows a few values that are missing from Figure 11-12. First, at ❶, notice that MRI uses a C union keyword to declare two alternative definitions for RArray. The first, an inner struct, defines len at ❷, capa at ❸, shared at ❹, and ptr at ❺. As with strings, MRI uses copy-on-write optimization with arrays, allowing two or more arrays to share the same underlying data. For arrays that share data, the shared value at ❹ refers to another RArray that contains the shared data.

The second half of the union at ❻ defines ary, a C array of VALUE pointers in RArray. This is an optimization that allows MRI to save the array data for arrays with three or fewer elements inside the RArray structure itself, avoiding the need to allocate the separate memory segment at all. MRI optimizes four other C structures in a similar way: RString, RObject, RStruct (used by the Struct class), and RBignum (used by the Bignum class).

Arrays Inside of Rubinius

Now let's see how Rubinius saves the same Fibonacci array internally. We learned earlier that Rubinius represents each Ruby object with a corresponding C++ object. This representation is true of arrays as well. For example, Figure 11-13 shows the C++ object that Rubinius would use to represent fibonacci_sequence.

Array			
ObjectHeader	total_ = 6	tuple_	start_ = 0

Figure 11-13: Rubinius uses C++ objects to represent arrays.

The combined four blocks represent an instance of the Array C++ class. Rubinius creates a C++ array object each time you create an array. From left to right, the fields are as follows:

- ObjectHeader contains technical information that Rubinius keeps track of inside each object, including a class pointer and an array of instance variables. ObjectHeader corresponds to the RBasic C structure in MRI and is one of the C++ superclasses of the Array C++ class inside the Rubinius virtual machine.
- total_ is the length of the array, which is 6 for fibonacci_sequence.
- tuple_ is a pointer to an instance of another C++ class, called Tuple, that contains the array data.
- start_ indicates where the array data starts inside the tuple object. (The tuple may contain more data than your array needs.) Initially, Rubinius sets this to 0.

Rubinius doesn't save the array data in the C++ array object. It saves it in a tuple object, as shown in Figure 11-14.

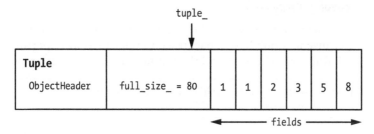

Figure 11-14: Rubinius saves array data in tuple objects.

Each tuple contains the same object header information as arrays. Rubinius saves this header information in every C++ object. Following the object header, tuple objects contain a value called full_size_, which keeps track of the size of this tuple object in bytes. Following this value, Rubinius saves the actual data values in a C++ array called fields. These data values are our six Fibonacci numbers, as shown at the right of Figure 11-14.

NOTE   *Array data values are saved in the tuple C++ object. If we had created a larger array, Rubinius would have used a larger tuple object. If we change the size of an array, Rubinius allocates another tuple of the appropriate size or, as we'll see in Experiment 11-2, it can optimize certain array methods in order to avoid allocating new objects and speed up your program.*

Experiment 11-2: Exploring the Rubinius Implementation of Array#shift

We've seen that Rubinius uses C++ objects to represent arrays, but remember that Rubinius uses a combination of Ruby and C++ code to implement methods in the Array class. In this experiment, we'll learn more about how arrays work by looking at how Rubinius implements the Array#shift method.

But first a quick review of what Array#shift does. As you may know, calling shift removes one element from the beginning of an array and *shifts* the remaining elements to the left, as shown in Listing 11-9.

```
fibonacci_sequence = [1, 1, 2, 3, 5, 8]
p fibonacci_sequence.shift
❶ => 1
p fibonacci_sequence
❷ => [1, 2, 3, 5, 8]
```

Listing 11-9: Array#shift removes the first element from an array, shifting the remaining elements over.

At ❶ Array#shift returns the first element of fibonacci_sequence. We can see from the output at ❷ that Array#shift also removes the first element from the array, shifting the other five elements. But how does Ruby implement Array#shift internally? Does it actually copy the remaining array elements to the left, or does it copy them into a new array?

Reading Array#shift

First, let's find out where the Array#shift method is located inside Rubinius. Because we don't have a backtrace to refer to as in Experiment 11-1, we can ask Rubinius where to find the method using source_location.

```
p Array.instance_method(:shift).source_location
 => ["kernel/common/array.rb", 848]
```

This output tells us that Rubinius defines the Array#shift method at line 848 in the file *kernel/common/array.rb* in the Rubinius source tree. Listing 11-10 shows the Rubinius implementation of Array#shift.

```
❶ def shift(n=undefined)
    Rubinius.check_frozen

❷   if undefined.equal?(n)
      return nil if @total == 0
❸     obj = @tuple.at @start
      @tuple.put @start, nil
      @start += 1
      @total -= 1

      obj
```

```
❹   else
      n = Rubinius::Type.coerce_to(n, Fixnum, :to_int)
      raise ArgumentError, "negative array size" if n < 0

      Array.new slice!(0, n)
    end
end
```

Listing 11-10: The implementation of Array#shift *inside the Rubinius kernel*

At ❶ shift takes an optional parameter n. If shift is called without a parameter n, as in Listing 11-9, it will remove the first element and shift the remaining elements by one position. If you provide a parameter n to shift, it will remove n elements and shift the remaining elements n positions to the left. At ❷ Rubinius checks whether the parameter n was supplied. If n was specified, it jumps to ❹ and uses Array#slice! to remove the first n elements and return them.

Modifying Array#shift

Now let's see what happens when you call shift with no parameters. How does Rubinius shift the array by one element? Unfortunately, the Tuple#at method called at ❸ is implemented by the C++ code inside the Rubinius virtual machine. (You won't find a definition for at in the Ruby *kernel/common/ tuple.rb* file.) This means we won't be able to read the entire algorithm in Ruby.

We can, however, add Ruby code to Rubinius to display information about the array data when we call shift. Because the Rubinius kernel is written with Ruby, we can change it like any other Ruby program! First, we'll add a few lines of code to Array#shift, as shown in Listing 11-11.

```
    if undefined.equal?(n)
      return nil if @total == 0

❶    fibonacci_array = (self == [1, 1, 2, 3, 5, 8])
❷    puts "Start: #{@start} Total: #{@total} Tuple: #{@tuple.inspect}" if
      fibonacci_array

      obj = @tuple.at @start
      @tuple.put @start, nil
      @start += 1
      @total -= 1

❸    puts "Start: #{@start} Total: #{@total} Tuple: #{@tuple.inspect}" if
      fibonacci_array

      obj
    end
```

Listing 11-11: Adding debug code to the Rubinius kernel

At ❶ we check whether this array is our Fibonacci array. Rubinius uses this method for every array in the system, but we want to display only information about our array. Then, at ❷ we display the values of @start, @total, and @tuple. Under the hood, @tuple is a C++ object, but in Rubinius it also functions as a Ruby object, allowing us to call its inspect method. At ❸ we display the same values once they've been changed by the Array#shift code.

Now we need to rebuild Rubinius to include our code changes. Listing 11-12 shows the output produced by the rake install command. (Run this at the root of the Rubinius source code tree.)

```
$ rake install

--snip--

   RBC kernel/common/hash.rb
   RBC kernel/common/hash19.rb
   RBC kernel/common/hash_hamt.rb
❶  RBC kernel/common/array.rb
   RBC kernel/common/array19.rb
   RBC kernel/common/kernel.rb

--snip--
```

Listing 11-12: Rebuilding Rubinius

The Rubinius build process recompiled the *array.rb* source code file at ❶, along with many other kernel files. (RBC refers to the Rubinius compiler.)

NOTE *Don't try to use this sort of code change in a production environment.*

Now to rerun Listing 11-9 using our modified version of Rubinius. Listing 11-13 shows the output interspersed with our original code.

```
   fibonacci_sequence = [1, 1, 2, 3, 5, 8]
   p fibonacci_sequence.shift
❶  Start: 0 Total: 6 Tuple: #<Rubinius::Tuple: 1, 1, 2, 3, 5, 8>
❷  Start: 1 Total: 5 Tuple: #<Rubinius::Tuple: nil, 1, 2, 3, 5, 8>
   => 1
   p fibonacci_sequence
   => [1, 2, 3, 5, 8]
```

Listing 11-13: Using our modified version of Array#shift

At ❶ and ❷ our new Ruby code inside Array#shift displays the internal contents of fibonacci_sequence: the @start, @total, and @tuple instance variables. Comparing ❶ with ❷, we can see how Array#shift works internally.

Rubinius hasn't allocated a new array object; it's reused the underlying tuple object. Rubinius has done the following:

- Changed @total from 6 to 5 because the length of the array has decreased by 1

- Changed @start from 0 to 1, which allowed it to continue to use the same value for @tuple; now the array contents start at the second value (index 1) in @tuple, not the first (index 0)

- Changed the first value in @tuple from 1 to nil because the first value is no longer used by the array

Creating new objects and allocating new memory can take a long time because Rubinius might have to ask for memory from the operating system. Its reuse of the underlying data in the tuple object, without copying or allocating memory for a new array, allows Rubinius to run faster.

Figures 11-15 and 11-16 summarize how Array#shift works. Figure 11-15 shows the array before calling Array#shift: @start pointed to the first value in the tuple, and @length was 6.

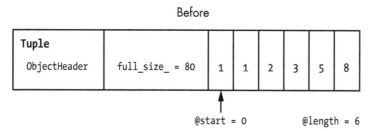

Figure 11-15: The tuple holding our Fibonacci numbers before calling Array#shift

Figure 11-16 shows the tuple after calling Array#shift; Rubinius has simply changed the values of @start and @length and set the first value in the tuple to nil.

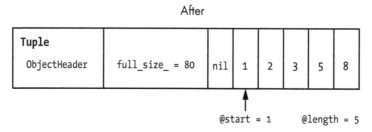

Figure 11-16: The same tuple after calling Array#shift

As you might guess, MRI uses a similar optimization for Array#shift by keeping track of where the array data starts in the original array. However, the C code it uses is more complex and difficult to understand. The Rubinius kernel gives us a much clearer view of this algorithm.

Summary

We've learned in this chapter that Rubinius uses a virtual machine implemented with C++ to run your Ruby code. Like YARV, the Rubinius virtual machine was custom designed to run Ruby programs, and it uses a compiler to convert your Ruby program into bytecode internally. We saw that these Rubinius instructions resemble YARV instructions; they operate on stack values in a similar way.

But what sets Rubinius apart from other Ruby implementations is its Ruby language kernel. The Rubinius kernel implements many built-in Ruby classes, such as Array, using Ruby code. This innovative design provides a window into Ruby internals—you can use Rubinius to learn how Ruby works internally without having to know C or Java. You can learn how Ruby implements strings, arrays, or other classes simply by reading the Ruby source code in the Rubinius kernel. Rubinius isn't just a Ruby implementation; it's a valuable learning resource for the Ruby community.

*The garbage collector is
where Ruby objects are born
and where they die.*

12

GARBAGE COLLECTION IN MRI, JRUBY, AND RUBINIUS

Garbage collection (GC) is the process high-level languages like Ruby use to manage memory for you. Where do your Ruby objects live while you're using them? How does Ruby clean up objects your program no longer uses? Ruby's GC system solves these problems.

Garbage collection is not unique to Ruby. The first implementation of garbage collection was in the Lisp programming language, invented by John McCarthy around 1960. Like Ruby, Lisp manages memory for you automatically using garbage collection. Since its invention, garbage collection has been the subject of decades of computer science research and has become an important feature of numerous computer languages, including Java, C#, and, of course, Ruby.

Computer scientists have invented many different algorithms for performing garbage collection. As it turns out, MRI uses the same GC algorithm John McCarthy invented over 50 years ago: *mark-and-sweep garbage collection.* JRuby and Rubinius, on the other hand, use a different algorithm, invented just a few years later in 1963: *copying garbage collection.* They also employ another innovation called *generational garbage collection* and can even perform GC tasks in a separate thread while your application continues to run using *concurrent garbage collection*. In this chapter we'll touch on the basic ideas behind these complex GC algorithms. The MRI, JRuby, and Rubinius garbage collectors use more complex versions of these algorithms, but the same fundamental principles apply.

Garbage Collectors Solve Three Problems

Despite its name, garbage collection is not only the process of cleaning up garbage objects. Garbage collectors, in fact, solve three problems:

- They *allocate* memory for use by new objects.
- They *identify* which objects your program is no longer using.
- They *reclaim* memory from unused objects.

Ruby's GC system is no different. When you create a new Ruby object, the garbage collector allocates memory for that object. Later, Ruby's garbage collector determines when your program has stopped using the object so it can reuse that memory to create new Ruby objects. Allocating memory and reclaiming memory are two sides of the same coin; it makes sense for Ruby's garbage collector to perform both tasks.

Garbage Collection in MRI: Mark and Sweep

A great place to start learning about garbage collection is MRI's relatively simple GC algorithm, which is similar to the one used by John McCarthy in 1960 with his groundbreaking work on Lisp. Once we understand how the algorithm works, we'll look at the more complex garbage collection in JRuby and Rubinius and explore how MRI is adopting some of their techniques.

MRI's *mark-and-sweep* algorithm hands your program memory for new objects until the available memory, or *heap*, is exhausted, at which point MRI stops your program and *marks* the objects that variables or other objects in your code still hold a reference to as *live objects*. Ruby then *sweeps* up the remaining objects, called *garbage objects*, allowing their memory to be reused. Once this process is complete, Ruby allows your program to continue again.

The Free List

Standard MRI Ruby uses McCarthy's original allocation solution, which is called the *free list*. Figure 12-1 shows what a free list looks like conceptually.

Figure 12-1: A conceptual view of the free list inside MRI

Each white square in the diagram represents a small piece of memory that is available for creating new objects. Think of this diagram as a linked list of unused Ruby objects. When you create a new Ruby object, MRI pulls a free memory block from the head of the list and uses it to create a new Ruby object, as shown in Figure 12-2.

Figure 12-2: Ruby has taken the first memory block from the free list and used it to create a new Ruby object.

The gray box in this figure is an allocated, live object. The remaining white boxes are still available. Internally all Ruby objects are represented by a C structure called RVALUE. MRI uses a C *union* inside RVALUE to encompass all of the C structures we've seen so far in MRI, such as RArray, RString, RRegexp, and so on. In other words, each square could be any kind of Ruby object or an instance of a custom Ruby class (via RObject). The contents of each object, such as the characters in a string, are often stored in a separate memory location.

As your program starts to allocate more new objects, MRI takes more new RVALUE structures from the free list, and the list of unused values shrinks, as shown in Figure 12-3.

Figure 12-3: As your program creates more objects, MRI starts to use up the free list.

MRI'S USE OF MULTIPLE FREE LISTS

When MRI starts to execute a Ruby script, it allocates memory for use in the free list. It sets the length of the initial free list to about 10,000 RVALUE structures, which means that MRI can create 10,000 Ruby objects without allocating more memory. As more objects are needed, MRI allocates more memory, placing more empty RVALUEs onto the free list.

Rather than create a single, long linked list with 10,000 elements, Ruby divides the allocated memory into subsections known as *heaps* in the MRI source code, each about 16k in size. It then creates a free list for each of these heaps, initially creating 24 lists of 407 objects each, using some of the remaining memory for other internal data structures.

Because there are multiple free lists, MRI repeatedly returns RVALUE structures from one free list until it's empty and then steps to another free list, returning more structures from that second list. In this way, MRI iterates over the available free lists until they are all empty.

Marking

As your program runs, it creates new objects, and eventually MRI uses up all remaining objects on the free list. At that point, the GC system stops your program, identifies objects that your code is no longer using, and reclaims their memory for allocation to new objects. If no unused objects are found, Ruby asks the operating system for more memory; if there is none to be had, Ruby throws an out-of-memory exception and stops.

Objects that your program allocated but that are no longer being used are known as *garbage objects*. To identify garbage objects, MRI traverses pointers in your objects' C structures, following references from one to another in order to find all active objects (see Figure 12-4). MRI knows your code is no longer using an object if it finds no references to them.

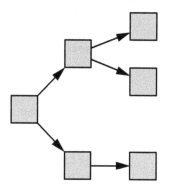

Figure 12-4: Ruby follows pointers, or references, from one object to another, starting with a root object on the left.

The gray box on the left is a *root object*, a global variable that you create or an internal object that Ruby knows your application must be using. There are typically many root objects at any given time. The arrows represent references from this root object to other objects, which in turn may contain references to other objects. This network of objects and references is known as the *object graph*. MRI marks each Ruby object that it finds as it traverses the object graph, stopping your program during the marking process in order to insure that no new object references are created.

Once the marking process completes, the heap contains a series of objects, both marked and unmarked, as shown in Figure 12-5. The marked objects are *live*, which means your code is actively using them. The unmarked objects are garbage, meaning Ruby can release or reclaim their memory. Your code is still using the marked objects, so their memory must be preserved.

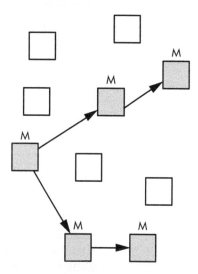

Figure 12-5: MRI has marked five active objects (gray) with five garbage objects remaining in the heap (white).

How Does MRI Mark Live Objects?

MRI saves the information about marked and unmarked objects using a technique known as *bitmap marking*. Bitmap marking refers to the technique of saving the live object marks as a series of bits in a data structure known as the *free bitmap* (see Figure 12-6). MRI uses a separate memory structure to hold the free bitmap and doesn't save the marks near the objects.

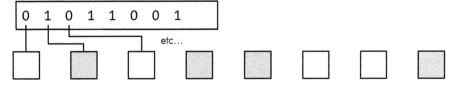

Figure 12-6: MRI saves the GC mark flags in a separate data structure known as the free bitmap.

The reason to use a separate memory structure for the mark bits has to do with a Unix memory optimization technique called *copy-on-write* (see page 265). Similar to how Ruby shares memory between different strings that contain the same letters, copy-on-write allows Unix processes to share memory that contains the same values. By saving the mark bits separately, MRI maximizes the amount of memory that will contain the same values across processes. (In Ruby 1.9 and earlier, the mark bits were saved inside each RVALUE structure, causing the garbage collector to modify almost all of Ruby's shared memory while marking live objects and rendering the copy-on-write optimization ineffective.)

Sweeping

Having identified garbage objects, it's time to reclaim them. Ruby's GC algorithm places the unmarked objects back on the free list, as shown in Figure 12-7.

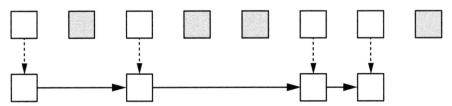

Figure 12-7: While sweeping, MRI places unused RVALUE structures back on the free list.

The process of moving unused objects back onto the free list is referred to as *sweeping* the objects. Normally this process runs very quickly because MRI doesn't actually copy objects; it simply adjusts the pointers in each RVALUE to create the free linked list (the solid arrows in Figure 12-7).

Lazy Sweeping

Beginning with version 1.9.3, MRI introduced an optimization known as *lazy sweeping*. The lazy sweep algorithm reduces the amount of time a program is stopped by the garbage collector. (Remember, during the normal mark and sweep, MRI stops executing your code.)

Lazy sweeping sweeps only enough garbage objects back to the free list to create a few new Ruby objects and to allow your program to continue, thus reducing the amount of time required to sweep. Ruby sweeps all of the garbage RVALUE objects found in only one of MRI's internal heap structures back to that heap's free list. If no garbage objects are found in the current heap, Ruby tries a lazy sweep on the next heap and works its way through the remaining heaps. (We'll see this algorithm at work in Experiment 12-1.)

Lazy sweeping can reduce the amount of time your program is paused waiting for garbage collection; however, it doesn't reduce the overall amount of garbage collection work to do. Lazy sweeping amortizes the same total amount of sweeping work over multiple GC pauses.

THE RVALUE STRUCTURE

You can find the definition of the RVALUE C structure in the *gc.c* MRI source code file, which contains the implementation of MRI's garbage collector. Listing 12-1 shows part of the RVALUE definition.

```
   typedef struct RVALUE {
❶   union {
❷     struct {
         VALUE flags;        /* always 0 for freed obj */
         struct RVALUE *next;
       } free;
❸     struct RBasic  basic;
       struct RObject object;
       struct RClass  klass;
       struct RFloat  flonum;
       struct RString string;
       struct RArray  array;
       struct RRegexp regexp;

   --snip--

     } as;
   #ifdef GC_DEBUG
       const char *file;
       int   line;
   #endif
   } RVALUE;
```

Listing 12-1: Part of the RVALUE definition from gc.c

Notice at ❶ that RVALUE uses a union to hold one of many different types of values internally. The first possible value is the free structure, defined at ❷, which represents RVALUEs still on the free list. MRI includes every other possible type of Ruby object in the union starting at ❸: RObject, RString, and so forth.

Disadvantages of Mark and Sweep

The chief disadvantage of mark and sweep is that it requires your program to stop and wait while the marking and sweeping processes take place. Beginning with version 1.9.3, however, MRI's lazy sweeping technique shortens the GC pauses somewhat.

Another disadvantage is that the time required to perform a mark-and-sweep garbage collection is proportional to the total size of the heap. During the marking phase, Ruby needs to visit every active object in your program. During the sweeping phase, Ruby needs to iterate over all of the unused garbage objects left in the heap. As the number of objects created by your program and the total heap size grows, both tasks become more time intensive.

The final issue with mark and sweep is that all of the free list elements—all of the unused objects available for your program to use—must be the same size. MRI doesn't know ahead of time when you allocate a new object whether it will be a string, an array, or a simple number. This is why the RVALUE structure MRI uses in the free list must encompass any possible type of Ruby object.

Experiment 12-1: Seeing MRI Garbage Collection in Action

You've learned how the MRI GC algorithm works at a theoretical level. Let's switch gears now to see how MRI performs actual garbage collection. The script in Listing 12-2 creates 10 Ruby objects.

```
10.times do
  obj = Object.new
end
```

Listing 12-2: Creating 10 Ruby objects using Object.new

If it's true that MRI assigns unused space from the free list to new objects, Ruby should remove 10 RVALUE structures from the free list and assign them to these 10 new objects when we run Listing 12-2. To see this in action, we use the ObjectSpace#count_objects method, as shown in Listing 12-3.

```
  def display_count
❶   data = ObjectSpace.count_objects
❷   puts "Total: #{data[:TOTAL]} Free: #{data[:FREE]} Object: #{data[:T_OBJECT]}"
  end

  10.times do
    obj = Object.new
❸   display_count
  end
```

Listing 12-3: Using ObjectSpace#count_objects to display information about MRI's heap

Now we call `display_count` at ❸ each time around the loop. `display_count` uses `ObjectSpace#count_objects` at ❶ to display information at ❷ about the total number of objects, the number of free objects, and the number of RObject structures active each time around the loop.

Running Listing 12-3 gives the output shown in Listing 12-4.

```
Total: 17491 Free: 171 Object: 85
Total: 17491 Free: 139 Object: 86
Total: 17491 Free: 132 Object: 87
Total: 17491 Free: 125 Object: 88
Total: 17491 Free: 118 Object: 89
Total: 17491 Free: 111 Object: 90
Total: 17491 Free: 104 Object: 91
Total: 17491 Free: 97 Object: 92
Total: 17491 Free: 90 Object: 93
Total: 17491 Free: 83 Object: 94
```

Listing 12-4: The output produced by Listing 12-3

The `Total:` field displays the value that MRI returns for `ObjectSpace.count_objects[:TOTAL]`. This value (17491) is the total number of objects currently active inside Ruby. It includes objects we create; objects Ruby creates internally while parsing, compiling, and executing our program; and objects on the free list. This number does not change when we create new objects because it already includes the entire free list.

The `Free:` field displays the value returned by `ObjectSpace.count_objects[:FREE]` for the length of the free list. Notice that the value drops by about 7 each time around the loop. We create only one object per iteration, but Ruby creates 6 other objects each time around the loop while running the code in the `display_count` method.

The `Object:` field displays the count of RObject structures currently active in Ruby. Notice that this value increases by 1 each time around the loop, even though we don't keep an active reference to the new objects. That is, we don't save the value returned by `Object.new` anywhere. The RObject count includes active and garbage objects.

Seeing MRI Perform a Lazy Sweep

Now if we increase the number of iterations from 10 to 30 and rerun Listing 12-3, we see the following output in Listing 12-5.

```
Total: 17493 Free: 166 Object: 85
Total: 17493 Free: 134 Object: 86
Total: 17493 Free: 127 Object: 87
Total: 17493 Free: 120 Object: 88

--snip--

Total: 17493 Free: 29 Object: 101
Total: 17493 Free: 22 Object: 102
Total: 17493 Free: 15 Object: 103
```

```
❶ Total: 17493 Free: 8 Object: 104
❷ Total: 17493 Free: 246 Object: 104
  Total: 17493 Free: 239 Object: 105
  Total: 17493 Free: 232 Object: 106
  Total: 17493 Free: 225 Object: 107
```

Listing 12-5: Running Listing 12-3 with 30 iterations instead of 10

This time the free list count drops to 8 at ❶. Then at ❷ the free count increases to 246, but the object count remains at 104. This must be a full garbage collection. But it's not! If Ruby had collected all available garbage objects, it would have reduced the RObject count when it increased the free count because all of our objects become garbage immediately. What's going on here?

This was a lazy sweep. Ruby first marked all active objects, indirectly identifying the garbage ones. Instead of moving all the garbage objects to the free list, however, it swept only a portion of them: the garbage objects it found in one of its internal heap structures. The free count increased, but the RObject count remained the same because MRI reused an RObject structure created by one of the previous iterations in order to create the new object.

Seeing MRI Perform a Full Collection

We can see the effect of a full garbage collection by triggering one manually with the GC.start method (see Listing 12-6).

```
def display_count
  data = ObjectSpace.count_objects
  puts "Total: #{data[:TOTAL]} Free: #{data[:FREE]} Object: #{data[:T_OBJECT]}"
end

30.times do
  obj = Object.new
  display_count
end

❶ GC.start
❷ display_count
```

Listing 12-6: Triggering a full garbage collection

Here, we again iterate 30 times, creating new objects and calling display_count. Then, we call GC.start at ❶, which triggers MRI to run a full garbage collection. Finally, at ❷ we call display_count again to display the same technical information. Listing 12-7 shows the new output.

```
--snip--

   Total: 17491 Free: 26 Object: 101
   Total: 17491 Free: 19 Object: 102
   Total: 17491 Free: 12 Object: 103
❶ Total: 17491 Free: 251 Object: 103
   Total: 17491 Free: 244 Object: 104
   Total: 17491 Free: 237 Object: 105
   Total: 17491 Free: 230 Object: 106
   Total: 17491 Free: 223 Object: 107
   Total: 17491 Free: 216 Object: 108
   Total: 17491 Free: 209 Object: 109
   Total: 17491 Free: 202 Object: 110
   Total: 17491 Free: 195 Object: 111
   Total: 17491 Free: 188 Object: 112
   Total: 17491 Free: 181 Object: 113
❷ Total: 17491 Free: 9527 Object: 43
```

Listing 12-7: The output generated by Listing 12-6

Most of Listing 12-7 shows output similar to Listing 12-5. The total remains the same, while the free count gradually decreases. At ❶ we see the lazy sweep occur again, increasing the free count to 251. But at ❷ we see a dramatic change. The total number of objects remains at 17491, but the free count jumps to 9527 and the number of objects reduces dramatically to 43!

From this observation, we know the following:

- The free count increased dramatically at ❷ because Ruby swept all of the garbage objects onto the free list in one large operation. This garbage included the objects our code created in previous iterations as well as objects that Ruby created internally during the parsing and compilation phases.

- The RObject count reduced to 43 because all of the objects created in previous iterations were garbage (because we didn't save them anywhere). The 43 count includes only objects Ruby created internally and none of the objects our code created. If we had saved our new objects somewhere, the RObject count would have remained the same. (We'll try this next.)

Interpreting a GC Profile Report

So far in this experiment we've allocated just a few objects from the free list. Of course, your Ruby programs will typically create many more than 30 objects. How does MRI's garbage collector behave when we create thousands or even millions of objects? How can you find out how much time is being taken by the garbage collector in a complex Ruby application?

The answer is to use the GC::Profiler class. If you enable it, MRI's internal GC code will collect statistics about each GC run. Listing 12-8 shows how to use GC::Profiler.

❶ GC::Profiler.enable

```
10000000.times do
  obj = Object.new
end
```

❷ GC::Profiler.report

Listing 12-8: Displaying a GC usage profile using `GC::Profiler` *(gc-profile.rb)*

We first enable the profiler at ❶ by calling GC::Profiler.enable. The following code creates 10 million Ruby objects. At ❷ we display the GC profile report by calling GC::Profiler.report. Listing 12-9 shows the report generated in Listing 12-8.

```
$ ruby gc-profile.rb
GC 1046 invokes.
Invoke Time(sec)    Use Size(byte)    Total Size(byte)    Total Object    GC Time(ms)
         0.036            690920              700040              17501       0.694000
         0.039            695200              700040              17501       0.433999
         0.041            695200              700040              17501       0.585000
         0.046            695200              700040              17501       0.577000
         0.049            695200              700040              17501       0.466000
         0.051            695200              700040              17501       0.516999
         0.054            695200              700040              17501       0.419000
         0.056            695200              700040              17501       0.535000
         0.059            695200              700040              17501       0.410000
         0.062            695200              700040              17501       0.426999
--snip--
```

Listing 12-9: A portion of the GC profile report generated in Listing 12-8

To save space, I've removed the first column from the report, a simple counter. Here's what the other columns mean:

- *Invoke time* shows when the garbage collection occurred, measured as seconds after the Ruby script started to run.
- *Use size* shows how much heap memory is used by all live Ruby objects after each collection is finished.
- *Total size* shows the total size of the heap after collection—in other words, the memory taken by live objects plus the size of the free list.
- *Total object* shows the total number of Ruby objects, either live or on the free list.
- Finally, *GC time* shows the amount of time each collection took.

Notice in this experiment that, aside from *invoke time,* none of the values change. The amount of memory used by live Ruby objects, the total size of the heap, and the total number of objects all remain the same. This is because we don't save the new Ruby objects anywhere. They all immediately become garbage. The *GC time* value fluctuates somewhat but more or less remains the same. The amount of time required by the collector to sweep all of the new objects back to the free list remains about the same because the collector sweeps about the same number of objects each time.

However, if we save all of the new objects in an array, they will remain live and not become garbage. Listing 12-10 shows code that saves each object into a single, large array.

```
GC::Profiler.enable

❶ arr = []
  10000000.times do
❷   arr << Object.new
  end

GC.start

GC::Profiler.report
```

Listing 12-10: Saving 10 million Ruby objects in an array (gc-profile-array.rb)

Here, we create an empty array at ❶ and save each of the new objects in it at ❷. Because the array holds a reference to all of the new objects, they remain active. The garbage collector can't reclaim memory from any of them. Listing 12-11 shows the GC profile report produced by Listing 12-10.

```
$ ruby gc-profile-array.rb
```
❶ GC 17 invokes.

Invoke Time(sec)	Use Size(byte)	Total Size(byte)	Total Object	GC Time(ms)
0.031	690920	700040	17501	0.575000
0.034	708480	716320	17908	0.689000
0.037	1261680	1269840	31746	1.077000
0.043	2254280	2262920	56573	1.994999
0.054	4044200	4053720	101343	3.454999
0.074	7266080	7277160	181929	5.288000
0.108	13058920	13072840	326821	9.417000
0.170	23489240	23508320	587708	14.465000
0.279	42267080	42311720	1057793	26.015999
0.478	76096560	76157840	1903946	45.910000

Listing 12-11: Ruby has to increase the heap size to accommodate all the new, live objects.

This time the profile report is very different! The garbage collector can't free any of the new objects because they remain active in the array. This means Ruby has no choice but to repeatedly allocate more memory to hold them. When you read Listing 12-11, notice that all three important values—*use size, total size,* and *total object*—increase exponentially. This increase is why at ❶ we see the garbage collector was called only 17 times. (Ruby also ran a few collections before we called GC::Profiler.enable as it parsed and compiled our script.) Each time the collector more or less doubled the size of the heap, allowing the script to continue to run for longer and longer periods of time. Instead of running many collections quickly, as we saw in Listing 12-9, Ruby ran just a few slow collections.

If we draw a graph of the time required for each collection (*GC Time*) against the total size of the heap (*Total Heap Size*), as shown in Figure 12-8, we can draw another interesting conclusion.

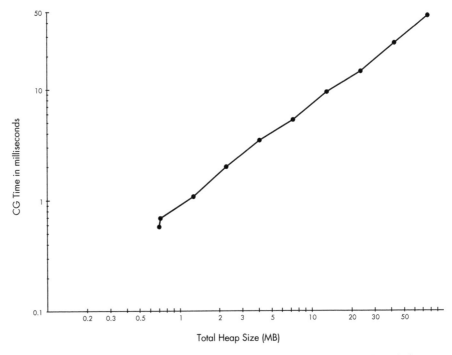

Figure 12-8: The time required to perform mark and sweep increases linearly with the heap size.

Figure 12-8 uses a logarithmic scale for both the x-axis (*Total Heap Size*) and the y-axis (*GC Time*). Because Ruby doubled the heap size during each collection, the data points are more or less evenly spaced across the logarithmic x-axis scale. They are also evenly spaced along the logarithmic y-axis because the time increases exponentially.

Most importantly, note the data points form a straight line: This straight line means the time required to perform a garbage collection increases linearly as a function of the total heap size. As you create more Ruby objects, it takes longer to mark them. Sweeping also takes longer when there are more garbage objects; however, in this example, we don't see any sweep time because all our objects remain live.

Garbage Collection in JRuby and Rubinius

Because JRuby uses the Java Virtual Machine (JVM) to implement Ruby, it's able to use the JVM's sophisticated GC system to manage memory for Ruby objects. In fact, garbage collection is one of the primary benefits of using the JVM platform: The JVM garbage collector has been refined over many years.

The Rubinius C++ virtual machine also includes a sophisticated, efficient garbage collector that uses some of the same underlying algorithms as the JVM. One of the benefits of choosing Rubinius as your Ruby platform is its sophisticated GC system.

The garbage collectors used by JRuby and Rubinius differ from MRI's garbage collector in three ways:

- Instead of using a free list, they allocate memory for new objects and reclaim memory from garbage objects using an algorithm called *copying garbage collection*.
- They handle old and young Ruby objects differently using *generational garbage collection*.
- They use *concurrent garbage collection* to perform some GC tasks at the same time that your application code is running.

NOTE *Although the GC systems used by JRuby and Rubinius are dramatically different from MRI's mark-and-sweep garbage collector, MRI has begun to incorporate some of these ideas as well. Specifically, the GC system in Ruby 2.1 has begun to use generational garbage collection.*

In the following sections, we'll explore the basic algorithms underpinning copying, generational, and concurrent garbage collection, as we learn more about how garbage collection works in Rubinius and JRuby.

Copying Garbage Collection

In 1963, three years after John McCarthy built the first Lisp garbage collector, Marvin Minsky developed a different way of allocating and reclaiming memory known as *copying garbage collection*. (Minsky's research was also originally used for Lisp. The algorithm was later refined by Fenichel and Yochelson in 1969 and by Baker in 1978.) Instead of using a free list to track available objects, copying garbage collectors allocate memory for new objects from a single large heap or memory segment. When that memory segment is used up, these collectors *copy* only the live objects over to a second memory segment, leaving the garbage objects behind. The two segments are then swapped, immediately reclaiming all of the memory from the garbage objects. (Rubinius and the JVM both use complex algorithms based on this original idea.)

Bump Allocation

When you allocate memory for a new object using a copying garbage collector, such as the collectors in the JVM and Rubinius, the garbage collector uses an algorithm called *bump allocation*. Bump allocation allocates adjacent memory segments from a large, continuous heap by *bumping*, or incrementing, a pointer to keep track of where the next allocation will occur. Figure 12-9 shows how this process works for three repeated allocations. (The large rectangle represents the Rubinius or JVM heap.)

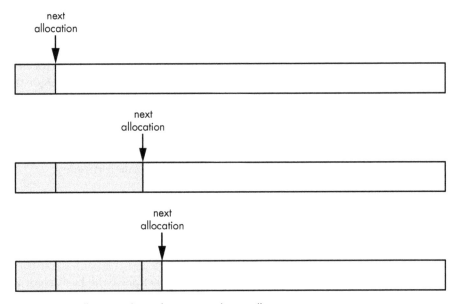

Figure 12-9: Allocating three objects using bump allocation

A copying collector keeps a pointer that tracks where in the heap the next allocation will occur. Each time the collector allocates memory for a new object, it returns some memory from the heap and moves this pointer to the right. As more objects are created, the memory allocated from the heap also moves to the right. Notice, too, that the new objects are not all the same size; each object uses a different number of bytes. As a result, the objects are not spaced evenly across the heap.

The advantages of this technique are that it's very fast and simple to implement and it provides good *locality of reference*, meaning that related values in your program should be located near each other in memory. Locality is important because if your code repeatedly accesses the same area of memory, your CPU can cache that memory and access it much more quickly. If your program often accesses very different areas of memory, the CPU must continually reload the memory cache, slowing down your program's performance.

Another benefit of copying garbage collection is the ability to create objects of different sizes. Unlike the RVALUE structure in MRI, JRuby and Rubinius can allocate new objects of any size.

The Semi-Space Algorithm

The real benefit and elegance of copying garbage collectors becomes evident when the initial heap is used up and a garbage collection occurs. Copying garbage collectors identify live and garbage objects the way that mark-and-sweep collectors do—by traversing the object graph following object references or pointers. Once the garbage objects have been identified, however, copying garbage collectors work very differently.

Copying garbage collectors actually use two heaps: one to create new objects with bump allocation and a second, empty one, as shown in Figure 12-10.

Figure 12-10: The semi-space algorithm uses two heaps, one initially empty.

The heap at the top contains the objects already created and is known as the *from-space*. Note that the objects in the from-space were already marked as live (gray with an *M*) or garbage (white). The lower heap is the *to-space*, and it's initially empty. The algorithm I'm about to describe is known as the *semi-space* algorithm because the total available memory is divided between the from-space and the to-space.

When the from-space becomes completely full, copying garbage collectors copy all of the live objects down into the to-space, leaving the garbage objects behind. Figure 12-11 shows the copying process.

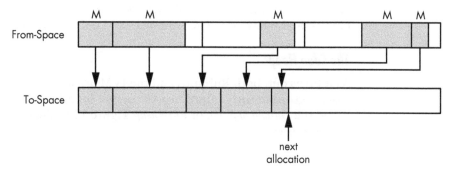

Figure 12-11: The semi-space algorithm copies only live objects to the second heap.

The from-space again appears at the top of the diagram and the to-space below. Notice how the live objects are copied down into the to-space. The arrows pointing down indicate this copying process. A pointer similar to the one used for bump allocation keeps track of where the next live object should be copied to.

Once the copying process is finished, the semi-space algorithm swaps heaps, as shown in Figure 12-12.

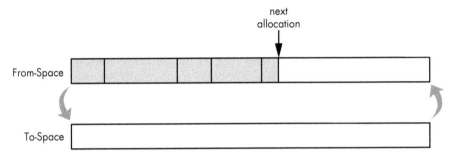

Figure 12-12: After copying the live objects, the semi-space algorithm switches heaps.

In Figure 12-12, the to-space has become the new from-space and is now ready to allocate more memory for new objects using bump allocation. You might expect the algorithm to be slow because so much copying is involved, but it's not, because only active, live objects are copied. Garbage objects are left in place and then reclaimed.

NOTE   *All of the live objects were copied to the left side of the heap; this allows the garbage collector to allocate the remaining unused memory most efficiently. This compaction of the heap is a natural result of the semi-space algorithm.*

While the semi-space algorithm is an elegant way to manage memory, it is somewhat memory inefficient. It requires the collector to allocate twice as much memory as it actually uses because all of your objects might remain active and could be copied into the second heap. The algorithm is also somewhat difficult to implement because when the collector moves live objects, it also has to update references and pointers to them internally.

The Eden Heap

As it turns out, both Rubinius and the JVM use a variation of the semi-space algorithm with a third heap structure for allocating new objects called the *Garden of Eden*, or *Eden heap*. Figure 12-13 shows the three memory structures.

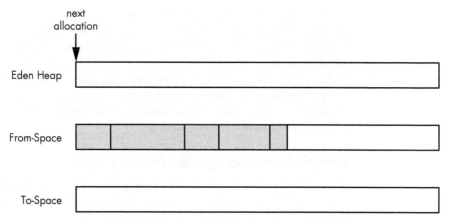

Figure 12-13: The Eden heap is for allocating memory for brand-new objects.

The Eden heap is where the JVM and Rubinius allocate memory for new objects; the from-space contains all of the live objects copied in the previous garbage collection process; and the to-space remains empty until the next garbage collection runs. Each time the garbage collection process runs, the collector copies your objects from both the Eden heap and from-space into the to-space, thereby allowing more memory to be available for new objects because the Eden heap will always be empty after each semi-space copy operation.

Generational Garbage Collection

Many modern garbage collectors, including the collectors in the JVM and the Rubinius VM, use *generational GC* algorithms, a technique that treats new objects differently than older ones. A new, or *young*, object is one that your program has just created, while an old, or *mature*, object is one that your program is continuing to use. The time that an object has to remain active for in order for it to be considered mature is usually measured by the number of times the garbage collection system has run.

The Weak Generational Hypothesis

The reason objects are categorized as either young or mature is based on the assumption that most young objects will have a short lifetime while mature objects are likely to continue to live for a long time. This assumption is known as the *weak generational hypothesis*. In simple terms, new objects are likely to die young. Because young and mature objects have different life expectancies, different GC algorithms are appropriate for each category, or *generation*.

For example, consider a Ruby on Rails website. To generate a web page for each client request, a Rails application creates many new Ruby objects. However, once a web page has been generated and returned to the client, all of those Ruby objects are no longer needed and the GC system can reclaim their memory. At the same time, the application might also create a few Ruby objects that live between requests, such as ones that represent a controller, some configuration data, or a user session. These few mature objects would have a longer lifetime.

Using the Semi-Space Algorithm for Young Objects

According to the weak generational hypothesis, young objects are created continually by your program but also become garbage quite frequently. Because of this, both the JVM and Rubinius run the GC process more frequently for young objects than for mature ones (you'll see just how much more frequently in Experiment 12-2). The semi-space algorithm is ideal for young objects because it copies only live objects. When the Eden heap fills up with new objects, the garbage collector identifies most of them as garbage because new objects usually die young. Because there are fewer live objects, the collector has less copying to do. The JVM refers to these objects as *survivors* and calls the from-space and the to-space *survivor spaces*.

Promoting Objects

When a new object becomes old (that is, when it has survived a certain number of runs of the GC system), it is *promoted*, or copied, into the mature generation heap during the semi-space copy process, as shown in Figure 12-14.

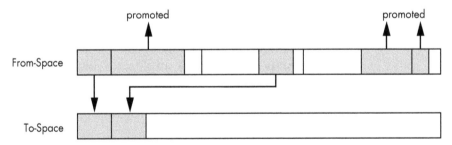

Figure 12-14: Generational garbage collectors promote old objects from the young heap to the mature one.

Notice that the from-space contains five active objects, shown as gray rectangles. Two of these are copied down to the to-space by the semi-space algorithm, but the other three are promoted. Their age has exceeded the *new object lifetime* because they have remained active for a certain number of GC runs.

In Rubinius, the new object lifetime is set to 2 by default, meaning that a young object becomes mature once the GC system has run twice with your code still holding a reference to that object. (This means that Rubinius will copy a live object twice between the from- and to-space, using the semi-space algorithm.) Over time, Rubinius adjusts the object lifetime value, based on various statistics, to optimize garbage collection as much as possible.

The JVM's garbage collector internally calculates the new object lifetime, attempting to keep the from- and to-space heaps about half full. If these heaps start to fill up, the new object lifetime will decrease, and objects will be promoted more quickly. If the spaces are mostly empty, the JVM will increase the new object lifetime, allowing new objects to remain there longer.

Garbage Collection for Mature Objects

Once your objects are promoted into the mature collection, they will likely live on for a long time due to the weak generational hypothesis. As a result, both the JVM and Rubinius need to run garbage collection on the mature generation much less frequently. Garbage collection on the mature generation runs once the heap allocated for mature objects fills up. Because most new objects don't live past the new object lifetime, the mature collection fills up slowly.

The JVM offers many command-line options that allow you to configure the relative or absolute sizes of young and mature generation heaps (the JVM documentation refers to the mature generation as the *tenured generation*). The JVM also maintains a third generation for internal objects created by the JVM itself: the *permanent generation*. Garbage collection on the young generation is called a *minor collection*, and on the tenured generation, it's a *major collection*.

Rubinius uses a sophisticated GC algorithm called *Immix* for the mature generation of objects. Immix attempts to reduce the amount of total memory used and the amount of heap fragmentation by collecting active objects into continuous regions. Rubinius also uses a third generation for very large objects and collects them using a standard mark-and-sweep process.

NOTE *MRI Ruby version 2.1 implements a generational GC algorithm for standard Ruby like the one the JVM and Rubinius have used for years. Its primary challenge is also detecting which mature objects reference young ones (see "References Between Generations" on page 316). MRI uses a solution common to many implementations of generational GC: it tracks each time a mature object references a young one using write barriers. However, implementing write barriers in MRI is complex because existing C extensions won't contain them.*

REFERENCES BETWEEN GENERATIONS

In addition to the new object lifetime, generational garbage collectors have to track another important detail: young objects that are active because of a reference from an old object. Because collections on the young generation will not mark mature objects, the collector might assume that certain young objects are garbage when they are not. Figure 12-15 shows an example of the problem.

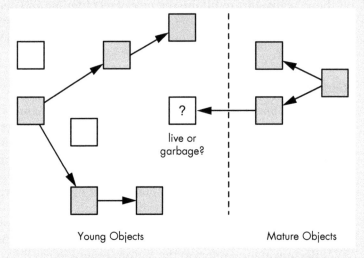

Young Objects   Mature Objects

Figure 12-15: Generational garbage collectors need to find mature objects that reference young objects.

The young collection contains several live objects (gray) and garbage objects (white). During the young object marking phase, the generational garbage collector follows only references from young objects in order to speed up the process, which occurs frequently. Notice, however, the center object marked with a question mark: Is it live or garbage? There are no references to it from other young objects, but there is a reference to it from a mature object. If Rubinius or the JVM were to run the semi-space algorithm on the young objects at left after marking them, the center object would be incorrectly considered garbage and its contents overwritten!

Write Barriers

Generational garbage collectors can solve this problem using *write barriers*. These are bits of code that keep track of when your program adds a reference from a mature object to a young one. When the garbage collector encounters such a reference, it considers that one mature object to be another root for use in marking young objects, thereby allowing the object in question to be considered live and to be copied properly by the semi-space algorithm.

Concurrent Garbage Collection

Both Rubinius and the JVM use another sophisticated technique to reduce the amount of time your application spends waiting for garbage collection: *concurrent garbage collection*. When using concurrent garbage collection, the garbage collector runs at the same time as your application code. This eliminates, or at least reduces, pauses in your program due to garbage collection because your application doesn't have to stop and wait while the garbage collector runs.

Concurrent garbage collectors run in a separate thread from the primary application. Although in theory this could mean that your application will slow a bit because part of the CPU's time has to be spent running the GC thread, most computers today contain microprocessors with multiple cores, which allow different threads to run in parallel. This means one of the cores can be dedicated to running the GC thread, leaving the other cores to run the primary application. (In practice, this still might slow down your application because fewer cores are available.)

NOTE   *MRI Ruby 2.1 also supports a form of concurrent garbage collection by performing the sweep portion of the mark-and-sweep algorithm in parallel while your Ruby code continues to run. This helps to reduce the amount of time your application is paused while garbage collection runs.*

Marking While the Object Graph Changes

Marking objects while your application is running presents one large obstacle for concurrent garbage collectors: What if your application changes the object graph while the collector is marking it? To better understand this problem, see the example object graph in Figure 12-16.

This figure shows a small set of objects being marked by a concurrent garbage collector. On the left is a root object, and to the right are various child objects referenced by the root object. All of the live objects are marked with *M* and shown in gray. The garbage collector, indicated by the large arrow, has already marked the live objects and is now processing the objects near the bottom. The collector is about to mark the two remaining white objects at the bottom right.

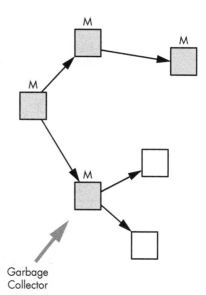

Figure 12-16: A garbage collector marking an object graph

Now suppose your application, which is also running while the marking process is underway, creates a new object and adds it as a child of one of the previously marked objects. Figure 12-17 shows the new situation.

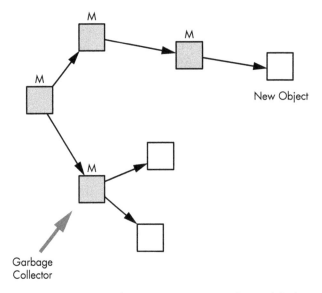

Figure 12-17: Your application creates a new object while the marking process is underway.

Notice that one of the live, marked objects points to a new object that hasn't been marked yet.

Now suppose the garbage collector finishes marking the object graph. It has marked all of the live objects, meaning that any remaining objects are assumed to be garbage. Figure 12-18 shows how the object graph appears at the end of the marking process.

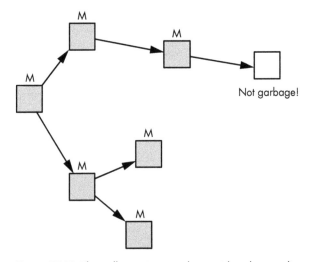

Figure 12-18: The collector incorrectly considers the new live object to be garbage.

The garbage collector has finished marking all live objects, but it missed the new object. The collector will now reclaim its memory, but the application will have lost valid data or will have garbage data added to one of its objects!

Tricolor Marking

The solution to this problem is to maintain a *mark stack*, or a list of objects that still need to be examined by the marking process, as shown in Figure 12-19.

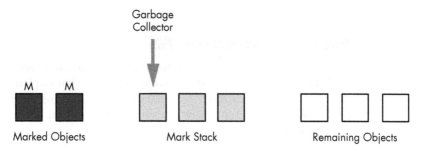

Figure 12-19: The marking process works through the objects in the mark stack.

Initially all of the root objects are placed on the mark stack. As the garbage collector marks objects, it moves them from the mark stack to the list of marked objects on the left, and it adds any child objects it finds to the mark stack. When the mark stack is exhausted, the garbage collector is finished; it has identified all live objects and any remaining objects on the right are assumed to be garbage. But with this scheme, if the application modifies one of the objects during marking, the collector can move the modified object back to the mark stack, even if it was previously marked, as shown in Figure 12-20.

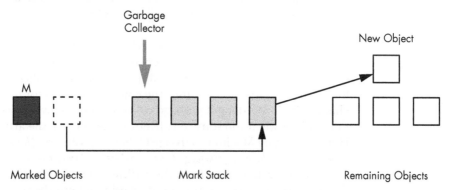

Figure 12-20: The collector moves a marked object back to the mark stack because the application modified it.

The application has added a new object to the system, as shown at right in the figure's remaining objects list. This time, however, the collector notices that an existing object was modified because it now contains a reference to the new object and it moves the modified object to the mark stack in the center. As a result, the collector will eventually find and mark the new object as it works through the mark stack.

This modified marking algorithm is known as *tricolor marking*: Objects already processed are considered "black"; objects on the mark stack, "gray"; and the remaining objects, "white," as shown in Figures 12-19 and 12-20.

NOTE *Concurrent garbage collectors can use write barriers to detect when an application changes the object graph. Write barriers are used by both generational and concurrent garbage collectors.*

Three Garbage Collectors in the JVM

In order to support different types of applications and server hardware, the JVM includes three separate garbage collectors that implement concurrent garbage collection differently. You can use command-line parameters to choose which collector to run in your JRuby program. The three collectors are as follows:

Serial   This collector stops your application and performs garbage collection while your application is waiting. It doesn't use concurrent garbage collection at all.

Parallel   This collector performs many GC tasks, including minor collections, in a separate thread while your application is running.

Concurrent   This collector performs most GC tasks in parallel with your application. It's optimized to reduce GC pauses as much as possible, but its use may slow down your application's overall throughput.

NOTE *In addition to these three, a variety of new, experimental garbage collectors are also available for the JVM. One of these is the garbage-first (G1) collector, and another is the continuously concurrent compacting (C4) collector.*

Unless you direct it to do otherwise, the JVM automatically selects one of these garbage collectors, depending on the type of hardware being used. For most computers, the JVM uses the parallel collector by default; for server-class machines, it uses the concurrent collector instead. You can change the JVM's default garbage collection choice by using command-line options when you start your JRuby program. See the article "Java SE 6 HotSpot Virtual Machine Garbage Collection Tuning" (*http://www.oracle .com/technetwork/java/javase/gc-tuning-6-140523.html*) for more details.

The ability to choose from these different GC algorithms and to further tune the behavior of the collector using many other configuration options is one of the great benefits of using JRuby. The effectiveness and performance of a garbage collector depends on your application's behavior as well as the underlying algorithms used.

To help make sense of the myriad GC-related options provided by the JVM, Charles Nutter, one of the lead developers behind the JRuby project, suggests using the following rules of thumb:

- When in doubt, stick with the JVM's default settings. These settings work well in most cases.
- If you have a lot of data that need to be collected frequently or periodically, the concurrent or experimental G1 collectors may do a better job than the parallel collector.
- Try to improve your code so it uses less memory before tuning garbage collection. Tuning the JVM's garbage collector when you are allocating too much memory solves only half the problem.

Experiment 12-2: Using Verbose GC Mode in JRuby

Experiment 12-1 explored garbage collection in MRI. In this experiment, we'll see how garbage collection works in JRuby by asking the JVM to display technical information about what the JVM's garbage collector is doing. Listing 12-12 shows the code from Experiment 12-1 that creates 10 Ruby objects.

```
10.times do
  obj = Object.new
end
```

Listing 12-12: Creating 10 Ruby objects using Object.new (jruby-gc.rb)

When we run this simple program using the -J-verbose:gc option, the JVM displays internal debugging information about garbage collection. Here's the command to use:

```
$ jruby -J-verbose:gc jruby-gc.rb
```

But this command doesn't produce any output. Perhaps we aren't creating enough objects to trigger a garbage collection.

Let's increase the number of new objects to 10 million, as shown in Listing 12-13.

```
10000000.times do
  obj = Object.new
end
```

Listing 12-13: Creating 10 million Ruby objects using Object.new (jruby-gc.rb)

The new output is shown in Listing 12-14.

```
$ jruby -J-verbose:gc jruby-gc.rb
[GC 17024K->1292K(83008K), 0.0072491 secs]
[GC 18316K->1538K(83008K), 0.0091344 secs]
[GC 18562K->1349K(83008K), 0.0006953 secs]
[GC 18373K->1301K(83008K), 0.0006876 secs]
[GC 18325K->1289K(83008K), 0.0004180 secs]
[GC 18313K->1285K(83008K), 0.0006950 secs]
[GC 18309K->1285K(83008K), 0.0006597 secs]
[GC 18309K->1285K(83008K), 0.0007186 secs]
[GC 18309K->1285K(83008K), 0.0005617 secs]
[GC 18309K->1285K(83008K), 0.0006873 secs]
[GC 18309K->1285K(83008K), 0.0004944 secs]
[GC 18309K->1285K(83008K), 0.0006644 secs]
[GC 18309K->1285K(83008K), 0.0006448 secs]
[GC 18309K->1285K(83008K), 0.0007203 secs]
```

Listing 12-14: The output produced by running Listing 12-13 with -J-verbose:gc

The JVM displays a line of information each time garbage collection occurs while running our Ruby program. There are 14 GC events shown here. Each line contains the following information:

[GC... The *GC* prefix means this event was a minor collection. The JVM cleaned up only new objects in the Eden heap or young objects in the survivor spaces.

17024K->1292K These values show the amount of data used by live objects before (left of the arrow) and after (right of the arrow) the garbage collection. In this example, the amount of space taken up by live objects in the young collection dropped from about 17MB or 18MB to about 1.3MB each time.

(83008K) The value in parentheses shows the total size of the JVM heap for this process. This value has not changed.

0.0072491 secs This value shows the amount of time taken to perform each garbage collection.

Listing 12-14 shows that the JVM's young heap repeatedly fills up as we create more Ruby objects. Notice that each time the JVM garbage collector usually takes less than 1 millisecond to clean up the many thousands of garbage objects.

Notice, too, that there were no major garbage collections. Why? Because we don't save our Ruby objects. Listing 12-13 creates 10 million objects but doesn't use them, so the JVM's garbage collector determines that they are all garbage and reclaims their memory immediately before they are promoted to become mature objects.

Triggering Major Collections

In order to trigger major collections, we need to create some mature objects by creating Ruby objects that don't die young but that live on for some time. We can achieve this by saving our new objects in an array, as we did in Experiment 12-1. Listing 12-15 repeats the same script again here for convenience.

```
❶ arr = []
  10000000.times do
❷   arr << Object.new
  end
```

Listing 12-15: Saving 10 million Ruby objects in an array

Notice at ❶ that we create an empty array and then insert all 10 million new objects into it at ❷. Because the array contains a reference to all objects, the objects will all remain live.

Now let's rerun our experiment using the -J-verbose:gc command. Listing 12-16 shows the result.

```
$ jruby -J-verbose:gc jruby-gc.rb
❶ [GC 16196K->8571K(83008K), 0.0873137 secs]
  [GC 25595K->20319K(83008K), 0.0480336 secs]
  [GC 37343K->37342K(83008K), 0.0611792 secs]
  [GC 37586K(83008K), 0.0029985 secs]
  [GC 54366K->54365K(83008K), 0.0617091 secs]
  [GC 65553K->65360K(83008K), 0.0586615 secs]
  [GC 82384K->82384K(100040K), 0.0479422 secs]
  [GC 89491K(100040K), 0.0124503 secs]
  [GC 95890K->95888K(147060K), 0.0795343 secs]
  [GC 96144K(147060K), 0.0030345 secs]
  [GC 130683K->130682K(148020K), 0.0941640 secs]
  [GC 147706K->147704K(165108K), 0.0925857 secs]
  [GC 150767K->151226K(168564K), 0.0226121 secs]
❷ [Full GC 151226K->125676K(168564K), 0.5317203 secs]
  [GC 176397K->176404K(236472K), 0.0999831 secs]

--snip--
```

Listing 12-16: The beginning of the output produced by running Listing 12-15 with -J-verbose:gc

Notice at ❷ that the output [Full GC...] first appears after 13 young collections. (The output continues past what is shown in Listing 12-16.) This tells us that many Ruby objects were promoted, filling up the mature generation and forcing a mature collection to run.

We can draw some other interesting conclusions from this output. First, the size of the young collection gradually grew from the first GC run at ❶ to the mature collection at ❷. This tells us that the JVM was automatically increasing the total heap size as more objects were created. Notice that the total heap size value in parentheses started at around 83MB and grew to over 200MB, as shown in bold. Also, each young collection was still relatively fast at under 0.1 seconds, though much slower than the ones we saw in Listing 12-14, which took less than 1 millisecond. Remember that the semi-space algorithm copies only live objects. This time all of our Ruby objects remained alive, and the JVM had to copy them repeatedly. Finally, notice that the mature, or full, collection at ❷ took about 0.53 seconds, which was much longer than any of the young collections.

Further Reading

There's a vast amount of information available on the topic of garbage collection. To learn more about John McCarthy's original free list implementation, see his article on Lisp: "Recursive Functions of Symbolic Expressions and Their Computation by Machine, Part 1" (*Communications of the ACM*, 1960).

For a taste of modern GC research, you can read about the Immix algorithm used by Rubinius in Stephen M. Blackburn and Kathryn S. McKinley's "A Mark-Region Garbage Collector with Space Efficiency, Fast Collection, and Mutator Performance" (*ACM SIGPLAN Notices*, 2008). The following article from Oracle both explains the JVM's overall GC algorithm and serves as a good reference for the many command-line options you can use to customize and tune the JVM's garbage collector's behavior: "Java SE 6 HotSpot Virtual Machine Garbage Collection Tuning" (*http://www.oracle.com/technetwork/java/javase/gc-tuning-6-140523.html*).

Finally, two definitive sources on GC algorithms in general and how they have changed over the years are Jones and Lins's *Garbage Collection: Algorithms for Automatic Dynamic Memory Management* (Wiley, 1996) and Jones, Hosking, and Moss's, *The Garbage Collection Handbook: The Art of Automatic Memory Management* (CRC Press, 2012).

Summary

This chapter has covered one of the most important but least understood areas of Ruby internals: garbage collection. We learned that garbage collectors allocate memory for new objects and clean up unused garbage objects. We examined the basic algorithms used by MRI, Rubinius, and JRuby for garbage collection and discovered that MRI allocates and reclaims memory using a free list, while Rubinius and the JVM use the semi-space algorithm. We also saw how Rubinius and JRuby employ concurrent and generational GC techniques, which MRI starts to use in Ruby 2.1.

But we've only scratched the surface of garbage collection. Since its invention in 1960, many complex GC algorithms have been developed; indeed, garbage collection is still an active area of computer science research. The GC implementations in MRI, Rubinius, and JRuby are likely to continue to evolve and improve over time.

The Ruby core
community welcomes
your challenge.

YET MORE RUBY VIRTUAL MACHINES
by Koichi Sasada

As a developer of YARV: Yet Another Ruby VM, I am thankful to have a chance to write about YARV in this appendix. Many pages of this book describe the internals of YARV, and the book has been read by people all over the world. I am greatly honored by that as a software developer, although it humbles me to have found several inefficiencies in YARV's implementation while reading the book. In this appendix, I will give some supplemental information and background on the design and implementation of YARV.

YARV: Yet Another Ruby VM

I started the development of YARV during the New Year's holiday in 2004. I had already been interested in a virtual machine for Ruby at that time. I built a simple prototype in about a week. (I must have had plenty of time to kill back then.) According to the first announcement ([ruby-dev:22494]), it was capable of running a program to calculate Fibonacci numbers.

In its early stages of development, I implemented YARV as an extension library for Ruby 1.8. Instead of replacing the whole runtime engine, I designed it to be used by Ruby 1.8 as a VM to run specific programs. In other words, it was another Ruby implementation on top of the Ruby 1.8 implementation. This architecture allowed us to test YARV with relative ease using Ruby 1.8, which was sufficiently stable. We could continue using the base mechanisms of Ruby 1.8, such as GC, C APIs, and so on. After finishing a substantial part of the development, the Ruby 1.8 core was removed and replaced with YARV all at once, in order to support features such as threads. However, we kept using infrastructure code, such as GC, after that. The Ruby interpreter (MRI/CRuby) is known to have an affinity with the C programming language. YARV inherits that characteristic as well. Then a new version of Ruby containing YARV at its core was released as Ruby 1.9. As of this writing in 2014, YARV has been used as the Ruby VM since then.

People often point out that YARV is not "Yet Another" anymore, because it is the official VM now. Though we still use the name because it is well known, we make it a rule not to use "YARV" in filenames or class names. When I started working on YARV, there had already been several proposals for the development of new virtual machines for Ruby. RiteVM by Matz, the creator of Ruby, and ByteCodeRuby were the most well-known projects then, as far as I can remember. That led me to prefix the name of our VM with "Yet Another." Of course, I named it so hoping it would become popular. There are many examples of software programs that have "Yet Another" in their names and nevertheless became popular; for example, yacc. By the way, RiteVM is now the name of the mruby VM which Matz is actively developing.

Design Principles of YARV

We chose to implement YARV for the Ruby 1.9 specification, instead of 1.8. At the time, Ruby 1.9 was the next version, and we were discussing its specification, so we targeted YARV at that specification. We also had the option of implementing it for Ruby 1.8, thereby supporting a large number of users instantly. But some of the Ruby 1.8 features seemed difficult to implement with the stack machine that YARV is based on. So I decided to implement my VM for the newer spec, while negotiating with Ruby developers to change the parts of the specification that were hard to implement. This strategy worked well, and YARV became one of the interpreters to run Ruby 1.9. I think that was one of the reasons that it was finally merged in as an official VM.

This book correctly explains YARV's design details. I would like to add, however, that it was not very straightforward to get to the current design. One of the things I remember being an issue was the stack structure of the virtual machine. The book describes YARV as a "double stack machine," but it used only one stack at first. Actual microprocessors allocate a calculation area and a function call frame one after another on a single stack. YARV used a similar architecture at first, but it became too complicated. Later I concluded that it should have two stacks, even if I had to give up some efficiency. YARV's operation became too complex, especially when implementing the extraction of a block as a closure. Because this book cleverly avoids such hairy details, readers fortunately do not have to confront this sort of complexity. But I am glad I have chance to explain that, because it was one of the most difficult parts to implement. By the way, having two stacks means that the cost of checking for stack overflows also doubles. So I implemented them both in the same memory block: one going from bottom to top and the other going from top to bottom. This trick somewhat reduced the cost of checking for stack overflows, because we only have to check the positions of two stack pointers once.

YARV Development Prehistory

I'd like to describe the history of how I came to develop YARV. Because earlier I had been interested in programming language processors, I had the experience of implementing two Java virtual machines. That gave me some knowledge of what was required to implement virtual machines intended for object-oriented programming languages. At the time, Mr. Nobuo Yamashita was periodically holding meetups to read the book *The Structure and Interpretation of Computer Programs* (SICP). By attending those meetings, I acquired knowledge and insight about implementations of Scheme. This insight was important because Ruby's block design was based on Lisp functions, as Chapter 8 of this book points out.

December 2002 saw the publication of *Ruby Source Code Kanzen Kaisetsu* (commonly known as the *Ruby Hacking Guide*, or RHG) by Mr. Minero Aoki, which is a unique book that explains the entire Ruby source code. Mr. Masayoshi Takahashi held meetings to read RHG about once a month. We took turns in a reading group, but because the author Aoki-san himself was one of the members, the other members could talk with him in person when they had questions. In this way, we learned the implementation details of Ruby very well. Let me add that both of these meetups were held in the meeting rooms at Time Intermedia, Ltd., where Mr. Yamashita was working then. I attended the meetups several times a month, and I wish to express my deep gratitude to the people who provided such an environment for learning.

After reading RHG and learning more about the structure of Ruby's implementation, it became clear to me that the evaluation module Ruby used to run programs—the heart of the Ruby interpreter—was not efficient enough. I kept on studying and thinking about the ideal design of a virtual machine to run Ruby programs precisely and efficiently, which I finally implemented all at once during that New Year's holiday. I didn't foresee that it would be released as a part of Ruby 1.9. My first motivation was performance improvement—my source code surely reflected that. In hindsight, it was far too early for performance optimization.

Yet More Ruby Virtual Machines

This book explains the current architecture of YARV, which you might conclude is the correct way of implementing Ruby. But, as I have explained in this appendix so far, all of Ruby's implementations, including YARV, are not much different from any other software application: they are all developed through trial and error by humans. While this book covers Ruby 2.0, we have already made various improvements for Ruby 2.1. And we are working on even more improvements that will make the forthcoming Ruby 2.2 even better.

For example, keyword arguments will be more efficient. Chapter 4 explains the implementation of keyword arguments. Quickly summarizing: Ruby first passes a hash object containing keyword name-value pairs as a normal argument. Then, at compile time, the receiver implicitly expands code that reads the values from the argument hash. Users don't seem to be complaining about its performance for now. I assume keyword arguments are not widely used, because it is a new feature introduced in Ruby 2.0. But this implementation is not efficient. Hash objects are created every time, incurring object creation and GC costs. Also, reading from hash objects using the implicitly expanded code is slow, because it involves multiple method calls.

In order to address this problem, we are reimplementing how Ruby 2.2 handles keyword arguments to avoid creating hash objects as much as possible. Meanwhile, we are implementing a new design that will collect the names of keyword arguments at compile time, so that the caller need only pass the values at runtime. The callee will then recombine the values with the names collected by the compiler. This design change will allow Ruby to process keyword arguments 10 times faster. I would like to keep on improving the quality of Ruby's implementation, including runtime efficiency.

If you become interested in YARV and Ruby implementations after reading this book, and if you have ideas for improving them, I encourage you to develop your own "Yet Another Ruby Implementation." The Ruby core community will welcome your challenge.

Koichi Sasada
Heroku, Inc.
November 2014

INDEX

BMETHOD methods, 94
brace_block grammar rule, 21
branchunless YARV instruction, 85
built-in Ruby methods, calling, 97–99
bump allocation, 310
bytecode, 33
--bytecode (JRuby option), 256
bytecode instructions
    Java, 254
    Rubinius, 277, 278–279
ByteList (Java object), 264

C

C++, working together with Ruby,
    279–280
C4 (continuously concurrent
    compacting) collector, 320
caches, clearing Ruby's method, 143–144
calling
    attr_reader, 97–98
    attr_writer, 97–98
    blocks, 61–62, 194–196
    built-in Ruby methods, 97–99
    eval with binding, 238–240
    lambda more than once in the same
        scope, 216–217
    lambdas, 209–211
    methods with blocks, 71–72
    normal Ruby methods, 95–97
call stack, 56
catch tables, 88–90
CFP (control frame pointer), 57, 88, 95
CFUNC methods, 61, 94, 97
child grammar rule, 15
Class (C++ class), 280
Class (Ruby class), 117
class << metaprogramming syntax, 225
class_alloc C function, 155
classes
    Array, 284–291
    BasicObject, 259
    Binding, 208
    Enumerator, 284
    Fixnum, 110
    Hash, 169
    included, 137, 152–154
    Integer, 62, 72, 97, 142–143, 282–284
    Object, 133, 157–158, 231–232
    origin, 150
    Proc, 211–213
    Ripper, 9–12, 22–29
    Ruby, implementing with Java classes,
        257–259
    RubyVM::InstructionSequence, 44–45,
        51–53
    seeing methods and submodules,
        152–153

singleton, 130, 226–227
String, 263–271
class_eval method, 244
class instance variables, 120–122
class keyword, 221
class method, 111
class methods, 127–130
    defining
        using a new lexical scope, 224
        using an object prefix, 223
    scope of, 236
Class.new method, 113
class pointers, 106, 107, 109
class scope, 232–234
class variables, 120–124
clearing, Ruby's method caches, 143–144
climbing, environment pointer ladder
    in C, 74–75
closures, 191, 197
    blocks as, 192–198
    and current value of self, 241–242
    defining methods with, 246–248
    and metaprogramming, 236–244
code
    how JRuby executes, 255–257
    how JRuby parses and compiles,
        254–255
    that writes code, 236–238
codeloader.rb file, 283
compilation, 31
compile.c file, 42
compiling
    calls to blocks, 38–44
    keyword arguments, 49
    optional arguments, 48
    simple scripts, 34–38
compilers
    introduced in Ruby 1.9 and 2.0, 33–34
    Rubinius, 277, 290
compstmt grammar rule, 21
concurrent collector (in the JVM), 320
concurrent garbage collection, 205, 317
    in the JVM, 320–321
    marking objects, 317–318
    tricolor marking, 319–320
constants, 124–125
    creating, for a new class or module,
        159–160
    finding, 156–158, 160–161
    lookup algorithm, 162, 163–164
    table, 125
const_missing method, 164
const_tbl pointer, 126
continuously concurrent compacting
    (C4) collector, 320
control frame pointer (CFP), 57, 88, 95
copying, a stack frame to the heap,
    208, 209

copying garbage collection, 205, 309
> bump allocation, 310–311
> Eden heap, 312–313
> and semi-space algorithm, 311–312

copy-on-write
> for strings, 265–271
> in Unix, 300

core#define_method method, 53

count_objects method, 129

creating
> constants, for a new class or module, 159–160
> lambdas, 207–209
> refinements, 228
> unique and nonshared strings, 267

cref (C structure), 244, 245

cref pointer, 68, 78

D

default values, for arguments, 47

define_method method, 246

defining
> class methods
>> using a new lexical scope, 224
>> using an object prefix, 223
> methods
>> alternative ways of, 223–231
>> normal process of, 221–223
>> using singleton classes, 226–227
>> using singleton classes in a lexical scope, 227–228

def keyword, 221–223

defs/keywords file, 8

density (in a hash table), 175

disadvantages of mark and sweep, 302

displaying the local table, 51–53

--dump parsetree (Ruby option), 29

dup method, 265–266

dynamic variable access, 71–74

E

each method, 91

Eden heap, 312–313

ensure keyword, 90

Enumerator class, 284

environment, 197, 198

environment pointer (EP), 68, 194, 197

environment pointer ladder, 74–75

EP (environment pointer), 68, 194, 197

eql? method, 175

eval method, 78, 236–240

examples
> grammar rule, 14
> instance_eval, 240–241
> method lookup, 139–140
> Module#prepend, 146

executing
> calls to blocks, 61–62, 194–196
> if statements, 84–86
> simple scripts, 58–60

expanding hash tables, 174–175

experiments
> Array#shift, Rubinius implementation of, 288–291
> backtraces, comparing in MRI and Rubinius, 281–284
> class methods, where Ruby saves, 127–130
> closures, defining methods with, 246–248
> constant, which Ruby finds first, 162–164
> copy-on-write performance, measuring, 267–271
> for loops, how Ruby implements, 90–92
> garbage collection (MRI), seeing in action, 302–308
> hashes
>> inserting new element into, 177–179
>> retrieving values from, 172–173
>> using with object keys, 183–189
> instance variable, time required to save, 113–115
> JIT compiler, monitoring, 260–263
> keyword arguments, how Ruby implements, 99–103
> local table, displaying, 51–53
> local variables, changing after calling lambda, 214–217
> modules, modifying after including, 151–154
> Ruby scripts
>> parsing, 9–12
>> tokenizing, 9–12
> Ruby versions, benchmarking, 65–67
> self, how it changes with lexical scope, 231–236
> special variables, exploring, 75–78
> verbose GC mode in JRuby, using, 321–324
> while loops vs. passing blocks, speed of, 200–203
> YARV instructions, displaying, 44–45

extend method, 138

F

false value, 110

Fenichel, Robert R., 309

finding constants, 156–158, 160–161

first-class citizen, treating a function as, 203–213

Tuple (C++ class), 287
types of Ruby methods, 93–95

U

UNDEF methods, 94
unless keyword, 85
unnamed arguments, 47, 96
until...end loop, 85
using method, 229

V

VALUE pointer, 106, 107, 110, 204
values
    array, how Ruby saves, 285–291
    default, for arguments, 47
    expanding hash tables to
        accommodate more, 174–175
    false, 110
    FIXNUM_FLAG, 110
    nil, 110
    simple, 110–111
    special, 71
    string, how Ruby saves, 204–207,
        263–271
    true, 110
variable access
    dynamic, 71–74
    local, 67–70
variables, 67–74
    class, 120–124
    class instance, 120–122
    instance
        for generic objects, 111, 113
        time required to save, 113–115
    local, changing after calling lambda,
        214–217
    special. *See* special variables
visualizing copy-on-write, 269–270
visualizing two instances of one class, 108
vm_core.h file, 198
vm_exec.c file, 64
vm_getivar (C function), 99
vm.inc file, 63
vm_insnhelper.h file, 74
VM_METHOD_TYPE_ISEQ (C source code
        value), 95
VM_METHOD_TYPE_CFUNC (C source code
        value), 97
VM_METHOD_TYPE_REFINED (C source code
        value), 229
vm_setivar (C function), 98

W

weak generational hypothesis, 313–314
while...end loop, 85, 200–203
write barriers, 316

X

-Xbootclasspath (Java option), 253

Y

Yacc (Yet Another Compiler
        Compiler), 12
YARV (Yet Another Ruby Virtual
        Machine), 33, 56–62,
        327–330
YARV instructions, 34, 63–64
    branchunless, 85
    displaying, 44–45
    getlocal, 74–75
    jump, 85
    leave, 45, 60
    opt_lt, 85
    opt_plus, 38, 60
    opt_send_simple, 38, 60
    putobject, 59
    putself, 36, 58, 63
    send, 92–95, 247
    setlocal, 69
    taking a close look at, 63–64
    throw, 87
    trace, 45
Yet Another Compiler Compiler
        (Yacc), 12
Yet Another Ruby Virtual Machine
        (YARV), 33, 56–62, 327–330
Yochelson, Jerome C., 309
-y (Ruby option), 19

Z

ZSUPER methods, 94

The Electronic Frontier Foundation (EFF) is the leading organization defending civil liberties in the digital world. We defend free speech on the Internet, fight illegal surveillance, promote the rights of innovators to develop new digital technologies, and work to ensure that the rights and freedoms we enjoy are enhanced — rather than eroded — as our use of technology grows.

EFF.ORG

ELECTRONIC FRONTIER FOUNDATION

Protecting Rights and Promoting Freedom on the Electronic Frontier

UPDATES

Visit *http://nostarch.com/rum/* for updates, errata, and other information.

More no-nonsense books from **no starch press**

PERL ONE-LINERS
130 Programs That Get Things Done
by PETERIS KRUMINS
NOVEMBER 2013, 152 PP., $19.95
ISBN 978-1-59327-520-4

RUBY WIZARDRY
An Introduction to Programming for Kids
by ERIC WEINSTEIN
DECEMBER 2014, 352 PP., $29.95
ISBN 978-1-59327-566-2
two color

PYTHON FOR KIDS
A Playful Introduction to Programming
by JASON R. BRIGGS
DECEMBER 2012, 344 PP., $34.95
ISBN 978-1-59327-407-8
full color

ELOQUENT JAVASCRIPT, 2ND EDITION
A Modern Introduction to Programming
by MARIJN HAVERBEKE
DECEMBER 2014, 472 PP., $39.95
ISBN 978-1-59327-584-6

HACKING, 2ND EDITION
The Art of Exploitation
by JON ERICKSON
FEBRUARY 2008, 488 PP., $49.95
ISBN 978-1-59327-144-2
includes CD

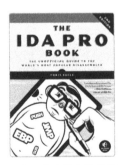

THE IDA PRO BOOK, 2ND EDITION
The Unofficial Guide to the World's Most Popular Disassembler
by CHRIS EAGLE
JULY 2011, 672 PP., $69.95
ISBN 978-1-59327-289-0

800.420.7240 OR 415.863.9900 | SALES@NOSTARCH.COM | WWW.NOSTARCH.COM

Lightning Source UK Ltd.
Milton Keynes UK
UKHW03f2200120418
320972UK00011B/245/P